SANYO
Automatic Microwave Cooking

A Benjamin **b** Company Book

Managing Editor: Virginia Schomp
Editor: Barbara Varnum
Editorial Assistants: Susan Jablonski, Pat Drew,
                      Glen Gilchrist, Dorothy Kincaid
Director, Consumer Education & Services: Thelma Pressman
Chief Home Economist: Betty Sullivan
Food Stylist: Carol Peterson
Art & Design: Thomas C. Brecklin
Typography: A-Line, Milwaukee
Photography: Teri Sandison, Los Angeles

Cookware and accessories courtesy of Williams Sonoma and Bullocks, Beverly
Center, Los Angeles

USER INSTRUCTIONS
PRECAUTIONS TO AVOID POSSIBLE EXPOSURE TO EXCESSIVE MICRO-WAVE ENERGY

(a) DO NOT ATTEMPT to operate this oven with the door open since open-door operation can result in harmful exposure to microwave energy. It is important not to defeat or tamper with the safety interlocks.

(b) DO NOT PLACE any object between the oven front face and the door or allow soil or cleaner residue to accumulate on sealing surfaces.

(c) DO NOT OPERATE the oven if it is damaged. It is particularly important that the oven door close properly and that there is no damage to the:
   (1) DOOR (bent)
   (2) HINGES AND LATCHES (broken or loosened)
   (3) DOOR SEALS AND SEALING SURFACES

(d) THE OVEN SHOULD NOT BE ADJUSTED OR REPAIRED BY ANYONE EXCEPT PROPERLY QUALIFIED SERVICE PERSONNEL.

Library of Congress Catalog Card Number: 78-71995
ISBN: 0-87502-129-8
Published by The Benjamin Company, Inc.
One Westchester Plaza
Elmsford, New York 10523
Printed in Japan
10 9 8 7 6 5 4 3 2

CONTENTS

I   What's It All About?   5
    An explanation of the Automatic Cusine-Master and how it works.

II   Look What You Can Do!   9
    The special advantages of microwave cooking.

III   Here's What You Need to Know   13
    About terms, techniques, and microwave cookware.

IV   Getting to Know Your Automatic Oven   27
    An explanation of typical features and what to expect.

V   Let's Use the Oven   32
    A step-by-step approach.

VI   On Your Own   35
    Converting conventional recipes and other tips.

VII   Off to a Good Start   39
    Appetizers for every occasion.

VIII   From Midday to Midnight   49
    Soups, sandwiches, and hot drinks for lunch or snacks.

IX   A Baker's Dozen   69
    Thirteen scrumptious baked items you'll repeat often.

X   Ring the Dinner Bell for Meat   77
    The family's favorites with beef, pork, veal, and lamb.

XI   Prime Time Poultry   105
    Chicken, turkey, cornish hens, and duck dressed up for you.

XII   Catch of the Day   121
    The best fish and seafood from lake, stream, and ocean.

XIII   A Visit to the Dairy Case   133
    Memorable meals with eggs and cheese.

XIV   The Grain Belt   141
    Great pasta, rice, and cereal recipes you'll love.

XV   Compliments for Your Meal   149
    Fresh-picked flavor from all kinds of vegetables.

XVI   Pour on the Praise   169
    A bevy of sauces to make a meal special.

XVII   How Sweet It Is!   181
    Cookies, cakes, pies, candies, and hmmm...

XVIII   From Freezer To Table — Fast!   199
    Specially-selected, frequently used frozen items.

XIX   Dinner's in the Oven   206
    The whole-meal method explained and illustrated.

    Index   219
    An especially helpful reference guide

What's It All About?

The key to success in learning to use your new and exciting Sanyo Automatic Cuisine-Master microwave oven is to understand how it works. It is not enough to simply install it, admire it, and stand in awe of its marvelous new technology. Your oven has so much to offer, and we have so much information to share with you, do take the time to read the few pages of introduction. These illustrated chapters will show and tell you all about the way the microwave works, why it works that way, what it can do, and how to get the most out of it.

A Cooking School

The greatest cook of all was once a beginner. Because most of us did not experience microwave cooking in our kitchens as we grew up, we do not have any information to draw upon. Microwave cooking may be different, but it is not complicated; all you need is a bit of practice. So, in these pages we have provided a quick course for you and brought our cooking school into your home. When you are comfortable with the principles and techniques, browse through the wonderful recipes in the chapters that follow, find one with ingredients you like, and you will be on your way to becoming a proficient microwave cook. As every good cook knows, "keeping in touch" with the food as it cooks insures success. As you prepare the recipes, do feel free to open the door to check on the food, just as you would with conventional cooking methods. Our sensors don't mind being interrupted; so you can turn, baste, and taste, just as you did before microwave cooking came along to simplify your life in the kitchen. This oven does not replace your vital ability to judge. It just does as much as is possible within the limits of today's technology. We haven't yet figured out how to cook the food and wash the dishes for you in the same appliance, but we're working on it!

To install your oven, follow the directions in the Use and Care Manual. A microwave oven operates on standard 110-120v household current. It requires little maintenance. While a conventional oven generates heat in the oven cavity, there is no heat generated in the microwave cavity; so food and grease do not bake on. No harsh cleaning tasks are necessary. Follow the Use and Care Manual for the few simple steps needed to keep the oven clean.

Conventional Cooking vs Microwave Cooking

In conventional cooking by gas or electricity, food on top of the stove cooks by heat applied to the bottom of the pan, and in the oven by hot air

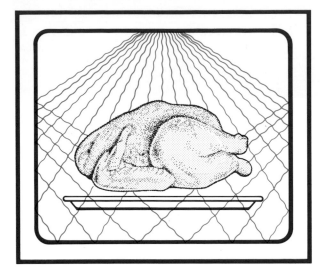

Microwaves bounce off oven walls and are absorbed by the food. There is no heat source and the air in the oven remains cool.

which surrounds the food. In microwave cooking, no energy is wasted in heating pots or air. Microwaves travel directly to the food. Inside the top of the oven is a magnetron vacuum tube which converts ordinary household current into high-frequency microwaves, similar to the microwaves in your radio or TV set. A stirrer-fan helps distribute the microwaves evenly throughout the oven. Microwaves are waves of energy, not heat. They are either reflected, passed through, or absorbed, depending upon the material contacted. For example, metal reflects microwaves; glass, pottery, paper, and most plastics allow the waves to pass through; and, finally, food absorbs microwaves. Very simply then, the absorbed microwave energy causes the food molecules to vibrate rapidly against each other, inducing friction, which in turn produces heat in the food. This is similar to the way heat is generated when you rub your hands together as fast as you can. Microwaves penetrate the food from the

outside, and the interior of the food cooks by conduction. Because we use cooking utensils that do not absorb microwave energy, but allow it to pass directly into the food, they do not become hot. However, they may absorb heat from the food itself and the occasional use of potholders may be necessary. The see-through panel in the oven door is made of a specially prepared material that contains a metal screen. The metal screen reflects the microwaves back into the cavity, yet enables you to observe the food as it cooks. Opening the microwave oven door turns the unit off automatically; so you can stir, turn, or check doneness with ease. And since there is no heat inside the cavity, no blast of hot air will greet you as with your conventional oven.

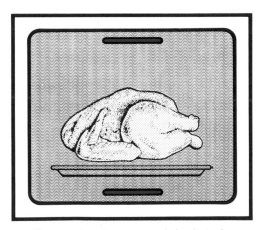

Conventional ovens cook by hot air.

Automatic Cooking

This oven adds a new dimension to microwave cooking. It is equipped with two types of sensors to measure, or sense, the temperature of the food and enable the oven to cook automatically. You do not select the time or power settings for automatic cooking. One sensor measures the *surface* temperature of the food being cooked by this method. The other measures the *internal* temperature of food cooked using the temperature probe. Though they cannot be used simultaneously, both sensors feed information to the oven's control center, a computer. Based on stored information, the computer determines how long a particular food needs to cook and regulates the power settings necessary for perfect doneness. Because the sensors measure what our eyes cannot see — surface and internal temperatures — they provide us with the ability to cook with greater accuracy than ever before.

Automatic Internal Temperature Sensor Cooking

Cooks have always devised ways to get at least a clue to the internal condition of food. A melon is thumped. A toothpick is inserted into a cake. A small cut is made in a steak. Of course, for years we have placed our trust in a meat thermometer when cooking a roast or a turkey to avoid the discovery of a mistake at the table. Now, taking this familiar thermometer several steps further, we rename it the internal temperature sensor, or temperature probe. And by connecting it to the oven's computer, we enable it to do a lot more than simply record the temperature of the food. With the aid of the computer, it actually determines when our meatloaf is done. It reheats soup or a sandwich to our preferred temperature. It has the oven stop and call us to the kitchen with a "beep" so we can turn over a roast, or baste a chicken. It will even keep food warm

for up to 1 hour after cooking is over. Much more reliable than a note on the refrigerator door! Detailed information about the internal-temperature sensor is provided on pages 30 and 31.

Automatic Surface Temperature Sensor Cooking

Years ago, the electric griddle was introduced and made it possible for us to measure and control the temperature of the *cooking* surface. Now, thanks to the space-age sensor in this oven, we can measure and control the temperature of the *food* surface. We no longer need to depend solely on our own built-in surface-heat sensors, our fingertips!

The surface-temperature sensor built into this oven uses the same principles used in space satellites. With the aid of a computer, satellites provide us with amazing views of the Earth at night. Areas of high population are outlined, even though they were in total darkness when the picture was taken. An infrared camera on board a satellite senses and records the heat radiated by big cities like New York, Chicago, or Los Angeles. It even "sees" the heat emitted by factories in remote locations. Like that camera, the infrared surface-temperature sensor in this oven "sees" the food through a lens and sends the surface temperature to the oven's "on-board" computer. The computer's stored data enables it to determine what surface temperature is required for the particular food item within the sensor's viewing area. Detailed information about the surface-temperature sensor is provided on pages 28 and 29.

The Recipes

The inside front and inside back covers present Quick Reference Guides for 59 basic food items. In addition, more than 300 recipes are included. Each recipe includes detailed instructions. In addition to over 170 recipes that use one of the automatic sensor-cooking methods, about 130 recipes use time and power settings you enter, and cook without the aid of the sensors. This is because some delicate foods require special attention from you. You see, you still are needed!

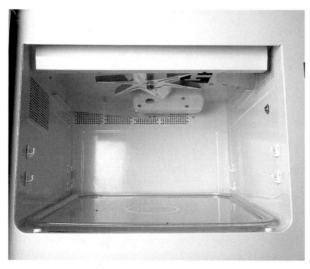

The stirrer-fan, surface-temperature sensor, probe receptacle, and other features are seen in this view. A wide-angle lens used for the photograph produces some distortion.

A Look Inside

You do not need a degree in science to understand the components of this unique equipment and how they work. In the photograph above, the spatter shield on the top of the oven cavity has been removed. The stirrer-fan is positioned in front. It is not controlled by a motor but spins as air flows through the oven. When the microwaves hit the stirrer-fan, it aids in distributing them evenly throughout the oven cavity. The magnetron tube is behind the "window" at the right of, and above, the stirrer-fan. This is where the microwaves enter the oven. Directly behind the stirrer-fan is the housing that contains the surface-temperature sensor. Its lens, recessed into the small, round opening on the left of the housing, only "sees" the area within the circle below on the glass tray. *Food must be placed over the circle when cooking with the surface-temperature sensor method.* You will also notice several screen-like areas that permit air to circulate within the oven and exhaust any steam from the food and, of course, the wonderful fragrances of food cooking. (Yes, though incredibly fast, microwave cooking produces the same appetizing aromas that bring the family to the kitchen to see "What's cooking." And they are often a clue to the fact that the food is almost ready to serve.) The receptacle for the internal-temperature sensor, the temperature probe, is at the right. The brackets on the walls are for the wire rack, used in whole meal cooking or to position some foods to improve cooking results. Finally, the tempered glass tray serves not only to catch spills, but also to elevate food, providing a space for the microwaves to bounce off the bottom of the oven and cook the underside of food.

In the next few pages, we would like to show you some of the wonderful things you can cook with your Sanyo Automatic Cuisine-Master microwave oven.

Look What You Can Do!

You can cook just about anything in the microwave oven, but some foods are so especially good done this way that we want to show several of them to you. The recipes for all the dishes illustrated here are included in the book. You'll find that the microwave oven not only cooks food superbly from scratch, but also reheats and defrosts with excellent results. Let's take a look.

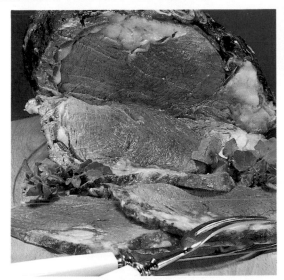

☐ *Roast beef* is juicy and rare, with less shrinkage than in the conventional oven. ☐ You can enjoy all kinds of *vegetables* at their wholesome best. Their true flavor and color are preserved. Potatoes are fluffy, cauliflower crisp, and broccoli the beautiful green it was born with. ☐ You'll want *scrambled eggs* for breakfast, lunch, and supper when you've tried them microwave-style. They're fluffier than in conventional cooking, and more pleasing to the eye as well as the palate. ☐ You'll think positively about *leftovers* after you try them reheated automatically in the microwave oven. Food will have that just-cooked taste and look whenever it is served.

☐ Cook luscious *chocolate cakes,* so tantalizingly moist, rich, and high. ☐ *Fruit,* such as this baked apple, can be prepared without water. Like vegetables, fruit retains that just-picked color and flavor. ☐ *Sauces* are a blessing to cook in the microwave oven, making constant stirring a thing of the past. Just imagine the convenience of mixing, cooking, and serving all in the same container.

Hollandaise sauce is smooth with just a few stirrings. ☐ The microwave oven can't be beat for *heating rolls and bread* so quickly they don't have a chance to be anything but perfect. And you can cook them right in the serving basket as long as there are no metal fasteners or trim. ☐ *Bacon* cooked in the microwave is incomparable — flat and crisp — and one slice takes less than a minute to

cook. It can be placed on a micro-proof bacon rack or between paper towels. □ *Candy* is a particular favorite with microwave cooks because it's as easy as pie. Chocolate and caramelized mixtures won't require constant stirring. Try this white chocolate Almond Bark or the Deluxe Mints and see for yourself. □ *Hot appetizers* are ready as needed, cooking quickly, with no mess and no pan to clean. Just cook them directly on paper plates or in a serving dish. Rumaki (bacon-wrapped chicken livers and water chestnuts) and Stuffed Mushrooms make delectable hors d'oeuvres. □ All kinds of *casseroles* cook without sticking to the dish in the microwave oven and they are still at their flavorful best later, thanks to just a few minutes of microwave reheating.

☐ Explore the pleasures of cooking *seafood* in your microwave oven. Fish fillets and steaks are moist and tender, their natural juices enhancing their delicate flavor. ☐ And for a pick-me-up that's really quick, there's no equal to a *bowl of soup,* a *cup of coffee,* or a *mug of cocoa* served directly from the oven. ☐ *Melt* *chocolate* and *soften butter or cream cheese* in seconds and save the time and the mess of double boilers and burned pans.

Now that you've had a sampling of what this appliance can do, let's take a look at what you need to know in order to start cooking.

In this chapter you will find everything you need to know to make microwave cooking easy, efficient, and pleasurable. Once you know the principles, the techniques will become second nature. Read this basic information with its accompanying illustrations carefully. As you begin to use the oven, you can always refer back to this handy guide whenever a question arises about a cooking term or method. Here you will learn why some foods cook faster than others, what you should know about timing and temperature, which cooking utensils are appropriate, how to cook most efficiently, and much more.

Because of the unique qualities of microwave energy, microwave cooking uses certain terms and methods that are different from those of conventional cooking. For example, in microwave cooking, many foods complete cooking during standing time, either in the oven or after being removed from the oven. In addition, how food is arranged in the cooking dish is important to its being cooked evenly throughout. You will also be introduced to some of the special considerations, such as positioning of the dish in the oven, called for when you are cooking with the surface-temperature sensor method.

You may wonder why you need to know all this when the oven performs so many tasks automatically. Fair question. If you restrict your cooking to those recipes that use the auto-matic temperature sensors, you may not need as much detail. But the fact is that the sensors cannot do everything. You'll also need to be familiar with this basic information to adapt recipes for personal preferences (do any two people like their scrambled eggs exactly alike?) and to use recipes from magazines and other cookbooks. In any event, study now can eliminate frustration later. Let's go to school.

ABOUT TIMING

Time is an important element in microwave cooking. But isn't that statement true for all cooking? You, the cook, have to be the judge as you consider your family's preferences and use your own instincts. Chances are, you can tell if a chicken is done simply by looking at it. You might even scoff at the timing chart given on a package because you know that a particular food always seems to need more or less time. It is important to know that even though the microwave oven is a superb product of computer technology, it is no more or less precise than any other cooking system. Nevertheless, because of the speed with which most foods are cooked, timing is more crucial in microwave cooking than in conventional cooking. One minute can cause a significant difference. When you consider that a cooking task requiring one hour in a conventional oven generally needs only one-quarter of that time in a microwave oven, you can understand why microwave cooking requires a somewhat different approach to timing. Where an extra minute in conventional cooking is seldom critical, in microwave cooking one minute can be the difference between overcooked or undercooked food. As you become familiar with your oven, you will recognize when to begin to check for doneness. Remember that it is better to undercook and add more cooking time than to overcook — then it's too late.

Cooking times for the preset temperature sensor recipes are determined automatically, of course. The approximate cooking times given with the automatic recipes are not precise and will vary, based on the quantity of food, starting temperature, and other factors.

Cooking time increases when the quantity of food is increased. Timing is determined automatically when the surface-temperature sensor is used. Note that one potato must be placed over the circle on the glass tray for the sensor to operate properly.

Cooking times could always be precise if a way could be found to guarantee that all foods would be exactly the same each time we cook them, and if the electric company would guarantee not to alter our power (there are frequent changes in the voltage levels reaching our homes). The fact is that one potato or one steak varies from another in density, moisture or fat content, shape, weight, and temperature. This is true of all food. The cook must be ready to adjust to the changes, to be flexible and observant. This discussion really comes down to the fact that you, not the microwave oven, are the cook.

While the oven can measure the surface or internal temperature when one of the sensors is used, it can't make judgments; so you must. All of the recipes have been meticulously kitchen tested by expert home economists. As in all fine cooking, however, microwave cooking needs and benefits from your personal touch. As you cook, feel free to alter the timing (using the LOWER or HIGHER pads with surface-temperature sensor cooking) to suit your preferences.

QUANTITY

The larger the volume of food there is, the more time is needed to cook it. One potato cooks in about 5 minutes; 3 potatoes may cook in 11 minutes; and 5 potatoes in about 18 minutes. Therefore, if the quantity in a recipe is changed, an adjustment in the timing is necessary. The oven automatically calculates timing adjustments for the preset sensor recipes.

You do not have to make any changes in the settings when making quantity adjustments.

When changing the quantity of a recipe that does not use one of the sensors, follow this general rule: When doubling, increase the cooking time by approximately 50 percent. When cutting a recipe in half, reduce the time by approximately 40 percent.

Shape and Size

Thin food cooks faster than thick food; thin sections faster than thick. Small pieces also cook faster than large pieces. For even cooking, place thick pieces toward the outside of the dish, since the outside areas cook faster than the inside areas. For best results, try to cook pieces of similar size and shape together.

Height

As in conventional cooking, areas that are closer to the energy source cook faster. In most microwave ovens, the energy source is at the top of the oven. Food close to the top may require shielding with pieces of aluminum foil and is usually turned over once for even cooking.

Density

Dense foods, like potatoes, roast beef, and carrots, take longer to cook than porous foods, such as cakes, ground beef, and apples, because it takes the microwaves longer to penetrate the denser texture. For example, a 2-pound roast will take longer than a 2-pound meat loaf.

A beef roast takes longer to cook than meatloaf of equal weight because the roast has a higher density (above right). Irregularly-shaped food, such as cut-up chicken, requires special arrangement in the dish to cook evenly. For surface-temperature sensor cooking, dish is positioned with thigh over circle on glass tray (top left). Food close to the energy source at the top of the oven is usually turned over during cooking. Portions may also be shielded with foil for part of the cooking time (above left).

Moisture Content

Moist food cooks faster than dry food because microwave energy is easily absorbed by the moisture within the food. For example, 1 cup of sliced zucchini will cook faster than 1 cup of carrots because of the higher water content in the zucchini. In fact, the amount of free moisture within a food helps determine how rapidly it cooks.

Sugar and Fat Content

Food high in sugar and fat heats quicker than items low in these ingredients, because microwave energy is attracted by sugar and fat. For example, the fruit or cheese filling of a sweet roll will heat faster than the roll itself and will be hotter, since sugar and fat reach higher temperatures than food low in sugar or fat content.

Relatively moist food, such as zucchini, takes less time to cook than drier food, such as carrots (left). Frozen and refrigerated food takes longer to cook than food at room temperature (center). A sweet roll heats a bit faster than a dinner roll (right).

Delicate Ingredients

This term is used to refer to food that cooks so quickly in the microwave oven that it can overcook — toughening, separating, or curdling. For example, mayonnaise, cheese, eggs, cream, dairy sour cream, etc. Other food may "pop," such as snails, oysters, and chicken livers. For this reason, a lower power setting is often recommended for proper cooking. However, when these ingredients are mixed with other food, as in a casserole, stew, or soup, you may use a higher power setting, because the increased volume automatically slows down the cooking.

Starting Temperature

As in conventional cooking, the temperature at which food is placed in the microwave oven affects the length of cooking time. More time is needed to cook food just out of the refrigerator than food at room temperature. For example, it takes longer to heat frozen green beans than canned green beans. Also, hot tap water will start boiling sooner than cold. Recipes in this book assume that food is at its normal storage temperature.

ABOUT UTENSILS

A wide variety of cookware and cooking implements can be used in the microwave oven. In order to indicate an item made of material that is safe and recommended for microwave cooking, we have created a new term, *microproof.* The Materials Checklist and *A Guide to Microproof Cookware* on the following pages will aid you in selecting the appropriate microproof utensil. Except for metal, most materials are microproof for at least a limited amount of cooking time. But unless specifically approved, items made of metal, even partially, are never to be used in the microwave oven, because they reflect microwaves, preventing them from passing through the cooking utensil into the food. In addition, metal that touches the oven sides will cause sparks, a static charge, known as arcing. Arcing is not harmful to you, though it will deface the oven. Metal twist ties or dishes or cups with gold or silver trim should not be used. See the Materials Checklist for those approved types of metal, such as pieces of aluminum foil, used as a shield over certain areas of food to prevent overcooking, or metal clips attached to frozen turkey.

When selecting a new piece of cookware, first check the manufacturer's directions. Also review the Materials Checklist and the *Guide to Microproof Cookware.* If you are still in doubt, try this test: Pour a cup of water into a glass measure and place in the oven next to the container or dish to be tested. Cook on HI for 1 minute. If the new dish feels hot, don't use it — it is absorbing microwave energy. If it feels warm, the dish may only be used for warming food. If it remains at room temperature, it is *microproof.*

The rapid growth of microwave cooking has created many new products for use in the microwave oven. Among these are microproof replacements for cookware formerly available only in metal. You'll find a wide variety at your store — cake, bundt, and muffin pans, roasting racks, etc. When you add these to traditional microproof cookware and the incredible array of microproof plastic and paper products, you'll find that microwave cooking enables you to select from many more kinds of cookware than are available for conventional cooking.

Selecting Containers

Containers should accommodate the food being cooked. Whenever possible use round or oval dishes, so that the microwaves are absorbed evenly into the food. Square corners in cookware receive more concentration of energy than the rest of the dish; so the food in the corners tends to overcook. Some cake and loaf recipes call for ring molds or bundt pans to facilitate more even cooking. This is because the center area in a round or oval dish generally cooks more slowly than the outside. Round cookware with a small glass inserted open end up in the center works just as well to eliminate undercooked centers. When a particular size or shape of container is specified in a recipe, it should be used. Varying the container size or shape may change

Unique roasting racks, browning dishes, and other cookware have been developed for microwave use (top left). Familiar items, such as molds and muffin pans, are now available in microproof materials (top right). A wide variety of glass, ceramic, and wood items are perfect for microwave use (above right). All kinds of paper products make microwave cooking especially easy (above left). Many plastics are safe for microwave use. Choose only plastics marked "for microwave use" and avoid plastic hot drink cups, such as Styrofoam, because they may melt (left).

the results. A 2-quart casserole in a recipe refers to a bowl-shaped cooking dish with its own lid. A 13×9-inch or 9-inch round baking dish refers to a shallow cooking dish. For liquids, large containers are specified to prevent them from boiling over. In selecting ring molds or bundt pans for surface temperature sensor cooking, those with very narrow centers work best. For best results, always try to use the dish cited in the recipe rather than substituting a different dish.

Materials Checklist

☐ CHINA, POTTERY: Ideal for microwave use. However, if they have metallic trim or glaze, they are not microproof and should not be used.

☐ GLASS: An excellent microwave cooking material. Especially useful for baking pies to check doneness of pie shells through the bottom. Since ovenproof glass is always safe, "microproof" is not mentioned in any recipe where a glass item is specified.

☐ METALS: *Not* suitable except as follows:

Small strips of aluminum foil can be used to cover areas on large pieces of meat or poultry that defrost or cook more rapidly than the rest of the piece — for example, a roast with jagged areas or thin ends, or the wing or breastbone of poultry. This method is known as *shielding* in microwave cooking.

Shallow aluminum frozen TV dinner trays with foil covers removed can be heated, provided that the trays do not exceed 3/4-inch depth. (However, microwaves can only reach the top surface of the food. TV dinners heat much faster if you "pop" the blocks of food out and arrange them on microproof dinner plates.)

Frozen poultry containing metal clamps may be defrosted in the microwave oven without removing the clamps. Remove the clamps after defrosting.

Trays or any foil or metal item must be at least 1 inch from oven walls.

☐ STRAW AND WOOD: Can be used for quick warming. Be certain no metal is used on the straw or wood items.

☐ PAPER: Approved for short-term cooking and for reheating at low settings. These must not be foil-lined. Extended use may cause the paper to burn. Waxed paper is a suitable covering.

☐ PLASTICS: Excellent products have been designed for microwave use. For best results, use only plastics marked for microwave use and follow the manufacturer's directions. Use plastic wrap specifically recommended for microwave use. Plastics which melt from the heat of the food should not be used.

☐ PLASTIC COOKING POUCHES: Can be used as long as they are marked for cooking. Slit the pouch so steam can escape.

Browning Dish

A browning dish, designed for microwave use only, is used to sear, grill, fry, or brown food. It is made to absorb microwave energy when the dish is preheated empty. A special coating on the bottom of the dish becomes very hot when preheated in the microwave oven. There are a variety of dishes available. Follow the manufacturer's instructions for care and use and for the length of time to preheat the dish.

After the dish is preheated, vegetable oil or butter may be added to enhance the browning and prevent food from sticking. After the food is placed on the preheated browning dish, the microwave energy is attracted to the food, rather than the dish. The hot surface of the dish browns the food. The food can be turned over to brown the other side. When cooking hamburger or moist foods, you may wish to pour off accumulated juices before turning the food over. The longer you wait to turn the food, the less browning occurs, since the dish cools off rapidly. You may need to drain the dish, wipe it out, and preheat it again. In doubling a recipe, such as fried chicken, wipe out the browning dish after the first batch, preheat the empty dish, and repeat the procedure. Since the browning dish becomes very hot, be sure to use potholders when handling it.

Used as a grill, the browning dish speeds cooking time. However, if you wish to use the dish to brown certain foods prior to adding them to a recipe, your recipe time will remain about the same. Some foods, such as eggs or sandwiches, require less heat for browning than other foods, such as chicken or meat.

Bottom Glass Tray

The bottom glass tray in the microwave oven is the primary cooking level. It is made of glass because microwaves penetrate the glass, and bounce off the oven bottom to cook the underside of the food. Glass is also easy to clean. Never operate the oven without the bottom tray in place. Food must be placed over the circle on the glass tray when cooking with the surface-temperature sensor method.

Middle Metal Rack

The removable middle metal rack of your oven is used mainly in whole meal cooking or when certain double quantities are cooked. The rack is made of specially engineered metal and is safe for the microwave oven. The microwaves bounce off the rack and are absorbed by the food. Generally, for more even and faster cooking, it is best to cook a few batches one after another rather than on two levels at the same time. The rack should be removed from the oven when not in use. *The rack cannot be used for automatic sensor cooking.*

Can We Help?

Sometimes, discovering the joys of a new appliance can be frustrating, can't it? I thought we'd take a moment at this point to let you know that we want you to become as comfortable and expert with your new oven as you are with your other kitchen appliances.

The "Cooking School" this book presents, coupled with your Use and Care Manual, may be all the help you need. But if you do have any questions that are not answered here or need additional assistance, please write me:

Thelma Pressman
Director, Consumer Education & Services
SANYO ELECTRIC, INC.
200 Riser Road
Little Ferry, New Jersey 07643
1-800-631-2501

A GUIDE TO MICROPROOF COOKWARE

ITEM	GOOD USE	GENERAL NOTES
China plates, cups	Heating dinners and drinks.	No metal trim.
Cooking pouches (plastic)	Cooking meat, vegetables, rice, other frozen food.	Slit pouch so steam can escape.
Corelle®	Heating dinners, soups, drinks.	Closed-handle cups should not be used.
Corning Ware® or Pyrex casseroles	Cooking main dishes, vegetables, desserts.	No metal trim.
Microwave browning dishes or grills	Searing, grilling, and frying small meat items; grilling sandwiches; frying eggs.	These utensils are specially made to absorb microwaves and preheat to high temperatures. They brown food that otherwise would not brown in a microwave oven.
Microwave roasting racks	Cooking roasts and chickens, squash and potatoes.	Special racks are available for cooking bacon.
Oven film and cooking bags	Cooking roasts or stews.	Substitute string for metal twist ties. Bag itself will not cause tenderizing. Do not use film with foil edges.
Paper plates, cups, napkins	Heating hot dogs, drinks, rolls, appetizers, sandwiches.	Absorbs moisture from baked goods and freshens them. Paper plates and cups with wax coatings should not be used.
Plastic wrap	Covering dishes.	Fold back edge to ventilate, allowing steam to escape.
Pottery and earthenware plates, mugs, etc.	Heating dinners, soups, drinks.	Some pottery has a metallic glaze. To check, use dish test (page 15).
Soft plastics, sherbet cartons	Reheating leftovers.	Used for very short reheating periods.
Thermometers	Measuring temperature of meat, poultry, and candy.	Use only approved microproof meat or candy thermometer in microwave oven. Microwave temperature probe is available with oven (page 28).
TV dinner trays (aluminum)	Frozen dinners or homemade dinners.	No deeper than $\frac{3}{4}$ inch. Food will receive heat from top surface only. Foil covering food must be removed.
Waxed paper	Covering casseroles. Use as a tent.	Prevents splattering. Helps contain heat where a tight seal is not required. Food temperature may cause some melting.
Wooden spoons, wooden skewers, straw baskets	Stirring puddings and sauces; for shish kabobs, appetizers, warming breads.	Can withstand microwaves for short cooking periods. Be sure no metal fittings on wood or straw.

ABOUT METHODS

The evenness and speed of micro-wave cooking are affected not only by the characteristics of the food itself, but also by certain methods, which are described here. Some of these techniques are used in con-ventional cooking as well, but they have a particular application in microwave cooking because of the special qualities of microwave energy. Many other important variables that influence cooking, defrosting, and reheating in the microwave oven are included here. Becoming familiar with these terms and methods will make microwave cooking easy and successful.

Arrangement

The way food is arranged in the oven and in the dish enhances even cooking and speeds in defrosting, heating, and cooking foods. The microwaves penetrate the outer portion of food first; therefore, foods should be arranged so that the denser, thicker areas are near the edge of the dish, and the thinner, more porous areas are near the center. For example, when cooking broccoli, split the heavy stalks to expose more area, then overlap with florets; or you can alternate florets of cauliflower with broccoli for an attractive dish. This gives even density to the food and provides even

Microwave arrangement methods create unique opportunities to cook and serve in the same dish. The cauliflower and broccoli dish, or any similar garden vegetable medley, is cooked, covered, using the surface-temperature sensor. Simply touch A7 and touch START. Shrimp, chicken legs, and tomatoes are shown properly arranged for microwave cooking. The dish must be placed in the oven with food over the circle on the glass tray when cooking with the surface-temperature sensor.

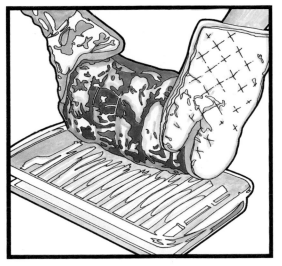

Use mitts to turn large food (above). Some recipes recommend rearranging food in the dish (top right). In microwave cooking, stir from the outside to the center (right).

cooking. Place shrimp in a ring with the tails toward the center. Arrange chicken legs like the spokes of a wheel with the bony ends toward the center. For surface-temperature sensor cooking, position the dish with the food item over the circle on the glass tray.

In microwave cooking, most items are arranged in a circle, rather than in rows. Muffins and potatoes are good examples of this technique. However, for surface-temperature sensor cooking, one item must be placed over the circle on the glass tray. To accomplish this, a microwave muffin ring, for example, is placed in the oven with one muffin cup — not the center of the ring — over the circle.

Turning Over

As in conventional cooking, large roasts, whole poultry, a ham, or hamburgers may require turning over to brown each side and to promote even heating. Food seared on a browning dish should be turned over. Microwave defrosting also frequently calls for food to be turned over.

Rearranging

Sometimes food that can't be stirred is repositioned in the dish to allow even heating. Move the center food to the outside of the dish and outer food toward the center. Some poultry and beef recipes profit from rearranging halfway through the cooking time.

Stirring

Less stirring is required in microwave cooking than in conventional cooking. When directed in a recipe, stir from the outside to the center because the outside cooks faster than the center. Stirring blends flavors and promotes even heating.

Rotating

A few foods, such as pies and cakes, that cannot be stirred, turned over, or rearranged, call for repositioning the cooking dish one-quarter or one-half turn to allow for even distribution of the microwave energy. Rotate only if the baked food is not cooking or rising evenly. Most foods do not need to be rotated.

Covering

Covers are used to trap steam, prevent dehydration, speed cooking time, and help food retain its natural moisture. Suitable tight coverings are microproof casserole tops, glass covers, plastic wraps, oven bags, and microproof plates and saucers. Boilable freezer bags may be used as cooking containers for the frozen food inside. Pierce top with a knife to ventilate before cooking. Remove coverings away from your face to prevent steam burns. Paper towels are especially useful as a light covering to prevent splatter and absorb moisture. Waxed paper helps to retain heat and moisture.

Shielding

Certain thin or bony areas, such as the wing tips of poultry, the head and tail of fish, or the breastbone of a turkey, cook faster than thicker areas. Covering these parts with small pieces of aluminum foil shields these areas from overcooking, since aluminum foil reflects the microwaves. Besides preventing thin parts of food from cooking more rapidly than thicker ones, shielding may be used during defrosting to cover those portions that defrost more quickly than others. Use aluminum foil only when recommended in recipes. Be careful not to allow the foil to come closer than 1 inch to the oven walls.

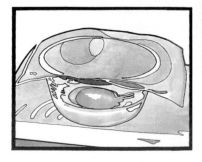

A one-quarter or one-half rotation is used for some muffins, cakes, and other foods (above left). Covers are as important in microwave cooking as in conventional cooking. Cover only when recipe recommends (left and above).

Standing Time

This term refers to the time food needs to complete cooking or thawing after microwave time is over. During the standing time, heat continues to be conducted from the outside to the center of the food. Food may remain in the oven for standing time (as it does with many of the preset recipes), or it may be placed on a heatproof counter. This procedure is an essential part of food preparation with the microwave oven. Some foods, such as roasts, require standing time to attain proper internal temperature for rare, medium, or well-done levels. Casseroles need standing time to allow the heat to spread evenly and to complete reheating or cooking. With cakes, pies, and quiches, standing time permits the center to finish cooking. During the standing time outside the oven, place food on a flat surface, such as a heat-resistant breadboard or countertop, not on a cooling rack as you would if cooking with a conventional oven.

Piercing

It is necessary to break the skin or membrane of certain foods, such as egg yolks, potatoes, liver, chicken giblets, eggplant, and squash. Because the skins or membranes retain moisture during cooking, they must be pierced before cooking to prevent bursting and to allow steam to escape. For example, pierce sausage casing in several places before cooking. A toothpick may be used for egg yolks; a fork is best for potatoes and squash.

Piercing helps steam escape (above right). The effect of standing time on roast beef (right). Use a flat surface for standing time, not a cooling rack (above).

Browning

Many foods do not brown in the microwave oven as much as they do in the conventional oven. Depending upon the fat content, most food will brown in 8 to 10 minutes in the microwave oven. For example, bacon browns in minutes because of its high fat content, but poultry will not brown even after 10 minutes. For food that cooks too quickly to brown, such as hamburgers, fried eggs, steaks, or cutlets, a special browning dish is available (page 19). The longer the cooking time, or the higher the fat content, the more browning will be achieved. You can also create a browned look on roasts, poultry, steaks, and other foods by brushing on a browning agent, such as gravy mix, soy sauce, dehydrated onion soup mix, paprika, etc. Cakes, bread, and pie shells do not brown as they do in conventional cooking. Using chocolate, spices, or dark flour helps attain the dark color. Otherwise, you can create appealing color by adding frostings, toppings, glazes, or dark spices such as cinnamon.

Adjusting for High Altitudes

As in conventional cooking, microwave cooking at high altitudes requires adjustments in cooking time for leavened products like breads and cakes. Other food may require a slightly longer cooking time to become tender, since water boils at a lower temperature. Usually, for every 3 minutes of microwave cooking time you add 1 minute for the higher altitude. Therefore, a recipe calling for 3 minutes needs 4 minutes and a recipe requiring 6 minutes needs 8 minutes. The wisest procedure is to start with the time given in the recipe and then check for doneness before adding additional time. Adding time is easy, but overcooking can be a real problem. Here, again, your judgment is vital.

Guide for Cook Control Settings

Main Setting	Suggested Cooking Uses
1	Raising bread dough; keeping casseroles and main dishes warm.
10 (warm)	Softening cream cheese.
20 (low)	Softening chocolate; heating breads, rolls, pancakes, tacos, tortillas, and French toast; clarifying butter; taking chill out of fruit; heating small amounts of food.
30 (defrost)	Thawing meats, poultry, and seafood; finish cooking casseroles, stews, and some sauces; cooking small quantities of most foods.
40 (braise)	Cooking less tender cuts of meat in liquid and slow-cooking dishes; finish cooking less tender roasts.
50 (simmer)	Cooking stews and soups after bringing to a boil; cooking baked custards and pasta.
60 (bake)	Cooking scrambled eggs, cakes.
70 (roast)	Cooking rump roast, ham, veal, and lamb; cooking cheese dishes; cooking eggs, and milk; cooking quick breads and cereal products.
80 (reheat)	Quickly reheating precooked or prepared foods; heating sandwiches.
90 (sauté)	Quickly cooking onions, celery, and green peppers; reheating meat slices quickly.
HI (max. power)	Cooking tender cuts of meat; cooking poultry, fish, vegetables, and most casseroles; preheating the browning dish; boiling water; thickening some sauces; cooking muffins. Cooking whole meal, i.e. two or three dishes at once.

Getting to Know Your Automatic Oven

The Sanyo Automatic Cuisine-Master microwave oven has 100 power settings. Just as in a conventional oven, these settings provide flexibility and control. Selection of the power setting is automatic, as is the timing, for the preset sensor recipes.

The oven control panel includes a Display Window at the top which provides a lighted readout of the time of day or of the oven's cooking functions. A series of touch pads, divided into 3 sections, is below the Display Window. A beep tone sounds when they are touched to confirm that the settings have been entered.

The top panel includes the 10 main preset sensor programs. Each program has several variations, activated by use of the numbered touch pads in the lower panel in combination with the sensor pads in the top panel. The HIGHER and LOWER touch pads are used to adjust cooking time on surface-temperature sensor recipes only. The touch pads to be used are identified at the top of and within the text of all automatic recipes.

The lower panel is the main control center of the oven, containing the START, STOP, and CLEAR pads. It also has the touch pads you use to select the power setting and timing for those recipes that do not use one of the automatic sensor programs. The *Guide* on page 26 lists the main power settings and gives them some familiar cooking terms. It also describes their most frequent uses in automatic recipes as well as in non-automatic recipes. Additional control panel information is available in your Use and Care Manual.

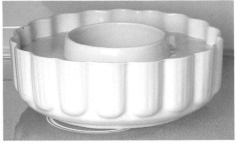

Muffin rings and ring molds are placed with food, not center of dishes, over circle on glass tray for surface-temperature sensor cooking (above and top right). Bundt pans and ring molds with narrow centers may be placed with center of dish over circle on glass tray (right). Additional information is on pages 28 and 29.

Surface-Temperature Sensor

This automatic cooking method determines the correct doneness of food by measuring the surface heat of the food. Information has been stored in the oven's computer enabling it to cause the oven to shut off or pause when the necessary surface temperatures have been reached. Instead of setting the cooking time and the power level desired to cook the food, all you do is select one of the surface-temperature sensor programs and touch START. The oven does the thinking for you. The sensor is built into the ceiling of the oven and reads the surface temperature without anything touching the food. *Food must, however, be placed over the circle on the glass tray for the sensor to function properly.* There are 8 main surface-temperature sensor programs, including DEFROST. Each has several variations, which you select by touching one of the main sensor touch pads and then one of the numbered touch pads located in the lower panel. *Automatic Cooking Guides* listing the principal uses for the 8 programs appear below and on page 29. More detailed *Guides* are in the appropriate chapters and inside the front and back covers.

Using the Surface-Temperature Sensor

The infrared sensor has been designed to operate with precision. To prevent a false reading, its circuitry is cooled during all operations of the oven (whether or not it is being used) and for approximately 3 minutes after the oven turns off. This is like leaving the fan on for a brief time after the lamp is turned off on a movie or slide projector. This "cool-down" period is an automatic function of the oven — you go right on with your cooking, knowing the fan is doing its job. There is no need to pause between cooking different foods. You can alter recipe quantity to suit your preference whenever the surface-temperature sensor is used.

AUTOMATIC DEFROSTING GUIDE

A0-0	Ground Meat
A0-1	Roasts
A0-2	Stew Meat, Steaks
A0-3	Chops, Bacon
A0-4	Chicken, Duck, Turkey Parts
A0-5	Whole Turkey, Whole Ham
A0-6	Whole Fish, Fish Steaks
A0-7	Fish Fillets, Shrimp

Automatic Cooking Guide
INSTANT FOODS

A2-0	Water (Instant Drinks)
A2-1	Milk, Cocoa
A2-2	Cereal
A2-3	Instant Soup
A2-4	Bacon

Automatic Cooking Guide
REHEAT

A1-0	Coffee, Tea
A1-1	Baby Food
A1-2	Bread Slices
A1-3	Rolls
A1-4	Deli Sandwiches, Pizza
A1-5	Plate of Food
A1-6	Casserole

Automatic Cooking Guide
CONVENIENCE FOODS

A3-0	Frozen Dinners
A3-1	Frozen Boil-in-Bag Foods
A3-2	Frozen Rice, Pasta
A3-3	Canned Chili, Stews, etc.
A3-4	Canned Soup
A3-5	Hot Dogs

**Automatic Cooking Guide
SEAFOOD**

A6-0   Whole Fish
A6-1   Fish Steaks, Fillets
A6-2   Shellfish
A6-3   Lobster

**Automatic Cooking Guide
VEGETABLES**

A7-0   Fresh, Firm
A7-1   Fresh, Delicate
A7-2   Fresh Corn-on-the-Cob
A7-3   Potatoes
A7-4   Frozen, Refrigerated
A7-5   Canned

**Automatic Cooking Guide
SLOW-COOK**

A8-0   Casseroles
A8-1   Homemade Soup
A8-2   Stews
A8-3   Pot Roasts, Swiss Steak, etc.

**Automatic Cooking Guide
DESSERTS**

A9-0   Cakes, Thin Batter
A9-1   Cakes, Heavy Batter or
　　　　 Fruit Added
A9-2   Cupcakes, Muffins
A9-3   Brownies, Other Bar Cookies
A9-4   Firm Fruit
A9-5   Delicate Fruit
A9-6   Pudding

Here are some additional details that can help make surface-temperature sensor cooking one of your best-liked features of this oven:

☐ Food must always be placed over the circle on the glass tray.

☐ The sensor works best when the food is as large as or larger than the circle.

☐ Food smaller than the circle must be placed exactly in the center of the circle (cups, rolls, etc.).

☐ Sensor programs often are combined within one recipe.

☐ Casseroles with *glass lids* are the best choice for automatic cooking. If you use a ceramic lid, be certain that it is microproof. If in doubt, test the lid using the method described on page 17.

☐ Cover food only when recommended in a recipe. Covering when not required can lead to false readings.

☐ Use a dish, casserole, glass measure, etc., only as large as needed for the food. A too-large dish can produce false readings.

☐ Use the HIGHER touch pad when specified and when you know you usually prefer a hotter drink or more than average doneness.

☐ Use the LOWER touch pad when specified and when you know you usually prefer a bit cooler drink or less than average doneness.

☐ Keep in mind that the sensor programs can be used for many cooking procedures in addition to those listed in the *Guides*. As you become experienced with the oven, you will undoubtedly discover your own new uses for the programs.

☐ For surface-temperature sensor cooking: Choose one of the 8 main programs. For example, touch A1. If a program other than A1-0 is desired, touch the appropriate number pad in the lower panel. Touch HIGHER or LOWER pads, if desired. Touch START.

☐ If after cooking a large item for more than 20 minutes, you wish to defrost another item, better results will be obtained if you allow the glass tray to cool to room temperature.

THE AUTOMATIC INTERNAL-TEMPERATURE SENSOR

When inserted into food, the internal-temperature sensor, the temperature probe, enables you to cook food to the exact internal temperature you want the food to reach, prior to standing time, to attain preferred doneness.

Two automatic programs are provided for the internal-temperature sensor. Probe temperatures, power settings, and pauses for turning or basting are preset for you. The A4 MEAT and A5 POULTRY programs give 12 options. The *Automatic Cooking Guides* on page 31 identify their main uses. As you become experi-enced in using your oven, do feel free to add your own recipes or food categories to our recommendations.

Automatic Probe Use

The temperature probe must be carefully and properly inserted in the food for accuracy. As a rule, the probe tip should be in the center of the dish, or in the thickest portion of the meat. Do not allow the probe to touch bone, fat, or any foil being used as a shield. After use, remove probe from the oven with potholders. Wash thin end in warm soapy water, rinse, and dry. Do not immerse in water or wash in a dishwasher.

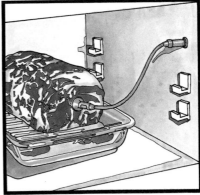

Proper positioning of the internal-temperature sensor, the temperature probe, assures good results.

Standing time is essential for most food to reach its best serving temperature. In microwave cooking, the temperature of most food rises about 5°F to 15°F during standing time. For example, after 10 minutes, the temperature of rare beef will reach 135°F.

Automatic Cooking Guide
TEMPERATURE PROBE
MEAT

A4-0   Meatloaf
A4-1   Beef Roasts, Rare
A4-2   Beef Roasts, Medium
A4-3   Beef Roasts, Well-Done
A4-4   Lamb Roasts, Medium
A4-5   Lamb Roasts, Well-Done
A4-6   Pork Roasts, Well-Done
A4-7   Precooked Hams

Automatic Cooking Guide
POULTRY

A5-0   Whole Chicken, Duckling
A5-1   Chicken, Halved or Quartered
A5-2   Whole Turkey
A5-3   Turkey Parts, Cornish Hen

Here are some detailed instructions that will be helpful to you in using the temperature probe:

☐ Place temperature probe in the food with the first inch of probe secured in the center of the food. Probe should not touch bone or a fat pocket.

☐ Insert probe from the side or front of food, except when into casserole or cup, etc. In general, insert probe in as close to a horizontal position as possible.

☐ Plug probe into receptacle on side wall of oven.

☐ Make sure thin end of probe does not touch cooking container or sides of oven.

☐ Never operate oven with probe in cavity unless probe is inserted in food and plugged into oven.

☐ To Cook: Touch A4 MEAT or A5 POULTRY and the appropriate numbers in the lower panel. Touch START. (It is not necessary to touch "0" for A4-0 or A5-0.)

NOTE: Automatic cooking functions identified in charts and on oven control panel are representative. Some programs may be used to cook foods other than those listed. Follow recipe instructions.

Conventional Probe Use

Suggested Temperature Probe Settings is a guide to probe temperatures recommended when the automatic sensor method is not used.

When the food reaches the temperature you set, the oven automatically holds it warm up to 1 hour. You do not set the cooking time for any probe recipes. You do set the power level at which you want the food to be cooked. If a power setting is not chosen, the oven cooks at HI. The procedure: Touch TEMP CONTROL. Set temperature. If power setting other than HI is desired, touch COOK CONTROL and set power level. Touch START.

Suggested Temperature Probe Settings*

120°   Rare Beef, Precooked Ham
130°   Medium Beef
140°   Fish Steaks and Fillets, Well Done Beef
150°   Vegetables, Hot Drinks, Soups, Casseroles
155°   Veal
165°   Well Done Lamb, Well Done Pork
170°   Poultry Parts
180°   Well Done Whole Poultry
200°   Cake Frosting

---

* Refer to individual Cooking Guides (see Index) for specific instructions.

Let's Use the Oven

Now it's time for some practical experience using all the features of your new Sanyo Automatic Cuisine-Master microwave oven. First, a quick hot drink, then an easy lunch. Finally, you'll see how really convenient automatic sensor cooking is with tonight's (or tomorrow's) vegetable. You've already read the introductory chapters and reviewed your Use and Care Manual, right? No cheating! Let's begin.

Lesson One

A quick pick-me-up

Take your favorite mug. Be sure there is no gold or silver trim or metallic glaze. If you're not certain about the mug being microproof, test as directed on page 17.

1. Fill mug with water and place in oven over circle on glass tray. Close oven door.

2. Touch CLEAR pad to erase any previous data. *(Not usually a necessary step.)*

3. Touch A1. Touch START. *(Oven cooks: HI, about 2 minutes.)*

4. Beep will be heard when 2 minutes end. The oven turns off automatically.

5. Open door. Remove mug. Handle will be cool enough to hold though cup itself will be warm from heated water.

6. Stir in instant coffee or tea. That's all there is to it with the automatic surface-temperature sensor method.

For non-automatic cooking, Step Three would be revised as follows:

☐ Touch TIME pad . Touch pads 2-0-0. Touch START. Oven is set to cook 2 minutes on HI. *(It is not necessary to use COOK CONTROL pad because oven automatically cooks on HI unless a different power level is entered.)*

Lesson Two
Soup and Sandwich Lunch

1. Pour soup into microproof 8- to 12-ounce soup mug.
2. Place mug in oven. Insert temperature probe in mug. Plug probe into receptacle.

3. Touch TEMP CONTROL. Touch pads 1-5-0. Touch COOK CONTROL. Touch pads 8-0. Touch START. Oven is set to heat soup to 150°F at power level 80.

6. Score hot dog in several places on two sides. Place on microproof plate. Place in oven with hot dog over circle on glass tray.

4. Observe Display Window. When 100°F appears, open door. Oven stops automatically. Stir soup. Close door. Touch START. Oven will heat soup to 150°F.

5. At Hold, open door. Remove probe and set soup aside, covered, while preparing hot dog.

7. Touch A3. Touch 5. Touch START. *(Oven cooks: 80, about 45 seconds.)*

8. At PAUSE, add hot dog to bun. Touch START. *(Oven cooks: 80, about 15 seconds.)*

Serve the soup and bring the mustard. Bon appetit!

We have demonstrated heating soup using the internal-temperature sensor, the temperature probe. The automatic surface-temperature sensor method is A3-4. Your choice next time.

2. Oven will beep when cooking sequence for bacon and onion is ended. Add beans to casserole and cover with casserole lid.

3. Touch A7. Touch 4. Touch HIGHER. Touch START. *(Oven cooks: HI, about 5 minutes.)*

4. Oven will beep and PAUSE will appear in Display Window. Add dressing and stir through. Touch START. *(Oven cooks: HI, about 4 minutes.)*

5. Let green beans stand 3 minutes, covered. Stir before serving.

These few lessons have given you just a hint to the simple and easy operation of this oven. You're ready now to go "on your own." The next chapter reads quickly, or you can come back to it later if you just can't wait to get to the recipes. We'll understand!

Lesson Three

Green Beans Italiano

We have selected this recipe because it gives you important information on the many ways this oven can become invaluable. In minutes, automatically, you can have a flavorful dish that raises vegetables from the ho-hum category to a treat the family will look forward to again and again.

3 slices bacon, chopped
1 small onion, chopped
2 packages (10 ounces each) frozen cut green beans
⅓ cup Italian dressing

1. Place bacon and onion in 2-quart microproof casserole. Place in oven over circle on glass tray. Cover with paper towel. Touch A2. Touch 4. Touch START. *(Oven cooks: HI, about 3 minutes.)*

You will undoubtedly want to cook some of your favorite conventional recipes in the microwave oven. With a little thought and experimenting you can convert many recipes. Before converting a recipe, study it to determine if it will adapt well to microwave cooking. Look for a recipe in the book that matches your conventional one most closely. For example, find a recipe with the same amount, type, and form of main ingredient, such as 1 pound ground meat or 2 pounds beef cut in 1-inch pieces, etc. Then compare other ingredients, such as pasta or vegetables. The microwave recipe will probably call for less liquid, because there is so little evaporation in microwave cooking.

At the beginning of each recipe chapter, hints on adapting recipes are provided. You will also notice that each preset recipe includes, in italics, the timing and power setting information as determined by the sensors and computer for the particular quantity used in that recipe, such as: *(Oven cooks: HI, 10 minutes; 50, 5 minutes.)* You can use that information as a guide in determining timing and power settings for those recipes you wish to adapt. Also use the following guidelines:

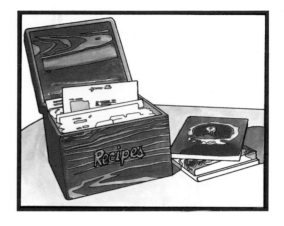

☐ Candies, bar cookies, meatloaf, and certain baked goods may not need adjustments in ingredients.

☐ In puddings, cakes, sauces, gravies, and some casseroles, liquids should be reduced.

☐ Most converted recipes will require adjustments in cooking time. Although a "rule of thumb" always has exceptions, you can generally assume that most microwave recipes are cooked in about one-quarter to one-third of the conventional recipe time. Check for doneness after one-quarter of the time before continuing to cook.

Now let's try converting a conventional recipe to the microwave oven. Suppose you have a favorite recipe for Chicken Marengo that you would like to prepare in your microwave oven. The closest recipe in this book turns out to be Chicken Cacciatore (page 114). Let's see how to convert that Chicken Marengo recipe.

Chicken Marengo
Conventional Style
4 to 6 servings

½ cup flour
1 teaspoon salt
½ teaspoon pepper
1 teaspoon tarragon
1 chicken (3 pounds), cut up
¼ cup olive oil
¼ cup butter
1 cup dry white wine
2 cups canned tomatoes
1 clove garlic, finely chopped
8 mushrooms (½ pound), sliced
  Chopped parsley

Preheat oven to 350°F. Mix flour, salt, pepper, and tarragon, and dredge chicken with seasoned flour. Reserve remaining flour.

In skillet heat oil and butter, and brown chicken. Place chicken in large casserole. Add reserved flour to the fat in skillet and, using a wire whisk, gradually stir in wine. When sauce is thickened and smooth, pour over the chicken and add the tomatoes, garlic, and mushrooms. Cover casserole and bake until chicken is tender, about 45 minutes. Before serving sprinkle with parsley.

Checking the Chicken Cacciatore recipe, you'll notice that the amount of liquid is quite a bit less than in the conventional Chicken Marengo recipe. That's because liquids do not reduce in microwave cooking and we don't want a thin sauce. Notice, too, that the onion is cooked first to be sure it is tender and that the flavor of the dish is fully developed. In converting, the Chicken Marengo recipe has the liquid reduced and the garlic is cooked first. Since the volume of food is about the same, the cooking times and power settings for Chicken Cacciatore are followed for Chicken Marengo Microwave Style. Here's the fully converted recipe:

Chicken Marengo
Microwave Style
4 to 6 servings

1 chicken (3 pounds), cut up
1 teaspoon salt
½ teaspoon pepper
1 teaspoon tarragon
1 clove garlic, minced
1 tablespoon butter
1 tablespoon olive oil
¼ cup flour
½ cup dry white wine
2 cups canned tomatoes
8 mushrooms (½ pound), sliced
  Chopped parsley

Rub chicken with salt, pepper, and tarragon and set aside. Place garlic, butter, and olive oil in 3-quart micro-proof casserole. Cook, covered, on HI, 1 minute. Add flour and stir until smooth, gradually adding wine. Stir in tomatoes and mushrooms. Cook, covered, on HI, 5 minutes; stir. Add chicken, immersing pieces in sauce. Cook, covered, on HI, 25 to 30 minutes, or until chicken is fork tender. Taste for seasoning, sprinkle with chopped parsley, and allow to stand, covered, 5 minutes before serving.

Butter, olive oil, and flour have been reduced since browning is not part of the microwave recipe. If you wish, however, add more butter and olive oil, dredge chicken in flour, and brown chicken in preheated browning dish. The white wine has been reduced to avoid a too thin sauce.

We've also included a simplified, automatic version of Chicken Marengo. See page 116.

About Low Calories

Scattered throughout the book are reduced-calorie suggestions and naturally low-calorie recipes. They are listed in the index so you can find them when you need them. In general, you can reduce calories in many recipes by making substitutions such as these:

☐ Bouillon or water for butter when sautéing or softening vegetables.

☐ Vegetables for potatoes or pasta.

☐ Lean meats for fatty ones.

☐ Skim milk for whole milk; skim milk cheeses like low-fat cottage, ricotta, and mozzarella for creamy fatty ones.

☐ Natural gravy with herbs for cream and butter sauces.

☐ Fruits cooked in their natural juices for fruit cooked with sugar added.

☐ Skinless chicken breast for regular cut-up chicken.

Cooking Casseroles

The microwave oven is exceptionally good for cooking casseroles. Vegetables keep their bright fresh color and crisp texture. Meat is tender and flavorful. Here are some general hints to help you:

☐ Casseroles are usually covered with plastic wrap or glass lids during cooking.

☐ Allow casseroles to stand 5 to 10 minutes before serving, according to size. Standing time allows the center of the casserole to complete cooking.

☐ You will obtain best results if you make ingredients uniform in size, stirring occasionally to distribute heat. If the ingredients are of different sizes, stir more often.

☐ Casseroles containing less tender meats need longer simmering on a lower power setting. The SLOW-COOK program, A8-0, eliminates the guesswork.

Reheating Casseroles

Most casseroles can be made ahead of time, refrigerated or frozen, then reheated later in the microwave before serving. The automatic surface-temperature sensor is used. Cover casserole with glass lid. Place in oven. Touch A1. Touch 6. Touch START. At Pause, stir. The reheating time, automatically determined by the sensor, will vary from a few minutes to about 20 minutes, depending upon the starting temperature.

Reheating Dinner Plates

How nice it will be to no longer worry about a hot meal for those late arrivals. A plate of food reheats quickly using the surface-temperature sensor. Arrange food on microproof plate with dense food, like meat and potatoes, around outside edge of plate, and less dense food, like green vegetables, toward the center. Cover plate with waxed paper. Place in oven. Touch A1. Touch 5. Touch START. It doesn't matter whether the plate of food has been refrigerated for a while or has just been filled from the table, the sensor will automatically calculate the correct reheating time.

Other Reheating Tips

As you can see, reheating is one of the major assets of this oven. Not only does most food reheat quickly, but it also retains moisture and its just-cooked flavor. The A1 REHEAT program will cover most of your reheating needs. However, you may find occasional uses for the following non-automatic reheating information:

☐ Use 80 except when otherwise specified. You can use the temperature probe for reheating casseroles, beverages, and other appropriate food. Insert probe into the largest or most dense piece of food and set temperature control at 150°F to 160°F.

☐ Dense food, such as mashed potatoes and casseroles, cooks more quickly and evenly if a depression is made in the center, or if the food is shaped in a ring.

☐ To retain moisture during reheating, cover food with plastic wrap or a microproof lid.

☐ Spread food out in a shallow container, rather than piling it high, for quicker and more even heating.

By the Way . . .

To get the greatest pleasure out of your microwave oven, keep in mind that certain food is best done by conventional means of cooking. For the following reasons we don't recommend using the microwave for:

☐ Eggs cooked in the shell, because the light membrane surrounding the yolk collects energy, which then causes a steam build-up that could explode the egg. Don't experiment. It's a mess to clean up!

☐ Deep-fat frying, because the confined environment of the oven is not suited to the handling of the food or oil and is not safe.

☐ Pancakes, because no crust forms. (But the oven is great for reheating pancakes, waffles, and similar items.)

☐ Toasting, because it also requires crust development.

☐ Popovers, because of the slow steam development necessary to make them rise.

☐ Home canning, because it is impossible to judge exact boiling temperatures inside a jar and you cannot be sure that the temperature and length of cooking are sufficient to prevent contamination of the food.

☐ Chiffon and angel food cakes, because they require steady, dry heat to rise and be tender.

☐ Heating bottles with small necks, like those for syrups and toppings, because they are apt to break from the pressure build-up.

☐ Large items, such as a 25-pound turkey or a dozen baking potatoes, because the space is not adequate and no time is saved.

☐ Do not attempt to make popcorn in a paper bag. The corn may dehydrate and overheat causing the paper bag to catch on fire. If you use a special microwave popcorn device, carefully follow the instructions provided with that product.

Off to a Good Start

Appetizers can be the most creative food of today's entertaining. They can be hot or cold, simple or fancy, light or hearty, depending upon the occasion. There are no rules; so you can let your imagination soar. Until now *hot* appetizers were the most troublesome and time-consuming for the host or hostess. But that's no longer true with the microwave oven. Parties are much easier and more enjoyable because the microwave eliminates all that last-minute hassle and lengthy cooking over a hot stove. You can assemble most appetizers and nibbles in advance, and at the right moment, just coolly "heat 'n serve!" This chapter presents many recipes for entertaining your guests, but you'll also be tempted to prepare delicious snacks and munchies just for the family. There's no doubt about it — appetizers cooked in the microwave oven are fun to make, fun to serve, and fun to eat.

Stuffed Mushrooms (page 47), Rumaki (page 47), and Quick Appetizer Pizza (page 46) are ready-to-cook (above and above right). To freshen corn chips and other snacks, just pop the serving bowl or basket in the oven on HI, 15 seconds; let stand 3 minutes (right).

Adapting Your Recipes

Most of the hot appetizers you've always wanted to make will adapt well to microwave cooking, except for those wrapped in pastry, since the coating does not become crisp.

Due to their usually delicate nature, most appetizers benefit from your personal attention in setting the time and power level required. The surface-temperature sensor works best on larger quantities and for reheating convenience appetizers.

The recipe for Rumaki (page 47) is an ideal guide for countless skewered appetizers containing seafood, chicken, vegetable, and fruit combinations. The enormous variety of finger foods, dippings, and canapés will provide you with continual tasty surprises. Here are some helpful tips:

☐ Appetizers and dips that contain cheese, mayonnaise, and other such delicate ingredients are usually heated on 70. A higher setting might cause separation or drying.

☐ The temperature probe set at 130°F on 70 provides an excellent alternative for heating hot dips containing seafood, cheese, or food to be served in a chafing dish or fondue pot.

☐ Because of its very delicate nature, a sour cream dip should be covered and heated with the temperature probe to 90°F on 50.

☐ Toppings for canapés can be made ahead, but do not place on bread or crackers until just before heating to assure a crisp base.

☐ Cover appetizers or dips only when the recipe specifies doing so. Use fitted glass lids, waxed paper, plastic wrap, or paper towels.

☐ You can heat two batches of the same or similar appetizers at one time by using both oven levels, the middle metal rack and bottom glass tray, for almost double the time of one batch. Watch closely; those on top may cook more quickly than those on bottom.

☐ Sensor program A1-6 uses power level 80 and has a built-in pause for stirring or adding ingredients. It is a perfect choice for appetizers prepared in casseroles or baking dishes.

COOKING GUIDE — CONVENIENCE APPETIZERS

Food	Amount	Cook Control Setting	Time	or	Automatic Sensor Method	Special Notes
Canned meat spread	4 oz.	80 (reheat)	30 - 45 seconds	or	A1-1 Higher	Transfer to small microproof bowl.
Canned sausages, cocktail sausages	5 oz.	80 (reheat)	1½ - 2 minutes	or	A1-4 Lower	Place in covered glass casserole.
Cocktail franks, pizza roll	4 servings	70 (roast)	45 - 60 seconds	or	A1-4	Place on paper towels. Roll will not crisp.
Cooked pizza, 10 inches, cut in 8 portions	1 wedge	80 (reheat)	45 - 60 seconds	or	A1-4	Place on paper towels or paper plate or leave in uncovered cardboard box, points toward center.
	4 wedges	80 (reheat)	1½ - 2 minutes	or	A1-4	
	Whole	70 (roast)	3¼ - 4 minutes	or	A1-4	
Dips, cream	½ cup	10 (warm)	1½ - 2½ minutes	or	A1-1	Cover with plastic wrap.
Egg rolls, pastry-covered	2 servings	70 (roast)	30 - 45 seconds	or	A1-3	Place on paper towels, do not cover.
Swiss fondue, frozen	10 oz.	80 (reheat)	5 - 6 minutes	or	A3-1 Lower	Slit pouch. Place on microproof plate. Stir before serving.

```
A8:0    LOWER
```

Swiss Fondue

Preset Cooking Time: about 21 minutes

>   4 cups (1 pound) shredded Swiss
>   cheese
>   1/4 cup all-purpose flour
>   1/4 teaspoon salt
>   Pinch pepper
>   1/4 teaspoon nutmeg
>   2 cups dry white wine
>   2 tablespoons kirsch
>   1 loaf French bread, cut
>   into cubes

Combine cheese, flour, salt, pepper, and nutmeg in 1½-quart microproof casserole. Stir to coat cheese with flour. Stir in wine. Cover and place in oven. Touch A8. Touch LOWER. Touch START. *(Oven cooks: HI, about 6 minutes.)*

At Pause, stir through several times. Touch START. *(Oven cooks: 50, about 10 minutes; stands: 0, 5 minutes.)*

Stir through several times to melt cheese. Blend in kirsch. Serve immediately with French bread cubes for dipping. (If fondue cools, cook on 30, 2 to 3 minutes, stirring several times.)

6 to 8 servings

Cheddar Cheese Canapés

Total Cooking Time: 30 seconds

>   1/2 cup (2 ounces) grated Cheddar
>   cheese
>   2 tablespoons half-and-half
>   2 tablespoons grated Parmesan cheese
>   1 tablespoon sesame seed
>   1/8 teaspoon Worcestershire sauce
>   1/8 teaspoon hot pepper sauce
>   12 crisp crackers or toast rounds
>   Chopped parsley

Combine Cheddar cheese, half-and-half, Parmesan cheese, sesame seed, Worcestershire, and hot pepper sauce until smooth. Spread 1 teaspoon mixture on each cracker. Arrange canapés on microproof plate. Place in oven. Cook on 70, 30 seconds.

Garnish with parsley and serve warm.

12 canapés

Cold Eggplant Appetizer

Total Cooking Time: 9 minutes

>   1 eggplant (1 pound)
>   1 small onion, minced
>   1/2 medium green pepper, seeded and
>   minced
>   1 clove garlic, minced
>   1 teaspoon lemon juice
>   1/4 teaspoon salt
>   1/8 teaspoon pepper
>   1 cup plain yogurt

Rinse eggplant; pierce skin in several places. Place on microwave roasting rack. Place in oven. Cook on HI, 7 minutes.

Set eggplant aside. Combine onion, green pepper, garlic, and lemon juice in small microproof bowl. Place in oven. Cook on HI, 2 minutes.

Cut eggplant in half lengthwise. Scoop pulp into serving bowl. Stir in onion mixture, salt, and pepper. Stir in yogurt. Cover and refrigerate. Taste and adjust seasoning before using. Serve with party rye, pumpernickel bread, or crackers.

2 cups

Cold Eggplant Appetizer is a delicious low-calorie topping for cut-up raw vegetables.

Liver and Sausage Pâté

Total Cooking Time: 12 minutes

- 1 pound chicken livers, rinsed and drained
- ½ pound mild Italian sausages, casings removed
- ⅓ cup diced onion
- 1 tablespoon bourbon
- ¼ cup heavy cream
- ½ teaspoon salt
- ¼ teaspoon nutmeg
- 2 packages (one 8-ounce and one 3-ounce) cream cheese, softened
- 2 tablespoons butter or margarine, softened
- 1½ tablespoons half-and-half

Butter 8×4-inch loaf pan. Line bottom and sides with waxed paper or aluminum foil. Cut each chicken liver into 4 pieces; discard membranes. Set livers aside. Break sausages into 4-cup glass measure. Place in oven. Cover with waxed paper. Cook on HI, 2 minutes.

Stir through sausages; cover. Cook on HI, 2 minutes.

Remove sausages from measure with slotted spoon. Drain on paper towels. Add chicken livers to drippings in measure. Place in oven. Cover with waxed paper. Cook on 50, 4 minutes.

Stir through chicken livers; cover. Cook on 50, 4 minutes. Purée onion and bourbon in blender or food processor. Add livers, sausages, heavy cream, salt, and nutmeg. Process thoroughly, stopping machine as necessary to scrape container. Pour into prepared loaf pan. Refrigerate at least 12 hours, or overnight.

Mix cream cheese, butter, and half-and-half in blender or food processor until smooth. Let stand at room temperature.

About 2 hours before serving, loosen pâté from pan and unmold onto serving platter. Carefully peel off waxed paper. Spread top and sides generously with cream cheese mixture. Refrigerate 1½ hours, or until cream cheese mixture is firm. Let stand at room temperature about 30 minutes before serving. Garnish with pimiento, capers, watercress, and green onions, if desired. Serve with assorted crackers and cocktail breads.

30 servings

Nachos

Total Cooking Time: 2 minutes

- 1 can (3⅛ ounces) jalapeño bean dip
- 1 bag (8 ounces) tortilla chips
- 1½ cups (6 ounces) grated Cheddar cheese
- 1 can (2¼ ounces) sliced jalapeño peppers

Spread bean dip lightly on chips. Top with cheese and peppers. Arrange 10 chips on microproof plate. Place in oven. Cook on 70, 40 seconds. Serve.

Arrange 10 more chips on another microproof plate. Place in oven. Cook on 70, 40 seconds. Serve.

Repeat with remaining 10 chips.

30 canapés

← Stuffed Mushrooms (page 47), Liver and Sausage Pâté

```
A1     6
```

Toasted Seasoned Pecans

Preset Cooking Time: about 8 minutes

  1 pound pecan halves
  1 tablespoon seasoned salt
  ¼ cup butter or margarine, cut
       into eighths

Place pecans in 1½-quart microproof casserole. Sprinkle with seasoned salt. Arrange butter evenly over pecans. Place in oven. Touch A1. Touch 6. Touch START. *(Oven cooks: 80, about 5 minutes.)*

At Pause, stir through several times. Touch START. *(Oven cooks: 80, about 3 minutes.)*

Let stand until cool.

1 pound

Tiny Meatballs

Total Cooking Time: 12 minutes

  1 pound lean ground beef
  ½ pound ground pork
  1 cup dry bread crumbs
  1 cup milk
  1 small onion, finely minced
  1 large egg, lightly beaten
  2 teaspoons soy sauce
  ½ teaspoon salt
  ¼ teaspoon pepper
  ¼ teaspoon allspice

Combine all ingredients in bowl. Shape into 1-inch balls. Arrange half of the meatballs in single layer on microwave roasting rack. Place in oven. Cook on 90, 6 minutes.

Transfer meatballs to chafing dish and keep warm. Arrange remaining meatballs on rack as above. Place in oven. Cook on 90, 6 minutes.

Add to chafing dish. Use toothpicks to spear meatballs. Serve hot with Curry Dipper (page 46).

60 meatballs

Meatballs can be prepared in advance and reheated on HI, 2 to 3 minutes.

Shrimp and Artichokes

Total Cooking Time: 5 minutes

  ½ pound small mushrooms
  1 jar (6 ounces) marinated
       artichoke hearts, drained
  ¼ cup lemon juice
  2 tablespoons olive oil
  2 cloves garlic, minced
  ½ teaspoon salt
  ½ teaspoon oregano
  ½ teaspoon dillweed
  ⅛ teaspoon pepper
  1 pound medium shrimp,
       shelled and deveined

Combine all ingredients except shrimp in microproof bowl; mix lightly; set aside. Arrange shrimp in single layer on round microproof plate, with tails toward center of plate. Place in oven. Cook on 70, 3 minutes. Observe and remove individual shrimp as they become pink. Set aside, covered, and keep warm.

Place artichoke mixture in oven. Cook on HI, 2 minutes. Remove from oven. Carefully stir in shrimp. Place in chafing dish to keep warm while serving.

about 6 servings

If using frozen shrimp, you may defrost using surface-temperature sensor method. Arrange shrimp on plate as instructed above and place in oven, with shrimp over circle on glass tray. Touch A0. Touch 7. Touch START. (Oven defrosts: 30, about 3 minutes; stands: 0, 5 minutes.)

NOTE: Automatic cooking functions identified in charts and on oven control panel are representative. Some programs may be used to cook foods other than those listed. Follow recipe instructions.

Shrimp and Artichokes, Tiny Meatballs, →
Toasted Seasoned Pecans, Nachos (page 43)

Party Nibblers

Total Cooking Time: 6½ minutes

      2 cups thin pretzel sticks
      2 cups crispy rice squares cereal
      2 cups crispy wheat squares cereal
      2 cups crispy oat circles cereal
   1½ cups (6 ounces) salted nuts
      7 tablespoons butter or margarine
      1 teaspoon Worcestershire sauce
    ½ teaspoon garlic powder
    ½ teaspoon onion powder
    ½ teaspoon celery salt

Combine pretzels, cereals, and nuts in 12×8-inch microproof baking dish; set aside. Place butter in 1-cup glass measure. Place in oven. Cook on HI, 1½ minutes.

Add Worcestershire and seasonings to butter; blend well. Drizzle over cereal mixture; toss lightly to mix. Place in oven. Cook on HI, 3 minutes.

Stir. Cook on HI, 2 minutes.

Let cool before serving or storing in airtight containers.

2½ quarts

Try changing combinations of ingredients or adding seasonings to suit your taste.

A2	3

Curry Dipper

Preset Cooking Time: about 4 minutes

      1 can (10¾ ounces) cream of
           mushroom soup, undiluted
   1½ tablespoons curry powder
      1 teaspoon lemon juice
      1 clove garlic, minced

Combine all ingredients in 4-cup glass measure and blend well. Place in oven. Touch A2. Touch 3. Touch START. *(Oven cooks: 80, about 4 minutes.)*

Serve hot with Tiny Meatballs (page 00), cubed sirloin, shrimp, or scallops.

1¼ cups

A1	4

Quick Appetizer Pizza

Preset Cooking Time: about 45 seconds

      1 English muffin, split and
           toasted
      2 tablespoons pizza sauce
      6 slices pepperoni
    ¼ cup (1 ounce) shredded
           mozzarella cheese

Spread each muffin half with 1 tablespoon pizza sauce. Top each with 3 slices pepperoni, then with cheese. Place both halves on microproof plate. Place in oven, with 1 muffin directly over circle on glass tray. Touch A1. Touch 4. Touch START. *(Oven cooks: 80, about 45 seconds.)*

Let stand 1 minute before serving.

2 servings

Crab Supremes

Total Cooking Time: 1½ minutes

      1 can (6½ to 7 ounces) crab
           meat, drained
    ½ cup finely minced celery
    ½ cup mayonnaise
      4 teaspoons sweet pickle relish
      2 teaspoons prepared mustard
      2 green onions, thinly sliced
    24 crisp crackers or toast rounds

Place crab meat in bowl; pick over and remove cartilage. Flake crab meat with fork. Add remaining ingredients except crackers. Spoon about 1 tablespoon mixture onto each cracker. Arrange 12 canapés on microproof plate. Place in oven. Cover with waxed paper. Cook on 70, 45 seconds.

Transfer canapés to serving platter. Arrange remaining canapés on microproof plate and place in oven. Cover with waxed paper. Cook on 70, 45 seconds.

Serve warm.

24 canapés

Rumaki

Total Cooking Time: 21 minutes

½ pound chicken livers, rinsed
   and drained
¼ cup soy sauce
½ teaspoon garlic powder
18 thin slices bacon, cut in half
1 can (8 ounces) sliced water
   chestnuts, drained

Cut livers into thirty-six 1-inch pieces; discard membranes. Combine soy sauce and garlic powder; set aside. Place 1 piece liver on 1 piece bacon. Top with 1 slice water chestnut. Roll up and fasten with toothpick; repeat with remaining liver pieces. Dip each rumaki in soy sauce mixture. Place 12 rumaki in circle on microwave roasting rack in microproof baking dish. Place in oven. Cover with paper towel. Cook on HI, 4 minutes.

Turn rumaki over. Cover. Cook on HI, 3 minutes. Remove from oven. Set aside and keep warm.

Repeat with remaining rumaki, cooking 12 at a time.

36 rumaki

Stuffed Mushrooms

Total Cooking Time: 4 minutes

24 medium mushrooms, stems removed
2 green onions, finely chopped
½ cup (2 ounces) shredded Cheddar
   cheese
⅓ cup dry bread crumbs
¼ cup butter or margarine, melted
½ teaspoon salt
½ teaspoon Italian herb seasoning
¼ teaspoon garlic powder
⅛ teaspoon pepper
½ teaspoon Worcestershire sauce

Chop mushroom stems finely; set caps aside. Combine chopped stems, green onions, and cheese; blend well. Add bread crumbs, butter, seasonings, and Worcestershire; blend well. Spoon mixture into caps, mounding slightly in center. Arrange on 10-inch round microproof plate. Place in oven. Cook on HI, 4 minutes.

24 appetizers

Crunchy Chicken Wings

Total Cooking Time: 29 minutes

14 chicken wings (about 3 pounds)
18 buttery crackers
½ cup grated Parmesan cheese
2 teaspoons parsley flakes
½ teaspoon garlic powder
½ teaspoon paprika
   Dash pepper
¼ cup butter or margarine

Cut chicken wings apart at both joints; discard tips. Pat dry with paper towels; set aside. Break crackers into blender or food processor container. Add remaining ingredients except butter. Cover and process until crackers are crumbed. Pour crumbs into plastic bag; set aside. Place butter in 9-inch microproof pie plate. Place in oven. Cook on HI, 1 minute.

Remove from oven. Dip chicken in butter, then shake in seasoned crumbs. Arrange half of the chicken over remaining butter in plate, with thickest parts toward outside of plate. Place in oven. Cover with paper towel. Cook on HI, 14 minutes.

Transfer chicken to serving platter and keep warm. Arrange remaining chicken in pie plate as above. Place in oven. Cover with paper towel. Cook on HI, 14 minutes.

28 pieces

Microwaves perform at their very best with sandwiches, hot drinks, soups, and chowders. For a quick pick-me-up all you need is a minute or two and a mug full of water for a cup of instant soup, or coffee. And, if you like to make soup from scratch without those endless hours of simmering and hovering that are required by conventional cooking, follow these microwave recipes.

Rise and shine with breakfast cocoa and wind down your day with after-dinner coffee swiftly and easily made in your microwave oven. What a convenience for coffee lovers! No more of that bitter mess when coffee is kept warm for more than 15 minutes in the conventional way. Brew your coffee as you normally do and pour what you want to drink now. Refrigerate the rest. Then, throughout the day, pour single cups as you wish. Place in the oven over the circle on the glass tray. Touch A1. Touch START. In a moment, truly fresh coffee.

Hot drinks or soup can be reheated using the surface-temperature sensor method. A soup mug is properly positioned over circle (above left). Two cups (or more) are arranged with one over circle, others placed in circular pattern around center cup (left). The internal-temperature sensor, the temperature probe, offers an alternate method for preparing soup. Note the probe position when a bowl or casserole is covered with plastic wrap: wrap is not pierced by the probe (above).

← *Country Vegetable Soup (page 51)*

Adapting Your Recipes

To convert your soup or hot drink recipes to the microwave method, find a similar recipe in this chapter and follow the sensor or time and power level settings used here. Most soup is cooked using the surface-temperature sensor method, program A8-1. Cooking begins at HI to heat the liquids rapidly, then reduces automatically to 50, providing slower cooking for flavor development and tenderization. The tips below will help you obtain excellent results.

☐ Soup is usually cooked covered. Large casseroles with lids are best as the lids can be removed easily to check on the food.

☐ It is always permissible to interrupt cooking by opening the oven door to stir or add ingredients. Simply touch START after closing door.

☐ Instead of soaking dried beans overnight, rinse beans in water. Place in micro-proof casserole. Add water. Cover and place in oven. Cook on HI, 20 minutes, or until water comes to a full boil. Set aside, covered, for 1 hour. Proceed to cook soup according to your recipe.

☐ Remember, since there is no heat in the microwave cavity, there is less evaporation of liquid than with stovetop simmering.

☐ Canned soup is heated using the surface-temperature sensor, program A3-4. Instant soup uses A2-3. Touch HIGHER or LOWER with either to adjust temperature to your preference.

☐ Be careful with milk-based liquids and 2- or 3-quart quantities. They can boil over quickly. Always choose a large microproof container. Fill individual cups of milk-based liquids no more than two-thirds full.

A8	1	LOWER

Chicken in the Pot

Preset Cooking Time: about 50 minutes

Boiling water
1 chicken (4 pounds), cut up
5 to 6 cups hot water
4 large carrots, cut into chunks
3 medium stalks celery, cut into chunks, with leaves
1 medium onion, cut into quarters
1 small parsnip, peeled and cut into chunks
1 tablespoon chicken bouillon granules
1/8 teaspoon pepper
Minced parsley

Pour boiling water over chicken to rinse; drain well. Arrange chicken and giblets, if available, in 4-quart microproof casserole. Add remaining ingredients except parsley. Add hot water, if necessary, to cover chicken. Cover and place in oven. Touch A8. Touch 1. Touch LOWER. Touch START. (Oven cooks: HI, about 25 minutes; 50, about 25 minutes.)

Let soup stand, covered, 15 minutes. Discard celery leaves. Divide parsley among individual soup bowls. Ladle soup over parsley.

4 to 6 servings

Always remove kidney from backs before cooking chicken for soup — it tends to make soup cloudy and adds a bitter taste.

The boiling water rinse reduces fat and helps eliminate foam. If desired, soup can be strained after cooking and broth served separately. Arrange chicken and vegetables on serving platter and sprinkle with parsley.

```
A8   1
```

Country Vegetable Soup

Preset Cooking Time: about 1 hour

 4 cups beef broth
 2 medium potatoes, peeled and
   cut into ½-inch cubes
 2 medium carrots, thinly sliced
 2 small onions, chopped
 1 can (12 ounces) whole-kernel
   corn, drained, or 1½ cups
   fresh corn
 1 cup shredded cabbage
 1 can (16 ounces) stewed tomatoes
 1 teaspoon salt
 ½ teaspoon thyme
 ⅛ teaspoon pepper
 1 bay leaf
 ⅓ cup chopped parsley

Combine all ingredients except parsley in 4-quart microproof casserole or soup tureen. Cover with plastic wrap. Place in oven. Touch A8. Touch 1. Touch START. *(Oven cooks: HI, about 20 minutes; 50, about 40 minutes.)*

Discard bay leaf. Divide parsley among 6 individual soup bowls and ladle soup over parsley. Serve with crackers or hard rolls.

6 servings

```
A2   3   HIGHER
```

Instant Soups, Soup Mixes

Preset Cooking Time: about 3 minutes

 1 envelope (1¼ ounces) instant
   soup mix
 ⅔ cup water

Combine soup mix and water in 8-ounce microproof mug or cup; blend well. Place in oven over circle on glass tray. Touch A2. Touch 3. Touch HIGHER. Touch START. *(Oven cooks: 80, about 3 minutes.)*

Let stand 3 minutes before serving.

1 serving

```
A0   6   &   A3   4
```

Mock Lobster Bisque

Preset Cooking Time: about 20 minutes

 1 pound frozen codfish or haddock
   fillets
 1 can (10¾ ounces) tomato soup,
   undiluted
 1 can (10¾ ounces) pea soup,
   undiluted
 1¼ cups milk
 ½ cup dry sherry

Place fillets in microproof baking dish. Place in oven. Touch A0. Touch 6. Touch START. *(Oven defrosts: 30, 3 minutes; stands: 0, 5 minutes.)*

Cut fillets into small chunks, reserving any liquid. Combine soups, milk, and sherry in 2-quart microproof casserole or soup tureen, stirring until smooth. Add fish and liquid. Cover and place in oven. Touch A3. Touch 4. Touch START. *(Oven cooks: 80, about 12 minutes.)*

Stir through several times before serving.

6 servings

```
A2   3
```

Cream of Mushroom Soup

Preset Cooking Time: about 8 minutes

 3 cups chopped mushrooms
 2½ cups chicken broth
 ½ teaspoon onion powder
 ¼ teaspoon salt
 ⅛ teaspoon garlic powder
 ⅛ teaspoon white pepper
 1 cup heavy cream, at room
   temperature

Combine all ingredients except cream in 2-quart microproof casserole or soup tureen. Cover. Place in oven. Touch A2. Touch 3. Touch START. *(Oven cooks: 80, about 8 minutes.)*

Stir in cream. Serve immediately.

6 servings

You can also use the temperature probe to cook this soup. Insert it into casserole and cook on HI, with the probe set at 150°F.

Canadian Green Pea Soup

Total Cooking Time: 11 minutes

>   1 can (2 ounces) mushroom stems
>   and pieces
>   1 tablespoon butter or margarine
>   2 cans (11¼ ounces each) green
>   pea soup, undiluted
>   1 cup grated carrots
>   ½ teaspoon salt

Drain mushroom liquid into 2-cup measure. Add water to equal 2 cups liquid; set aside. Place butter in 2-quart microproof casserole or soup tureen. Place in oven. Cook on 60, 1 minute.

Add mushrooms, soup, and mushroom-water mixture; stir with fork until blended. Add carrots and salt; blend well. Place in oven. Cover with waxed paper. Cook on 80, 10 minutes.

Serve hot with croutons or crackers.

4 to 6 servings

A1   6

Cream of Corn Soup

Preset Cooking Time: about 14 minutes

>   1 can (17 ounces) cream-style corn
>   1 can (13¾ ounces) chicken
>   broth
>   ⅔ cup water
>   ¼ cup thinly sliced zucchini
>   2 tablespoons water
>   1 tablespoon cornstarch
>   2 large eggs, lightly beaten
>   1 green onion, finely chopped

Combine corn, broth, ⅔ cup water, and zucchini in 2-quart microproof casserole or soup tureen. Cover and place in oven. Touch A1. Touch 6. Touch START. *(Oven cooks: 80, about 10 minutes.)*

At Pause, stir 2 tablespoons water and cornstarch until cornstarch is dissolved. Blend into soup. Touch START. *(Oven cooks: 80, about 4 minutes.)*

Gradually whisk eggs into soup in thin stream. Garnish with green onion and serve immediately.

4 servings

A8:0   HIGHER

Meatball Soup

Preset Cooking Time: about 30 minutes

>   ¾ pound lean ground beef
>   ½ cup cornmeal
>   1 large egg
>   1 can (28 ounces) whole tomatoes,
>   broken up
>   ½ cup water
>   1 small onion, diced
>   1 tablespoon chopped green
>   chilies
>   1 teaspoon chili powder
>   ½ teaspoon salt
>   ¼ teaspoon marjoram
>   ¼ teaspoon pepper
>   1 clove garlic, minced

Combine beef, cornmeal, and egg; blend well. Shape into ½-inch balls; set aside. Combine remaining ingredients in 2-quart microproof casserole or soup tureen. Cover and place in oven. Touch A8. Touch HIGHER. Touch START. *(Oven cooks: HI, about 5 minutes.)*

At Pause, drop meatballs into soup. Cover. Touch START. *(Oven cooks: 50, about 20 minutes; stands: 0, 5 minutes.)*

Stir soup gently before serving.

4 to 6 servings

Canadian Green Pea Soup →

Minestrone Soup

Total Cooking Time: 58 minutes

- 1 pound beef for stew, trimmed and cut into ½-inch cubes
- 5 cups hot water
- 1 medium onion, chopped
- ½ teaspoon basil
- ¼ teaspoon pepper
- 1 clove garlic, minced
- ½ cup thinly sliced carrots
- 1 can (16 ounces) whole tomatoes, broken up
- 1½ cups sliced zucchini
- 1 cup shredded cabbage
- 1 can (16 ounces) kidney beans, drained
- ½ cup uncooked vermicelli, broken into 1-inch pieces
- 2 tablespoons chopped parsley
- 1 teaspoon salt
  Grated Parmesan or Romano cheese

Combine beef, hot water, onion, basil, pepper, and garlic in 4-quart microproof casserole. Cover and place in oven. Cook on HI, 25 minutes.

Add carrots and tomatoes. Cover. Cook on HI, 8 minutes.

Add zucchini, cabbage, beans, vermicelli, parsley, and salt. Cover. Cook on 50, 25 minutes.

Let stand 5 minutes before serving. Sprinkle each serving generously with cheese.

6 to 8 servings

The temperature probe may be used after all ingredients have been added to casserole. Cook on 50, with the probe set at 150°F.

A7   4   HIGHER

Chilled Minted Pea Soup

Preset Cooking Time: about 7 minutes

- ¼ cup coarsely chopped fresh mint leaves
- ¼ cup chopped parsley
- ½ medium head lettuce, cored and chopped
- 2 green onions, chopped
- 2 packages (10 ounces each) frozen peas, thawed
- 1 can (13¾ ounces) chicken broth
- ½ teaspoon salt
- ¼ teaspoon white pepper
- ½ cup heavy cream
- 4 sprigs fresh mint

Combine chopped mint, parsley, lettuce, green onions, peas, broth, salt, and pepper in 2-quart microproof casserole or soup tureen. Place in oven. Touch A7. Touch 4. Touch HIGHER. Touch START. *(Oven cooks: HI, about 3 minutes.)*

At pause, stir through. Touch START. *(Oven cooks: HI, about 4 minutes.)*

Pour soup in batches into blender or food processor container. Cover and process on low speed until blended. Increase speed to high; purée. Stir in cream. Cover and chill before serving. Garnish each serving with mint sprig.

4 servings

French Onion Soup

Total Cooking Time: 21 minutes

- 3 large onions, cut into quarters and thinly sliced
- ¼ cup butter or margarine
- 2 teaspoons all-purpose flour
- 6 cups beef broth
- ¼ cup dry white wine
- ½ teaspoon salt
- ⅛ teaspoon white pepper
- Garlic powder
- 6 to 8 slices French bread, toasted and buttered
- 1 cup (4 ounces) shredded Swiss cheese

Place onions and butter in 3-quart microproof casserole. Place in oven. Cook on HI, 6 minutes.

Stir. Cook on HI, 6 minutes.

Stir in flour. Cook on HI, 1 minute.

Stir in broth, wine, salt, and pepper. Cover. Cook on HI, 8 minutes.

To serve, lightly sprinkle garlic powder on hot toast. Nearly fill soup bowls with hot soup; float toast on top. Cover toast generously with cheese and let stand until cheese melts.

6 to 8 servings

You may prefer to prepare this soup early in the day. If so, refrigerate before adding toast. To serve, cover soup and cook on HI, 5 minutes, stirring twice during heating. Serve as directed above.

A3	4	HIGHER

Canned Soup

Preset Cooking Time: about 5 minutes

- 1 can (10¾ ounces) soup, undiluted

Pour soup into 1½- to 2-quart microproof casserole. Stir in milk or water as directed on can. Place in oven. Touch A3. Touch 4. Touch HIGHER. Touch START. *(Oven cooks: 80, about 5 minutes.)*

Cover and let stand 3 minutes before serving.

2 servings

Hearty Cheese and Frank Soup

Total Cooking Time: 23 minutes

- ½ cup sliced celery
- 1 medium carrot, thinly sliced
- ¼ cup chopped onion
- ¼ cup butter or margarine
- 2 tablespoons all-purpose flour
- 2 cans (13¾ ounces each) chicken broth
- ½ pound frankfurters, sliced
- 2 cups (8 ounces) shredded Cheddar cheese
- 1½ cups milk or half-and-half

Combine celery, carrot, onion, and butter in 3-quart microproof casserole or soup tureen. Cover and place in oven. Cook on HI, 4 minutes.

Stir; cover. Cook on HI, 4 minutes.

Add flour and stir until smooth. Blend in broth and frankfurters. Cover. Cook on HI, 10 minutes.

Add cheese and stir until melted. Stir in milk. Cover. Cook on 50, 5 minutes.

6 servings

`A7:0   HIGHER   &   A3   4`

Tomato Soup Piquante

Preset Cooking Time: about 11 minutes

- ½ cup finely chopped celery
- 1 tablespoon butter or margarine
- 1 quart tomato juice
- 1 can (10½ ounces) beef consommé, undiluted
- 1 tablespoon dry sherry
- 1 teaspoon sugar
- ½ teaspoon thyme
- ½ teaspoon celery salt
- ⅛ teaspoon hot pepper sauce
- 4 to 6 slices lemon

Place celery and butter in 2-quart micro-proof casserole or soup tureen. Place in oven. Touch A7. Touch HIGHER. Touch START. *(Oven cooks: HI, about 3 minutes.)*

Add remaining ingredients except lemon. Cover. Touch A3. Touch 4. Touch START. *(Oven cooks: 80, about 8 minutes.)*

Let soup stand 3 minutes. Garnish with lemon slices before serving.

4 to 6 servings

This is one of several recipes that combine the benefits of two automatic cooking programs within one recipe. Simply follow the sequence given in the recipe for excellent results.

Japanese Cauliflower Soup

Total Cooking Time: 28 minutes

- 3 tablespoons butter or margarine
- ¼ cup all-purpose flour
- ⅛ teaspoon nutmeg
- 4 cups chicken broth
- 1 head cauliflower (2½ pounds), broken into florets
- ¼ cup heavy cream or undiluted evaporated milk
- 1 egg yolk
   Minced parsley

Place butter in 2-quart microproof casserole or soup tureen. Place in oven. Cook on HI, 2 minutes.

Add flour and nutmeg and stir until smooth. Blend in broth. Cover. Cook on HI, 7 minutes.

Stir in cauliflower. Cover. Cook on HI, 15 minutes.

Remove soup from oven and let stand 10 minutes. Purée in batches in blender or food processor. Return soup to casserole. Cover and place in oven. Cook on HI, 4 minutes.

Whisk cream and egg yolk until blended. Add small amount of soup to yolk mixture and blend well. Gradually whisk mixture back into soup. Sprinkle with parsley and serve immediately.

4 servings

You can make a lower-calorie soup by substituting whole or undiluted evaporated skim milk for the heavy cream.

If desired, 4 cups water and 4 teaspoons chicken bouillon granules can be substituted for the chicken broth.

New England Clam Chowder

Total Cooking Time: 19 minutes

- ¼ cup butter, melted
- ¼ cup all-purpose flour
- 2 cans (7½ ounces each) minced clams
- 2 slices bacon, diced
- 2 medium potatoes, peeled and cut into ½-inch cubes
- 1 medium onion, chopped
- 3 cups milk
- ½ teaspoon salt
- ⅛ teaspoon white pepper

Combine butter and flour; set aside. Drain clam liquid into 2-cup measure. Add water to equal 2 cups liquid; set aside. Place bacon in 3-quart microproof casserole or soup tureen. Place in oven. Cook on HI, 3 minutes.

Stir in potatoes and onion. Cover. Cook on 90, 10 minutes.

Add flour mixture, blending thoroughly. Stir in clam-water mixture, clams, milk, salt, and pepper. Cover. Cook on HI, 1 minute.

Stir through several times. Cover. Cook on HI, 5 minutes.

4 to 6 servings

Cold Fresh Tomato Soup

Total Cooking Time: 25 minutes

- 2 pounds ripe tomatoes, peeled and cut into eighths
- 2 cups dry white wine
- ½ cup chopped onions
- 1 tablespoon sugar
- 2 teaspoons paprika
- 1 teaspoon salt
- 1 strip (2 inches) lemon peel
- 1 sprig parsley
- 1 to 2 teaspoons lemon juice, to taste
- ½ cup dairy sour cream or plain yogurt

Combine tomatoes, wine, onions, sugar, paprika, salt, lemon peel, and parsley in 4-quart microproof casserole. Cover and place in oven. Cook on HI, 10 minutes.

Stir through several times. Cover. Cook on HI, 15 minutes.

Discard lemon peel and parsley. Pour soup into blender or food processor container and mix until smooth. Blend in lemon juice. Cover and refrigerate several hours before serving. Top each serving with dollop of sour cream.

4 to 6 servings

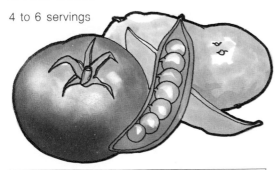

A2	1	HIGHER

Hot Milk

Preset Cooking Time: about 3 minutes

- 1 cup (8 ounces) milk

Pour milk into microproof mug or cup. Place in oven over circle on glass tray. Touch A2. Touch 1. Touch HIGHER. Touch START. *(Oven cooks: 70, about 3 minutes.)*

1 serving

This is an ideal way to heat milk for hot chocolate or any milk-based beverage.

A2:0

Irish Coffee

Preset Cooking Time: about 3 minutes

- 3 tablespoons Irish whiskey
- 1 tablespoon instant coffee powder
- 2 teaspoons sugar
  Whipped cream

Pour whiskey into 8-ounce microproof mug or cup. Add coffee and sugar. Stir in enough water to fill three-quarters full. Place in oven over circle on glass tray. Touch A2. Touch START. *(Oven cooks: HI, about 3 minutes.)*

Stir until sugar is dissolved. Top with whipped cream. Do not stir; coffee should be sipped through the layer of cream.

1 serving

A2:0

Russian Tea Mix

Preset Cooking Time: about 3 minutes

- 1 jar (9 ounces) powdered orange breakfast drink
- 1 package (3 ounces) lemonade mix
- 1½ cups instant unsweetened tea
- ⅓ cup sugar
- 1 teaspoon cinnamon
- 1 teaspoon ground cloves
- ¾ teaspoon ginger
- ¼ teaspoon nutmeg

Combine all ingredients. Store in covered jar or container until ready to use. To make 1 serving, place 2 to 3 teaspoons mix in 8-ounce microproof mug or cup. Add water or cider; blend well. Place in oven over circle on glass tray. Touch A2. Touch START. *(Oven cooks: HI, about 3 minutes.)*

Stir before serving.

64 servings

You can prepare up to 6 cups at a time and the oven will automatically calculate the required cooking time. Place 1 cup over circle on glass tray; arrange other cups in ring around center cup. If cooking 2 or 3 cups, place them with portions of all cups inside circle on glass tray.

A2	1

Cappuccino

Preset Cooking Time: about 4 minutes

- 2 cups milk
- ¼ cup semisweet chocolate pieces
- 2 teaspoons sugar
- 2 teaspoons instant coffee powder (preferably espresso)
- ½ cup brandy
  Whipped cream

Combine milk, chocolate, sugar, and coffee in 4-cup glass measure. Place in oven. Touch A2. Touch 1. Touch START. *(Oven cooks: 70, about 4 minutes.)*

Stir until sugar is dissolved. Pour into 4 mugs. Stir 2 tablespoons brandy into each. Top with dollop of whipped cream. Garnish with cinnamon or nutmeg, if desired.

4 servings

A2	3

Hot Buttered Rum

Preset Cooking Time: about 3 minutes

- ¼ cup rum
- 2 teaspoons brown sugar
- 1½ teaspoons unsalted butter
  Dash nutmeg
- 1 stick cinnamon

Combine rum and brown sugar in tall microproof mug or cup. Add water to fill two-thirds full. Place in oven over circle on glass tray. Touch A2. Touch 3. Touch START. *(Oven cooks: 80, about 3 minutes.)*

Add butter and stir until melted. Sprinkle with nutmeg and insert cinnamon stick as stirrer.

1 serving

You can increase the quantity of all beverages as desired. The oven will automatically determine the cooking time. Remember that at least 1 cup must always be positioned over the circle on the glass tray.

A2:0	HIGHER

Hot Devilish Daiquiri

Preset Cooking Time: about 5 minutes

- 1½ cups hot water
- 1 can (6 ounces) frozen lemonade concentrate, thawed
- 1 can (6 ounces) frozen limeade concentrate, thawed
- ¼ cup sugar
- 2 sticks cinnamon
- 8 whole cloves
- ½ cup light rum

Combine all ingredients except rum in 2-quart microproof bowl; blend well. Place in oven. Touch A2. Touch HIGHER. Touch START. *(Oven cooks: HI, about 5 minutes.)*

Remove from oven. Stir in rum. Ladle into punch cup, and serve. Garnish each serving with lemon slice and whole clove, if desired.

8 to 10 servings

A2	1

West Coast Cocoa

Preset Cooking Time: about 6 minutes

- ⅓ cup unsweetened cocoa powder
- ¼ cup sugar
- 3 cups milk
- 2 teaspoons grated orange peel
- ¼ teaspoon almond extract
- 4 sticks cinnamon

Combine cocoa and sugar in 4-cup glass measure. Stir in ½ cup milk to make smooth paste. Blend in remaining 2½ cups milk, orange peel, and almond extract, stirring until sugar is dissolved. Place in oven. Touch A2. Touch 1. Touch START. *(Oven cooks: 70, about 6 minutes.)*

Pour into mugs. Insert cinnamon sticks as stirrers.

4 servings

West Coast Cocoa, Cappuccino, →
Hot Devilish Daiquiri

A2:0

Spicy Apple Drink

Preset Cooking Time: about 9 minutes

- 1 quart apple cider
- ¼ cup firmly packed brown sugar
- 2 sticks cinnamon
- 8 whole cloves
- ½ medium lemon, thinly sliced
  Pinch mace
  Pinch nutmeg
- 1 medium orange, thinly sliced
  and seeded

Combine all ingredients except orange in 2-quart microproof bowl, stirring until brown sugar is dissolved. Place in oven. Touch A2. Touch START. *(Oven cooks: HI, about 9 minutes.)*

Strain into mugs. Garnish with orange slices before serving.

4 servings

A2:0

Hot Toddy

Preset Cooking Time: about 3 minutes

- 1 cup (8 ounces) water
- 2 tablespoons honey
- 1 tablespoon lemon juice
- 1 jigger (1½ ounces) brandy

Combine ingredients in large microproof mug or cup. Place in oven over circle on glass tray. Touch A2. Touch START. *(Oven cooks: HI, about 3 minutes.)*

1 serving

A2:0

Hot Water for Instant Beverages

Preset Cooking Time: about 2 minutes

- 1 cup (8 ounces) water

Pour water into microproof mug or cup. Place in oven over circle on glass tray. Touch A2. Touch START. *(Oven cooks: HI, about 2 minutes.)*

1 serving

This is an ideal way to heat water for tea, instant coffee, bouillon, etc.

A2:0

Hot Cranberry Punch

Preset Cooking Time: about 9 minutes

- 3 cups cranberry juice
- 1 cup apple juice
- ½ cup orange juice
- 3 tablespoons lemon juice
- 3 tablespoons sugar
  Whole cloves
- 1 stick cinnamon
- 1 orange, sliced and seeded

Combine juices, sugar, 4 cloves, and cinnamon in 2-quart microproof bowl. Cover and place in oven. Touch A2. Touch START. *(Oven cooks: HI, about 9 minutes.)*

Stir until sugar is dissolved. Strain into punch bowl; reserve cloves. Stick cloves into orange slices and float slices on punch as garnish.

8 servings

Rinsing the punch bowl with hot water is a quick way to warm it before adding punch.

A2:0   HIGHER

Tomato Warmer

Preset Cooking Time: about 7 minutes

- 2½ cups tomato juice
- 1 can (10½ ounces) beef broth
- ¼ cup lemon juice
- 1 teaspoon prepared horseradish
- 1 teaspoon parsley flakes
- ½ teaspoon celery salt
- ¼ cup dry sherry (optional)

Combine all ingredients except sherry in 4-cup glass measure. Place in oven. Touch A2. Touch HIGHER. Touch START. *(Oven cooks: HI, about 7 minutes.)*

Pour into 6 mugs. Stir 2 teaspoons sherry into each mug before serving.

6 servings

Adapting Your Sandwiches

The variety of sandwich combinations is endless and limited only by your imagination. The surface-temperature sensor is a marvelous convenience. Use A1-4 for most sandwiches, using the LOWER option for thin sandwiches and HIGHER for "Dagwoods." You can also have fun with the special A3-5 program. It includes a pause to add the top half of the bun, etc. Keep in mind that you can increase or decrease the quantity and the sensor will make timing changes automatically. Just be sure food is placed over the circle on the glass tray. Some further tips:

☐ A few thin slices of meat heat more quickly than one thick slice. The slower-heating thick slice can cause bread or roll to overcook before meat is hot. Try A3-5, adding the roll after the meat is hot, as we do with the Hot Dog recipe (page 65).

☐ The best breads to use for warmed sandwiches are day-old, full-bodied breads such as rye and whole wheat, and breads rich in eggs and shortening, like French or Italian and other white breads.

☐ Heat sandwiches on paper napkins, paper towels, or paper plates to absorb the steam and prevent sogginess. Cover with a paper towel to prevent splattering. More simply, you can wrap each sandwich in a paper towel. Remove wrapping immediately after warming.

☐ Moist fillings, such as that in a Sloppy Joe or a barbecued beef sandwich, should generally be heated separately from the rolls, to prevent sogginess.

☐ The browning dish can be used to enhance your grilled cheese, Reuben, or bacon sandwich. Brown the buttered outer side of bread before inserting filling.

A2   4   &   A3   5

Bacon Cheesewiches

Preset Cooking Time: about 3½ minutes

 ½ cup (2 ounces) grated Cheddar
   cheese
 1 tablespoon mayonnaise
 2 teaspoons catsup
 1 large hard-cooked egg,
   chopped
 2 slices bacon
 2 hamburger buns, split

Combine cheese, mayonnaise, catsup, and egg; set aside. Place bacon on paper towel-lined microproof plate. Place in oven. Cover with another paper towel. Touch A2. Touch 4. Touch START. (Oven cooks: HI, about 2 minutes.)

Break each slice of bacon in half; set aside. Spread half of the cheese mixture on bottom half of each bun. Place on microwave roasting rack. Place in oven, with 1 bun over circle on glass tray. Touch A3. Touch 5. Touch START. (Oven cooks: 80, about 1 minute.)

At Pause, place 2 bacon halves on each sandwich. Cover with tops of buns. Touch START. (Oven cooks: 80, about 30 seconds.)

2 sandwiches

A3   5

Coney Island Hot Dog

Preset Cooking Time: about 1½ minutes

 1 jumbo hot dog (3 ounces)
 1 hot dog bun, split
   Prepared mustard
 2 tablespoons drained sauerkraut
   Pickle relish, chili, grated
     cheese, chopped onion
     (optional)

Score opposite sides of hot dog in several places. Place on microproof plate. Place in oven, with hot dog over circle on glass tray. Touch A3. Touch 5. Touch START. (Oven cooks: 80, about 1 minute.)

At Pause, place hot dog in bun. Place in oven as above. Touch START. (Oven cooks: 80, about 30 seconds.)

Top with mustard, sauerkraut, and selected garnish.

1 serving

A1   6   LOWER

Beef Tacos

Preset Cooking Time: about 9 minutes

 1 pound lean ground beef
 1 small onion, chopped
 1 envelope (1¼ ounces) taco
   seasoning mix
 10 taco shells
 1½ cups (6 ounces) shredded Cheddar
   cheese
 2 cups shredded lettuce
 2 medium tomatoes, chopped
 1 avocado, peeled and diced
   Dairy sour cream (optional)
   Hot pepper sauce (optional)

Crumble beef into 2-quart microproof casserole. Add onion. Place in oven. Touch A1. Touch 6. Touch LOWER. Touch START. (Oven cooks: 80, about 6 minutes.)

At Pause, stir to break up beef; drain. Stir in seasoning mix. Touch START. (Oven cooks: 80, about 3 minutes.)

Remove beef mixture from oven. Divide among taco shells. Top each with cheese, lettuce, tomato, and avocado. Pass sour cream and hot pepper sauce separately.

10 tacos

If you like your taco shells warm, place them in the oven before filling. Touch A1. Touch 3. Touch START. (Oven cooks: 80, about 30 seconds.) Fill warmed shells with beef mixture and top as directed above.

Hot Ham and Swiss

Total Cooking Time: about 1 minute

 2 slices rye bread
   Butter or margarine
   Mayonnaise
 2 thin slices boiled ham
 1 slice Swiss cheese

Spread bread with butter and mayonnaise. Place ham and cheese between bread slices. Place on microwave roasting rack. Place in oven. Insert temperature probe at least 1 inch into center of sandwich. Cook on HI, with probe set at 110°F.

1 sandwich

Cheeseburgers

Total Cooking Time: 2½ minutes

- 1 pound lean ground beef
  Salt and pepper to taste
- 4 slices process American cheese
- 4 hamburger buns, split and
  toasted

Preheat microwave browning dish according to manufacturer's directions. While dish is preheating, season beef with salt and pepper. Shape into 4 patties. When browning dish is ready, immediately place patties on dish in oven. Cook on HI, 2 minutes.

Quickly turn patties over and add 1 slice cheese to each. Cook on HI, 30 seconds.

Serve on toasted buns with your favorite condiments.

4 cheeseburgers

A clever way to cook rare, medium, and well-done burgers at the same time is to simply make thicker patties for rare and thinner for well-done. It works, really!

A3	5

Roast Beef 'n Swiss Rolls

Preset Cooking Time: about 1¼ minutes

- 1½ tablespoons butter or margarine,
  softened
- ⅓ teaspoon prepared mustard
- ¼ teaspoon poppy seed
- ⅛ teaspoon onion powder
- 2 large hard rolls, split
- 2 thin slices roast beef
- 2 slices Swiss cheese

Combine butter, mustard, poppy seed, and onion powder. Spread rolls with butter mixture. Place 1 slice each beef and cheese on bottom halves of rolls. Place on microwave roasting rack. Place in oven, with 1 roll over circle on glass tray. Touch A3. Touch 5. Touch START. *(Oven cooks: 80, about 1 minute.)*

At Pause, cover with tops of rolls. Touch START. *(Oven cooks: 80, about 15 seconds.)*

2 sandwiches

A3	5

Precooked Sausages, Bratwurst, Polish Sausage, Knockwurst

Preset Cooking Time: about 2 minutes

- 1 sausage (3 ounces)
- 1 hot dog bun, split

Score opposite sides of sausage in several places. Place on microwave roasting rack. Place in oven, with sausage over circle on glass tray. Touch A3. Touch 5. Touch START. *(Oven cooks: 80, about 1½ minutes.)*

At Pause, remove sausage from rack. Drain rack and wipe clean with paper towel. Place sausage in bun. Place on microwave rack. Place in oven as above. Touch START. *(Oven cooks: 80, about 30 seconds.)*

1 serving

```
A3    5
```

Reuben Sandwich

Preset Cooking Time: about 1½ minutes

4 slices rye or pumpernickel bread
  Butter or margarine
6 ounces corned beef, thinly
  sliced
½ cup drained sauerkraut
2 heaping tablespoons Thousand
  Island dressing
2 slices Swiss cheese

Toast bread; spread lightly with butter. Layer remaining ingredients evenly over 2 slices toast. Place on microwave roasting rack. Place in oven, with 1 sandwich over circle on glass tray. Touch A3. Touch 5. Touch START. *(Oven cooks: 80, about 1 minute.)*

At Pause, top with remaining 2 slices toast. Touch START. *(Oven cooks: 80, about 30 seconds.)*

2 sandwiches

```
A3    5
```

Hot Dog

Preset Cooking Time: about 1 minute

1 hot dog (1.6 ounces)
1 hot dog bun, split
  Prepared mustard (optional)
  Pickle relish (optional)

Score opposite sides of hot dog in several places. Place on microproof plate. Place in oven, with hot dog over circle on glass tray. Touch A3. Touch 5. Touch START. *(Oven cooks: 80, about 50 seconds.)*

Place hot dog in bun. Top with mustard and relish. Place in oven as above. Touch START. *(Oven cooks: 80, about 10 seconds.)*

1 serving

Yes, of course, you can cook 2, 3, or 4 hot dogs. The surface-temperature sensor and the oven's computer will automatically increase the cooking time required.

Barbecued Beef-on-a-Bun

Total Cooking Time: 18¾ minutes

1 pound top round steak
¼ cup butter or margarine
1½ tablespoons cornstarch
¼ cup beef broth
¼ cup lemon juice
½ cup chili sauce
1 tablespoon brown sugar
1 tablespoon instant minced onion
1 tablespoon Worcestershire sauce
1 teaspoon prepared horseradish
½ teaspoon salt
¼ teaspoon paprika
¼ teaspoon hot pepper sauce
1 small clove garlic, minced
6 heated buns

Cut steak across grain into very thin strips; set aside. Place butter in 2½-quart microproof casserole. Place in oven. Cook on HI, 45 seconds.

Add steak; stir to coat. Cover. Cook on 50, 5 minutes.

Stir. Cover. Cook on 50, 3 minutes.

Dissolve cornstarch in broth and lemon juice. Add to steak. Add remaining ingredients except buns; blend well. Cover and place in oven. Cook on 50, 10 minutes.

Let stand 2 minutes before spooning onto buns. Serve hot.

6 sandwiches

It's hard to imagine a sandwich that is not improved by warming the buns first. While the beef mixture stands for 2 minutes, place 6 buns on microproof plate. Place in oven, with 1 bun over circle on glass tray. Touch A1. Touch 3. Touch HIGHER. Touch START. (Oven cooks: 80, about 1 minute.)

← *Reuben Sandwich*

```
  A3    5    LOWER
```

Croissant Rougemont

Preset Cooking Time: about 1 minute

    1   croissant
    1   thick slice (2 ounces)
            sharp Cheddar cheese,
            cut in half
    ¼   apple, sliced
        Cinnamon

Cut croissant in half lengthwise. Place bottom half on microproof plate. Top with half of the cheese. Top with apple and then with remaining cheese. Sprinkle with cinnamon. Place in oven with croissant over circle on glass tray. Touch A3. Touch 5. Touch LOWER. Touch START. *(Oven cooks: 80, about 45 seconds.)*.

At Pause, cover with top half of croissant. Touch START. *(Oven cooks: 80, about 15 seconds.)* Serve immediately.

1 serving

This splendid idea comes to us from our friends in Canada. Merci! It suggested a variety of simple-yet-elegant twists with croissants to us, and we'd like to share a few of them with you here.

```
  A3    5    LOWER
```

Chicken Croissant

Preset Cooking Time: about 2¼ minutes

    ¾   cup chopped cooked chicken
            (one-half breast)
    1   hard-cooked egg, chopped
    ¼   cup finely chopped celery
    3   tablespoons mayonnaise
    2   tablespoons thinly sliced
            green onion
    1   tablespoon chopped parsley
    ¼   teaspoon dillweed
        Salt and pepper
    2   croissants
    2   slices (1 ounce each)
            Monterey Jack cheese

Combine chicken, egg, celery, mayonnaise, green onion, parsley, dillweed, salt, and pepper in mixing bowl; blend well. Set aside.

Cut croissants in half lengthwise. Place bottom halves on microproof plate. Top each with half of the chicken mixture. Place 1 slice cheese on each croissant. Place in oven with croissants over circle on glass tray. Touch A3. Touch 5. Touch LOWER. Touch START. *(Oven cooks: 80, about 1¾ minutes.)*

At Pause, cover with top halves of croissants. Touch START. *(Oven cooks: 80, about 30 seconds.)*

2 servings

Here are some other suggestions for croissant fillings: tuna salad, ham salad, pastrami and sauerkraut (squeeze all moisture from sauerkraut), sliced hot dogs and chili, and spinach with mushrooms and cheese. Now it's your turn. Have some fun and surprise your luncheon guests.

```
  A3    5    LOWER
```

Croissant S'Mores

Preset Cooking Time: about 1 minute

    1   croissant
    1   chocolate candy bar
            (1½ ounces)
    5   large marshmallows, cut in
            half

Cut croissant in half lengthwise. Place bottom half on microproof plate. Break chocolate bar in thirds and place on croissant. Top with marshmallow halves. Place in oven over circle on glass tray. Touch A3. Touch 5. Touch LOWER. Touch START. *(Oven cooks: 80, about 45 seconds.)*

At Pause, cover with top half of croissant. Touch START. *(Oven cooks: 80, about 15 seconds.)*

1 serving

Watch the smiles all around when the after-school crowd tries this fun snack. It is so simple that it can be their own recipe. Prepare up to 5 at the same time. The oven automatically determines the correct cooking time.

Croissant Rougemont →
Spicy Apple Drink (page 60)

| A1 | 6 | LOWER | & | A3 | 5 |

Pizza Burgers

Preset Cooking Time: about 9 minutes

- ½ pound lean ground beef
- 1 tablespoon finely chopped onion
- ½ cup pizza sauce
- ¼ teaspoon salt
- Dash pepper
- ⅛ teaspoon cinnamon
- ½ cup (2 ounces) shredded mozzarella cheese, divided
- 4 hamburger buns, split

Crumble beef into 1½-quart microproof casserole. Add onion. Place in oven. Touch A1. Touch 6. Touch LOWER. Touch START. *(Oven cooks: 80, about 5 minutes.)*

At Pause, stir to break up beef; drain. Add pizza sauce, salt, pepper, and cinnamon; blend well. Place in oven. Touch START. *(Oven cooks: 80, about 3 minutes.)*

Stir in ¼ cup cheese. Arrange bottom halves of buns on microwave roasting rack. Top with beef mixture. Sprinkle with remaining cheese. Place in oven, with 1 bun over circle on glass tray. Touch A3. Touch 5. Touch START. *(Oven cooks: 80, about 45 seconds.)*

At Pause, cover with tops of buns. Touch START. *(Oven cooks: 80, about 45 seconds.)*

4 sandwiches

| A3 | 5 |

Hot Tuna Buns

Preset Cooking Time: about 3 minutes

- 1 can (6½ to 7 ounces) tuna, drained and flaked
- 1 cup chopped celery
- ¼ cup mayonnaise
- 2 tablespoons catsup
- 1 teaspoon lemon juice
- Salt and pepper
- 4 hamburger buns, split

Combine tuna, celery, mayonnaise, catsup, and lemon juice. Season with salt and pepper. Spoon mixture onto bottom halves of buns. Place microwave roasting rack in oven. Place sandwiches on rack, with 1 sandwich directly over circle on glass tray, 2 sandwiches toward front of oven, and remaining sandwich toward rear of oven. Touch A3. Touch 5. Touch START. *(Oven cooks: 80, about 2 minutes.)*

At Pause, top sandwiches wtih top halves of buns. Touch START. *(Oven cooks: 80, about 1 minute.)*

4 sandwiches

You can prepare 2 sandwiches using the A3-5 setting with the LOWER key. The oven will automatically adjust the cooking time.

| A1 | 6 | LOWER |

Italian Meatball Sandwich

Preset Cooking Time: about 16 minutes

- 1 pound lean ground beef
- 1 cup cooked rice
- 1 small onion, finely chopped
- 2 large eggs, lightly beaten
- 1 tablespoon Italian seasoning
- 1 jar (15 ounces) spaghetti sauce
- 1 loaf (1 pound) French or Italian bread, cut in half lengthwise
- Grated Parmesan cheese

Combine beef, rice, onion, eggs, and seasoning. Shape into 8 balls. Place 1 meatball on microwave roasting rack and arrange remaining meatballs in ring around center meatball. Place in oven, with center meatball over circle on glass tray. Touch A1. Touch 6. Touch LOWER. Touch START. *(Oven cooks: 80, about 9 minutes.)*

At Pause, transfer meatballs to microproof casserole. Top with sauce. Cover and place in oven. Touch START. *(Oven cooks: 80, about 7 minutes.)*

Spoon meatballs and sauce onto bottom half of loaf. Sprinkle generously with cheese. Cover with top of loaf, slice in half, and serve.

2 sandwiches

A Baker's Dozen

Quick breads, sweet rolls, muffins, and coffee cakes are easy to prepare in the microwave oven. Many breads turn out with excellent texture and flavor, but since there is no heat in the microwave oven cavity, a crust does not develop and they do not brown. We have selected recipes that are well-suited to microwave cooking and you may wish to experiment with your own. There are several recipes included that do well using the surface-temperature sensor method and they are great fun to prepare. Selection and placement of microwave muffin rings, ring molds, and bundt pans is important. To avoid problems, please review the illustrations on page 30. Then you will be ready to add your own baker's dozen to ours.

Breads, such as Zucchini-Nut Bread (page 73) may be tested for doneness just as in conventional cooking (above left). The surface-temperature sensor method is ideal for heating bread and rolls. Use A1-2 or A1-3 and place over circle on glass tray (above). Raising bread dough is a snap. A cup of water helps provide a moist environment (left).

Adapting Your Recipes

When adapting "quick bread" recipes, you will find it necessary to reduce the amount of leavening (baking powder or soda) by about one-quarter the normal amount. A bitter aftertaste is apparent if too much leavening is used in biscuits or muffins. Since foods rise higher in the microwave oven, you will not see a loss in volume from the reduction of baking soda or powder. If a recipe contains buttermilk or sour cream, do not change the amount of soda, since it serves to counteract the sour taste and does not act only as a leavening agent. When using a mix where leavening cannot be reduced, allow the batter or dough to stand about 10 minutes before cooking to reduce some of the gas. Yeast doughs need not be changed but may cook more evenly if cooked in a bundt pan or ring mold rather than the conventional loaf pan. And observe the following tips:

☐ To raise yeast dough, place 1 cup water in 2-cup glass measure. Cook on HI, 3 minutes, or until boiling. Place dough in oven next to water. Set Cook Control at "1" (lowest possible setting) and timer at 10 minutes. When timer beeps, leave dough in oven another 20 minutes, or until double in bulk.

☐ Fill paper-lined muffin cups only half full to allow for muffins rising higher.

☐ You can prepare your own "brown 'n serve" rolls. Bake them in the microwave oven. Brown in the conventional oven just before serving.

☐ When preparing yeast dough, use a glass measure and the temperature probe set at 120°F to heat liquids.

☐ If a baked item appears done to you, open door and check with tester or toothpick, just as you do in conventional cooking. Interrupting the cooking sequence does not change the program. Touch START to resume cooking.

☐ During cooking, some baked goods may begin to rise unevenly. When you notice this, open door and rotate dish about one-quarter turn. Uneven rising is seldom significant because many items are inverted onto a serving dish and the variation in rising disappears.

CONVENIENCE BREADS

Food	Amount	Automatic Sensor Method	Time	Special Notes
Hamburger buns, hot dog rolls, frozen:	1 lb.	A0-0	3½ - 4½ minutes	Use original microproof container, paper plate, or towels. Place on microproof rack, turn over after 2 minutes.
Room temperature	1	A1-3	5 - 10 seconds	Wrap in paper towel.
	2	A1-3	10 - 15 seconds	
	4	A1-3	15 - 20 seconds	
	6	A1-3	20 - 25 seconds	
Doughnuts, sweet rolls, muffins	1	A1-3	10 - 15 seconds	Place on paper plate or towel. Add 15 seconds if frozen.
	2	A1-3	20 - 25 seconds	
	4	A1-3	35 - 40 seconds	
	6	A1-3	45 - 50 seconds	
Whole coffee-cake, frozen:	10 - 13 oz.	A1-3 Higher	1½ - 2 minutes	Place on paper plate or towel.
Room temp.:	10 - 13 oz.	A1-3	1 - 1½ minutes	Place on paper plate or towel.
French bread, frozen:	1 lb.	A1-3	1½ - 2 minutes	Place on paper plate or towel.
Room temp.:	1 lb.	A1-3 Lower	20 - 30 seconds	
English muffins, waffles, frozen: 2	2	A1-2	30 - 45 seconds	Place on paper towels. Toast in toaster after defrosting, if desired.
Corn bread mix:	15 oz.	A9-2	12 - 14 minutes	Use 9" round dish, or microproof muffin tray. Turn dish if rising unevenly. Let stand 5 minutes before serving.

A9   1

Molasses Buttermilk Bread

Preset Cooking Time: about 11 minutes

- ½ cup all-purpose flour
- ½ cup whole wheat flour
- ½ cup cornmeal
- 1 teaspoon baking soda
- ½ teaspoon salt
- 1 cup buttermilk
- ⅓ cup molasses
- 2 tablespoons vegetable oil
- 1 large egg, lightly beaten
- ⅓ cup raisins or currants

Lightly grease 6-cup microproof ring mold. Combine flours, cornmeal, baking soda, and salt. Blend buttermilk, molasses, oil, and egg in separate bowl. Add to flour mixture, blending well. Stir in raisins. Pour batter into prepared mold. Place in oven, with batter positioned over circle on glass tray. Touch A9. Touch 1. Touch START. *(Oven cooks: 70, about 11 minutes.)*

Let stand 10 minutes before turning out of mold onto wire rack. Let cool completely before slicing.

10 to 12 servings

Caramel Nut Sticky Buns

Total Cooking Time: 4 minutes

- ⅓ cup firmly packed brown sugar
- 3 tablespoons butter or margarine
- 1 tablespoon water
- 1 teaspoon cinnamon
- ⅓ cup chopped walnuts or pecans
- 1 package (10 ounces) refrigerator biscuits, separated

Combine brown sugar, butter, water, and cinnamon in 4-cup microproof ring mold. Place in oven. Cook on HI, 1 minute.

Stir in nuts. Cut each biscuit into quarters. Place in brown sugar mixture. Stir carefully to coat each piece. Push biscuits toward outside of mold. Place in oven. Cook on HI, 3 minutes.

Let stand 2 minutes. Pull biscuits apart to serve.

6 servings

Raisin-Nut Ring

Total Cooking Time: 9 minutes

- 3 tablespoons butter or margarine
- ⅓ cup firmly packed brown sugar
- 2 tablespoons corn syrup
- ½ cup chopped walnuts or pecans
- ¼ cup raisins
- 1 package (10 ounces) refrigerator buttermilk biscuits, separated

Place butter in 6-cup microproof ring mold. Place in oven. Cook on HI, 1 minute.

Add brown sugar and corn syrup and spread evenly over bottom of mold. Sprinkle evenly with nuts and raisins. Cook on HI, 1 minute.

Arrange biscuits over nuts and raisins. Cook on 50, 7 minutes. If biscuits begin to rise unevenly, open door and rotate mold one-quarter turn; touch START.

Let stand 3 minutes before inverting mold onto serving plate. Let syrup drizzle down sides of ring before removing mold.

10 servings

A1   4   LOWER

Garlic Parmesan Bread

Preset Cooking Time: 1 minute

- ½ cup butter or margarine, softened
- 2 or 3 cloves garlic, minced, or 1 teaspoon garlic powder
- 1 loaf (1 pound) French, Italian, or sourdough bread
- ½ cup grated Parmesan cheese Paprika

Combine butter and garlic; set aside. Cut loaf into 1-inch thick slices without cutting all the way through. Spread slices with garlic butter. Sprinkle with cheese and paprika. Place loaf on microwave roasting rack. Place in oven. Touch A1. Touch 4. Touch LOWER. Touch START. *(Oven cooks: 80, about 1 minute.) Serve warm.*

12 servings

```
A9   1   LOWER
```

Zucchini-Nut Bread

Preset Cooking Time: about 14 minutes

    1 cup sugar, divided
    2 teaspoons cinnamon
    1 cup grated zucchini
    2 large eggs
  ½ cup vegetable oil
  ½ cup plain yogurt
    1 teaspoon vanilla
 1¾ cups all-purpose flour
  ⅔ cup chopped walnuts
    1 teaspoon baking soda
    1 teaspoon salt

Lightly grease 6-cup microproof ring mold. Combine 2 teaspoons each sugar and cinnamon. Sprinkle over greased surface of mold. Shake to spread evenly; discard excess. Combine remaining sugar, zucchini, eggs, oil, yogurt, and vanilla in mixing bowl. Beat in remaining ingredients. Pour into prepared mold. Place in oven, with batter positioned over circle on glass tray. Touch A9. Touch 1. Touch LOWER. Touch START. *(Oven cooks: 70, about 14 minutes.)* If bread begins to rise unevenly, open door and rotate dish one-half turn; touch START.

Let stand at room temperature 10 minutes before turning out of mold onto wire rack. Let cool completely before slicing.

12 to 18 servings

```
A9   2   LOWER
```

Raisin Bran Muffins

Preset Cooking Time: about 6 minutes

    1 large egg
    1 cup buttermilk
 1¼ cups all-purpose flour
    1 cup raisin bran cereal
  ¾ cup firmly packed brown sugar
  ¼ cup chopped nuts (optional)
  ¼ cup vegetable oil
    1 teaspoon baking soda
  ¼ teaspoon salt

Combine egg and buttermilk. Blend in remaining ingredients. Spoon half of the batter into 6 paper-lined microproof muffin cups, filling cups two-thirds full. Place in oven, with 1 muffin over circle on glass tray. Touch A9. Touch 2. Touch LOWER. Touch START. *(Oven cooks: HI, about 3 minutes.)*

Remove from oven. Fill 6 muffin cups and place in oven as above. Touch A9. Touch 2. Touch LOWER. Touch START. *(Oven cooks: HI, about 3 minutes.)*

Let stand 3 minutes before serving.

12 muffins

```
A9   2   LOWER
```

Oatmeal Muffins

Preset Cooking Time: about 7½ minutes

    3 tablespoons chopped walnuts or
          pecans
    2 tablespoons brown sugar
       Dash nutmeg
  ⅔ cup firmly packed brown sugar
  ½ cup vegetable oil
  ½ cup buttermilk or sour milk
    2 large eggs, beaten
    1 cup all-purpose flour
  ⅔ cup rolled oats
    1 teaspoon baking powder
  ½ teaspoon baking soda
  ½ teaspoon salt

Combine nuts, 2 tablespoons brown sugar, and nutmeg; set aside. Blend ⅔ cup brown sugar with oil, buttermilk, and eggs. Stir in remaining ingredients except nut mixture. Spoon one third of the batter into 6 paper-lined microproof muffin cups, filling cups half full. Sprinkle with one third of the nut mixture. Place in oven, with 1 muffin over circle on glass tray. Touch A9. Touch 2. Touch LOWER. Touch START. *(Oven cooks: HI, about 2½ minutes.)*

Repeat with remaining batter, cooking 6 muffins at a time. Let muffins stand 3 minutes before serving.

18 muffins

← *Zucchini-Nut Bread, Raisin Bran Muffins, Oatmeal Muffins*

A9:0

Honey Corn Bread Ring

Preset Cooking Time: about 13 minutes

       1 cup all-purpose flour
       1 cup cornmeal
     ¾ cup milk
     ⅓ cup honey
     ¼ cup shortening
       2 large eggs
       2 teaspoons baking powder

Lightly grease 6-cup microproof ring mold; set aside. Combine all ingredients; stir just until blended. Pour into prepared mold. Place in oven, with batter positioned over circle on glass tray. T ouch A9. Touch START. *(Oven cooks: 50, about 8 minutes; HI, about 5 minutes.)* If bread begins to rise unevenly, open door and rotate mold one-quarter turn; touch START.

16 servings

English Muffin Bread

Total Cooking Time: 9 minutes

          Cornmeal
       2 cups milk
     ½ cup water
       5 cups all-purpose flour,
             divided
       2 packages active dry yeast
       1 tablespoon sugar
       2 teaspoons salt
     ¼ teaspoon baking soda

Sprinkle two 8½ × 4½-inch microproof loaf pans with cornmeal. Shake out excess. Combine milk and water in 4-cup glass measure. Place in oven. Cook on HI, 3 minutes.

Mix 3 cups flour, yeast, sugar, salt, and baking soda in large bowl. Add warm milk mixture and beat well. Blend in remaining 2 cups flour and stir until dough is stiff. Divide dough between prepared loaf pans. Cover and let rise in warm, draft-free place 45 minutes. Place 1 loaf in oven. Cook on HI, 3 minutes. Rotate pan one-quarter turn. Cook on HI, 3 minutes.

Repeat with remaining loaf. Let stand 5 minutes before removing from pans. Slice loaves thinly and toast before serving.

16 to 20 servings

A9:0

Pineapple Zucchini Bread

Preset Cooking Time: about 16 minutes

     ¾ cup sugar
     ½ cup vegetable oil
       2 large eggs
       1 can (8¼ ounces) crushed
             pineapple
    1¾ cups all-purpose flour
       1 cup grated zucchini
       1 teaspoon cinnamon
     ½ teaspoon baking powder
     ½ teaspoon baking soda
     ½ cup chopped nuts
     ¼ cup graham-cracker crumbs

Grease bottom and sides of 8-cup microproof ring mold. Combine sugar, oil, and eggs. Add pineapple, flour, zucchini, cinnamon, baking powder, and baking soda; mix well. Stir in nuts. Turn into prepared mold. Sprinkle evenly with graham-cracker crumbs. Place in oven, with batter positioned over circle on glass tray. Touch A9. Touch START. *(Oven cooks: 50, about 10 minutes, HI, about 6 minutes.)* If bread begins to rise unevenly, open door and rotate mold one-half turn; touch START.

Let stand 10 minutes before turning out of mold onto wire rack. Cool completely before slicing.

12 to 18 servings

Honey Corn Bread Ring →
Pineapple Zucchini Bread

A9 2 LOWER

Blueberry Muffins

Preset Cooking Time: about 6 minutes

- 1½ cups all-purpose flour
- ⅓ cup firmly packed brown sugar
- 1 teaspoon cinnamon
- ½ teaspoon baking powder
- ½ teaspoon baking soda
- ½ teaspoon salt
- ¾ cup buttermilk
- ¼ cup vegetable oil
- 1 large egg
- ⅔ cup blueberries

Combine flour, brown sugar, cinnamon, baking powder, baking soda, and salt. Add buttermilk, oil, and egg; stir vigorously just until moistened. Fold in blueberries. Spoon half of the batter into 6 paper-lined microproof muffin cups, filling cups two-thirds full. Place in oven, with 1 muffin over circle on glass tray. Touch A9. Touch 2. Touch LOWER. Touch START. *(Oven cooks: HI, about 3 minutes.)*

Remove from oven. Fill 6 muffin cups and place in oven as above. Touch A9. Touch 2. Touch LOWER. Touch START. *(Oven cooks: HI, about 3 minutes.)*

Let muffins stand 2 minutes. Serve warm or cool.

12 muffins

A1 HIGHER & A9 3

Dandy Dumplings

Preset Cooking Time: about 22 minutes

- 1 cup all-purpose flour
- 1½ teaspoons baking powder
- ½ teaspoon salt
- 3 tablespoons shortening
- ½ cup milk
- 1 tablespoon minced parsley
- 2½ cups chicken, beef, or vegetable broth

Combine flour, baking powder, and salt. Cut in shortening until mixture is consistency of coarse meal. Stir in milk and parsley just until moistened; set aside. Pour broth into 1½-quart microproof casserole. Place in oven. Touch A1. Touch HIGHER. Touch START. *(Oven cooks: HI, about 4 minutes.)*

Immediately drop batter into boiling broth by rounded teaspoonfuls. Touch A9. Touch 3. Touch START. *(Oven cooks: HI, about 8 minutes.)*

At Pause, stir mixture carefully. Cover. Touch START. *(Oven cooks: HI, about 10 minutes.)*

Let stand 2 minutes. Transfer dumplings to serving dish with slotted spoon and serve immediately.

16 dumplings

A9:0

Sour Cream Coffeecake

Preset Cooking Time: about 9 minutes

- ½ cup chopped walnuts or pecans
- ⅓ cup firmly packed brown sugar
- 2 tablespoons all-purpose flour
- 2 tablespoons butter or margarine
- ¼ teaspoon cinnamon
- ⅛ teaspoon salt
- ½ cup butter or margarine, softened
- ½ cup sugar
- 2 large eggs
- ½ teaspoon vanilla
- 1½ cups all-purpose flour
- ½ teaspoon baking soda
- ½ teaspoon baking powder
- ½ cup dairy sour cream

Combine nuts, brown sugar, 2 tablespoons flour, 2 tablespoons butter, cinnamon, and salt until crumbly; set aside. Cream ½ cup butter and sugar with electric mixer until light and fluffy. Add eggs and vanilla and blend well. Sift 1½ cups flour, baking soda, and baking powder into another bowl. Beat flour into creamed mixture alternately with sour cream. Spread half of the batter in 8-inch round microproof baking dish. Sprinkle half of the nut mixture over batter. Carefully spread remaining batter on top. Sprinkle with remaining nut mixture. Place in oven. Touch A9. Touch START. *(Oven cooks: 50, about 5 minutes; HI, about 4 minutes.)* If your cake begins to rise unevenly, open door and rotate dish one-quarter turn; touch START.

Let stand 3 minutes before serving.

8 to 10 servings

Ring the Dinner Bell for Meat

Cooking meat in the microwave oven offers tremendous advantages over the conventional range. For juiciness and flavor, the microwave method excels. It also stretches your meat dollar by reducing shrinkage. And you can defrost, cook, and reheat in minutes while your kitchen remains cool and comfortable.

If some of your guests or family prefer beef rare and others medium, the microwave solves the problem. After the roast is carved, just seconds bring slices of rare roast to medium or well done. In addition, meat for the barbecue is enhanced by precooking in the microwave. You get that wonderful charcoal flavor without the long watchful cooking that often results in burned or blackened meat. Microwave roasting methods are similar to dry roasting in your conventional oven. This means that the better, tender cuts of meat are recommended for best results. Less tender cuts should be marinated or tenderized and cooked at low power settings. Easiest of all, both the temperature probe and the surface-temperature sensor contribute to automatic cooking of all kinds of meat recipes.

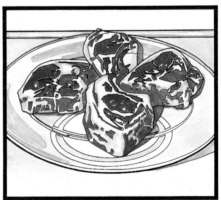

Pot Roast in Sherry (page 85) is just one of the excellent recipes that use the surface-temperature sensor method (above). Lamb chops are shown properly arranged on a plate and placed with meat, not bone, over circle on glass tray for defrosting using the A0-2 program (above right). The temperature probe is properly positioned in Rib Roast (page 86) for automatic cooking (right).

Browning Meat

You can enhance the color and flavor of ground beef patties, steaks, meatloaf, and roasts by using one of the following: microwave browning sauces and powders, powdered brown gravy mix, a liquid browning agent, Worcestershire sauce, soy sauce, steak sauce, paprika, dehydrated onion soup mix, or a microwave browning dish (page 19).

By trimming fat off roasts, and using only lean stewing meat for beef patties and meatloaf, you permit the microwave energy to go directly to the meat itself, rather than the fat. This will achieve more browning. Added fat is not required in microwave cooking.

Using the browning dish for Cheeseburgers (page 63).

Adapting Your Recipes

Guides on the following pages outline microwave thawing and cooking times, and power settings, for most standard meat products. The internal-temperature sensor, the temperature probe, offers many automatic cooking options as well as opportunities for you to select and set your own desired temperatures and power levels. The *Automatic Cooking Guide* for meat is on page 31. Automatic cooking options are also included in the *Guide* on pages 80-83. An *Automatic De-frosting Guide* is on page 79. Please also review the following tips for sure success in cooking meat.

☐ Less tender cuts, such as chuck, bottom round, rump, or brisket can be cooked using the surface-temperature sensor program, A8-3. If used in casseroles, choose A8-0. Stewing meat in liquid calls for A8-2.

☐ Ground beef can be prepared using the A1-6 program. It has a built-in pause for stirring to break up the beef.

☐ The automatic temperature probe program, A4, is best for all tender cuts of meat, as well as meatloaf and pork. Consult the *Guides* on pages 29 and 80-83.

☐ Recipe times here presume meat is at refrigerator temperature. If your meal requires lengthy preparation, during which the meat may reach room temperature, reduce cooking times.

☐ Baste, marinate, or season meat just as you would for conventional cooking.

☐ You can use a microwave roasting rack to elevate meat from its drippings during cooking.

☐ Check dishes that use relatively long cooking times to be sure liquid has not evaporated. Add liquid as necessary.

☐ Most ground beef recipes call for lean meat. If you are using regular ground beef, drain fat before adding sauce ingredients.

Using the Defrosting Guides

1. Remove meat from its original paper or plastic wrappings.
2. Place meat in microproof dish.
3. Defrost in the microwave oven only as long as necessary, since standing time will complete the thawing process. Separate items like chops, bacon, and hot dogs as soon as possible. If pieces are not thawed, distribute evenly in oven and continue defrosting.
4. Slightly increase the time for weights larger than on the chart. Do not double.
5. If you do not plan immediate cooking, follow the guide for only one-half to three-fourths of recommended time. Place meat in refrigerator until needed.

Automatic Defrosting Guide **MEAT**
A0-0 Ground Beef
A0-1 Beef, Lamb, Pork Roasts
A0-2 Steaks, Stewing Meat
A0-3 Chops, Bacon

DEFROSTING GUIDE — MEAT

Meat	Amount	Cook Control Setting	Time (in minutes/ pound)	Standing Time (in minutes)	or	Automatic Sensor Method	Special Notes
Beef							
Ground beef	1-lb.	30 (defrost)	5 - 6	5	or	A0-0	Turn over once. Remove thawed portions with fork. Return remainder.
	2-lbs.	30 (defrost)		5			
	1/4-lb. patty	30 (defrost)	1 per patty	2	or	A0-0	Defrost on plate
Pot roast, chuck	under 4 lbs.	30 (defrost)	3 - 5	10	or	A0-0	Turn over once.
	over 4 lbs.	70 (roast)	3 - 5	10	or	A0-1	Turn over once.
Rib roast, rolled	3 to 4 lbs.	30 (defrost)	6 - 8	30 - 45	or	A0-1	Turn over once.
	6 to 8 lbs.	70 (roast)	6 - 8	90	or	A0-1	Turn over twice.
Rib roast, bone in		70 (roast)	5 - 6	45 - 90	or	A0-1	Turn over twice.
Rump roast	3 to 4 lbs.	30 (defrost)	3 - 5	30	or	A0-1	Turn over once.
	6 to 7 lbs.	70 (roast)	3 - 5	45	or	A0-1	Turn over twice.
Round steak		30 (defrost)	4 - 5	5 - 10	or	A0-1	Turn over once.
Flank steak		30 (defrost)	4 - 5	5 - 10	or	A0-2	Turn over once.
Sirloin steak	1/2" thick	30 (defrost)	4 - 5	5 - 10	or	A0-2	Turn over once.
Tenderloin steak		30 (defrost)	4 - 5	8 - 10	or	A0-2	Turn over once.
Stew beef	2 lbs.	30 (defrost)	3 - 5	8 - 10	or	A0-2	Turn over once. Separate.
Lamb							
Cubed for stew		30 (defrost)	7 - 8	5	or	A0-2	Turn over once. Separate.
Ground lamb	under 4 lbs.	30 (defrost)	3 - 5	30 - 45	or	A0-2	Turn over once.
	over 4 lbs.	70 (roast)	3 - 5	30 - 45	or	A0-0	Turn over twice.
Chops	1" thick	30 (defrost)	5 - 8	15	or	A0-3	Turn over twice.
Leg	5 - 8 lbs.	30 (defrost)	4 - 5	15 - 20	or	A0-1	Turn over twice.
Pork							
Chops	1/2"	30 (defrost)	4 - 6	5 - 10	or	A0-3	Separate chops halfway through defrosting time.
	1"	30 (defrost)	5 - 7	10			
Spareribs, country-style ribs		30 (defrost)	5 - 7	10	or	A0-3 HIGHER	Turn over once.
Roast	under 4 lbs.	30 (defrost)	4 - 5	30 - 45	or	A0-3	Turn over once.
	over 4 lbs.	70 (roast)	4 - 5	30 - 45	or	A0-1	Turn over twice.
Bacon	1-lb.	30 (defrost)	2 - 3	3 - 5	or	A0-3	Defrost until strips separate.
Sausage, bulk	1 lb.	30 (defrost)	2 - 3	3 - 5	or	A0-0	Turn over once. Remove thawed portions with fork.
Sausage links	1 lb.	30 (defrost)	3 - 5	4 - 6	or	A0-3	Turn over once. Defrost until pieces can be separated.
Hot dogs		30 (defrost)	5 - 6	5	or	A0-3	

DEFROSTING GUIDE — MEAT

Meat	Amount	Cook Control Setting	Time (in minutes/ pound)	Standing Time (in minutes)	or	Automatic Sensor Method	Special Notes
Veal							
Roast	3 to 4 lbs.	30 (defrost)	5 - 7	30	or	A0-1	Turn over once.
	6 to 7 lbs.	70 (roast)	5 - 7	90	or	A0-1	Turn over twice.
Chops	1/2" thick	30 (defrost)	4 - 6	20	or	A0-3	Turn over once. Separate chops and continue defrosting.
Variety Meat							
Liver		30 (defrost)	5 - 6	10	or	A0-3	Turn over once.
Tongue		30 (defrost)	7 - 8	10	or	A0-1	Turn over once.

Using the Cooking Guide

1. Meat should be completely thawed before cooking.
2. Trim fat from meat. If recipe recommends, place on microwave roasting rack. Set in microproof baking dish.
3. Meat may be covered lightly with waxed paper to stop splatters.
4. Use the temperature probe for the most accurate cooking of larger cuts. Place probe sensor as horizontally as possible in the densest area, avoiding fat pockets or bone.
5. Unless otherwise noted, times given for steaks and patties will give medium doneness.
6. Ground meat to be used for casseroles should be cooked briefly first; crumble it into a microproof dish and cook covered with a paper towel. Then drain off any fat and add meat to casserole.
7. During standing time, the internal temperature of roasts will rise between 5°F and 15°F. Hence, standing time is considered an essential part of the time required to complete cooking.
8. Cutlets and chops that are breaded are cooked at the same time and cook control setting as shown on chart for unbreaded.

COOKING GUIDE — MEAT

Meat	Amount	First Cook Control Setting And Time	Second Cook Control Setting And Time	or	Automatic Sensor Method	Standing Time (in minutes)	Special Notes
Beef							
Ground beef	Bulk	HI (max. power) 2½ minutes per pound	Stir. HI (max. power) 2½ minutes per pound	or	A1-6	5	Crumble in dish, cook covered.
Ground beef patties, 4 oz., 1/2" thick	1	HI (max. power) 1 minute	Turn over. HI (max. power) 1 - 1½ minutes		not applicable		Shallow baking dish.
	2	HI (max. power) 1 - 1½ minutes	Turn over. HI (max. power) 1 - 1½ minutes				Shallow baking dish.
	4	HI (max. power) 3 minutes	Turn over. HI (max. power) 3 - 3½ minutes				Shallow baking dish.
Meatloaf	2 lbs.	HI (max. power) 12 - 14 minutes		or	A4-0	5 - 10	

COOKING GUIDE — MEAT

Meat	Amount	First Cook Control Setting And Time	Second Cook Control Setting And Time	or	Automatic Sensor Method	Standing Time (in minutes)	Special Notes
Beef rib roast, boneless		HI (max. power) Rare: 4 - 5 minutes per pound Medium: 5 - 6 minutes per pound Well: 6 - 7 minutes per pound	Turn over. 70 (roast) 3 - 4 minutes per pound 5 - 6 minutes per pound 6 - 7 minutes per pound	or	A4-1 A4-2 A4-3	10 10 10	Glass baking dish with microproof roasting rack.
Rib roast, bone in		HI (max. power) Rare: 3 - 4 minutes per pound Medium: 4 - 5 minutes per pound Well: 5 - 6 minutes per pound	Turn over. 70 (roast) 3 - 4 minutes per pound 3 - 5 minutes per pound 5 - 6 minutes per pound	or	A4-1 A4-2 A4-3	10	Glass baking dish with microproof roasting rack.
Beef rump, other less tender cuts		HI (max. power) 5 minutes per pound	Turn over. 50 (simmer) 10 minutes	or	A8-3	10 - 15	Casserole with tight cover. Requires liquid.
Beef brisket, boneless, fresh or corned	2½ - 3½ lbs.	HI (max. power) 5 minutes per pound	Turn over. 50 (simmer) 20 minutes per pound	or	A8-3	10 - 15	4-quart casserole Dutch oven with tight cover. Water to cover.
Top round steak		HI (max. power) 5 minutes per pound	Turn over. 50 (simmer) 5 minutes per pound		not applicable	10 - 15	Casserole with tight cover. Requires liquid.
Sirloin steak	3/4 to 1" thick	HI (max. power) 4½ minutes per pound	Drain dish and turn over. HI (max. power) 2 minutes per pound		not applicable	10 - 15	Shallow cooking dish or browning dish preheated
Minute steak or cube steak,	4, 6-oz. steaks	HI (max. power) 1 - 2 minutes	Drain dish and turn over. HI (max. power) 1 - 2 minutes		not applicable		Browning dish preheated on HI (max. power)
Tenderloin	4, 8-oz. steaks	HI (max. power) Rare: 5 minutes Med: 6 minutes Well: 9 minutes	Drain, turn steak. HI (max. power) 1 - 2 minutes 2 - 3 minutes 2 - 3 minutes		not applicable	10 - 15	Browning dish preheated on HI (max. power)
Rib eye or strip steak	1½ to 2 lbs.	HI (max. power) Rare: 4 minutes Med: 5 minutes Well: 7 minutes	Drain, turn steak. HI (max. power) ½ - 1 minute 1 - 2 minutes 2 - 3 minutes		not applicable	10 - 15	Browning dish preheated on HI (max. power)
Lamb Ground lamb patties	1 - 2 lbs.	HI (max. power) 4 minutes	Turn over. HI (max. power) 4 - 5 minutes		not applicable		Browning dish preheated on HI (max. power)
Lamb chops	1 - 1½ lbs. 1" thick	HI (max. power) 8 minutes	Turn over. HI (max. power) 7 - 8 minutes		not applicable		Browning dish preheated on HI (max. power)
Lamb leg or shoulder roast, bone in		70 (roast) Medium: 4 - 5 minutes per pound Well: 5 - 6 minutes per pound	Cover end of leg bone with foil. Turn over. 70 (roast) Medium: 4 - 5 minutes per pound Well: 5 - 6 minutes per pound	or or	A4-4 A4-5	5 10	12 × 7-inch dish with microproof roasting rack.

COOKING GUIDE — MEAT

Meat	Amount	First Cook Control Setting And Time	Second Cook Control Setting And Time	or	Automatic Sensor Method	Standing Time (in minutes)	Special Notes
Lamb roast, boneless		70 (roast) 5 - 6 minutes per pound	Turn over. 70 (roast) 5 - 6 minutes per pound	or	A4-4	10	12 × 7-inch dish with microproof roasting rack.
Veal: Shoulder or rump roast, boneless	2 - 5 lbs.	70 (roast) 9 minutes per pound	Turn over. 70 (roast) 9 - 10 minutes per pound	or	A4-3	10	12 × 7-inch dish with microproof roasting rack.
Veal cutlets or loin chops	1/2" thick	HI (max. power) 2 minutes per pound	Turn over. HI (max. power) 2 - 3½ minutes per pound		not applicable		Browning dish preheated on HI (max. power)
Pork: Pork chops	1/2" thick	HI (max. power) 6 minutes per pound	Turn over. HI (max. power) 5 - 6 minutes per pound		not applicable	5	Browning dish preheated on HI (max. power)
Spareribs		70 (roast) 6 - 7 minutes per pound	Turn over. 70 (roast) 6 - 7 minutes	or	A8-3	10	12 × 7-inch dish with microproof roasting rack.
Pork loin roast, boneless	3 - 5 lbs.	HI (max. power) 6 minutes per pound	Turn over 70 (roast) 5 - 6 minutes per pound	or	A4-6	10	12 × 7-inch dish with microproof roasting rack.
Pork loin, center cut	4 - 5 lbs.	HI (max. power) 5 - 6 minutes per pound	Turn over. 4 - 5 minutes per pound 70 (roast)	or	A4-6	10	13 × 9-inch dish with microproof roasting rack.
Ham, boneless, precooked		70 (roast) 5 - 7 minutes per pound	Turn over. 70 (roast) 5 - 7 minutes per pound	or	A4-7	10	12 × 7-inch dish with microproof roasting rack.
Center cut ham slice	1 - 1½ lbs.	70 (roast) 5 minutes per pound	Turn over. 70 (roast) 5 - 6 minutes per pound	or	A4-7	10	12 × 7-inch baking dish.
Smoked ham shank		70 (roast) 4 - 5 minutes per pound	Turn over. 70 (roast) 4 - 5 minutes per pound	or	A4-7	10	12 × 7-inch dish with microproof roasting rack.
Canned ham	3 lbs.	70 (roast) 5 - 6 minutes per pound	70 (roast) 5 - 6 minutes per pound	or	A4-7	10	12 × 7-inch dish with microproof roasting rack.
	5 lbs.	70 (roast) 4 - 5 minutes per pound	Turn over. 70 (roast) 4 - 5 minutes per pound	or	A47	10	12 × 7-inch dish with microproof roasting rack.
Sausage patties	12-oz.	HI (max. power) 2 minutes	Turn over. HI (max. power) 1½ - 2 minutes per pound		not applicable		Browning dish preheated on HI (max. power)
Sausage	16 oz.	HI (max. power) 3 minutes	Stir. HI (max. power) 1 - 2 minutes	or	A1-6		Crumble into 1½-quart dish, covered.
Pork sausage links	1/2 lb.	Pierce casing HI (max. power) 1 minute	Turn over. HI (max. power) 1 - 1½ minutes	or	A3-5		Browning dish preheated on HI (max. power)
	1 lb.	HI (max. power) 2 minutes	HI (max. power) 1½ - 2 minutes				

COOKING GUIDE — MEAT

Meat	Amount	First Cook Control Setting And Time	Second Cook Control Setting And Time	or	Automatic Sensor Method	Standing Time (in minutes)	Special Notes
Bratwurst, precooked		Pierce casing 70 (roast) 5 minutes per pound	Rearrange. 70 (roast) 4 - 5 minutes per pound	or	A3-5		Casserole.
Polish sausage, knockwurst, ring bologna		Pierce casing 80 (reheat) 2 - 2½ minutes per pound	Rearrange 80 (reheat) 2 - 2½ minutes per pound	or	A3-5		Casserole.
Hot dogs	1	80 (reheat) 25 - 30 seconds		or	A3-5		Shallow dish.
	2	80 (reheat) 25 - 40 seconds		or	A3-5		Shallow dish.
	4	80 (reheat) 50 - 55 seconds		or	A3-5		Shallow dish.
Bacon	2 slices	HI (max. power) 2 - 2½ minutes		or	A2-4		Dish; slices between paper towels
	4 slices	HI (max. power) 4 - 4½ minutes		or	A2-4		Dish; slices between paper towels
	6 slices	HI (max. power) 5 - 6 minutes		or	A2-4		Roasting rack, slices covered with paper towels
	8 slices	HI (max. power) 6 - 7 minutes		or	A2-4		Roasting rack, slices covered with paper towels

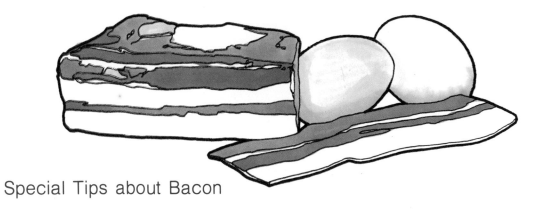

Special Tips about Bacon

☐ Cook bacon on a paper towel-lined plate, and cover with paper towels to prevent splatters and absorb drippings.

☐ To reserve drippings, cook bacon on a microwave roasting rack in a microproof baking dish or on a microwave bacon rack. Bacon can also be cooked, in slices or cut up, in a casserole and removed, if necessary, with a slotted spoon.

☐ For bacon that is soft rather than crisp, cook at the minimum timing.

☐ Bacon varies in quality. The thickness and amount of sugar and salt used in curing will affect browning and timing. Thicker slices take a bit longer to cook.

☐ Sugar in bacon causes brown spots to appear on the paper towels. If the bacon tends to stick a bit to the towel, it is due to an extra high amount of sugar.

☐ The surface-temperature sensor program for cooking bacon automatically is A2-4. If a dish is used, line and cover as described above. If using a microwave roasting rack, cover with a paper towel.

COOKING/DEFROSTING GUIDE — CONVENIENCE BEEF
For Automatic Sensor Method see Page 29

Food	Amount	Cook Control Setting	Time (in minutes)	or	Temperature Probe Setting	Special Notes
Barbecued beef, chili, stew, hash, meatballs, etc.	16 oz. or less (cans)	80 (reheat)	3 - 5	or	150°	Remove from cans to microproof plate or casserole, cover. Stir halfway through cooking time.
Peppers, cabbage rolls, chow mein, etc.	over 16 - 32 oz. (cans)	80 (reheat)	5 - 9	or	150°	
Barbecued beef, chili, stew, corned beef hash, meatballs, patties in sauce, gravy	8 - 16 oz. package (frozen)	HI (max. power)	5 - 11	or	150°	Remove from foil container to microproof casserole, cover. Slit plastic pouches
Dry casserole mixes, cooked hamburger added	6½ - 8 oz. package	HI (max. power)	18 - 22	or	150°	Remove mix from package to 3-quart microproof casserole. Cover. Stir once.

Horseradish-Onion Beef Roast

Total Cooking Time: 21 minutes

- 1 beef round rump roast, boneless (3½ pounds)
- ½ cup prepared horseradish
- 1 tablespoon steak sauce
- 1 clove garlic, minced
- 1 envelope (1½ ounces) onion soup mix, divided
- ¼ cup cold water
- 2 tablespoons all-purpose flour
  Dash pepper

Remove string from roast. Cut roast in half horizontally without cutting all the way through; open gently. Slash inside of roast all over without cutting all the way through. Combine horseradish, steak sauce, and garlic. Spread over cut surfaces of roast. Press cut surfaces together; tie roast securely with string. Place in shallow 2½- to 3-quart microproof baking dish. Sprinkle with half of the soup mix. Place in oven. Cover with waxed paper. Cook on 70, 10 minutes.

Turn roast over. Cover. Cook on 70, 7 minutes.

Transfer roast to warmed serving platter. Cover with aluminum foil to keep warm while preparing gravy. (Internal temperature of roast will rise to 140°F, medium rare.)

Pour drippings into 4-cup glass measure; skim fat. Add water to equal 1 cup liquid. Combine remaining soup mix, ¼ cup cold water, and flour; blend well. Stir into drippings. Place in oven. Cook on HI, 2 minutes.

Whisk through several times. Cook on HI, 2 minutes.

Add pepper; stir vigorously. Slice roast. Pass gravy separately.

6 to 8 servings

A3	3	HIGHER

Barbecued Beef, Chili, Stew, Hash, Meatballs

Preset Cooking Time: about 8 minutes

- 1 can (16 ounces) barbecued beef, chili, stew, hash, or meatballs

Pour beef mixture into microproof casserole. Place in oven. Touch A3. Touch 3. Touch HIGHER. Touch START. *(Oven cooks: 80, about 4 minutes.)*

At Pause, stir. Touch START. *(Oven cooks: 80, about 4 minutes.)*

1 to 2 servings

A8	3

Boiled Beef Carbonnade

Preset Cooking Time: about 1 hour 19 minutes

- 1 lean beef heel or round roast (3 pounds)
- 1 small onion, sliced
- 1 medium carrot, sliced
- 5 peppercorns
- 1/8 teaspoon white pepper
- 1 bay leaf
- 1 can (12 ounces) beer
  Salt

Place roast, onion, carrot, peppercorns, pepper, and bay leaf in 4-quart microproof casserole. Pour in beer. Add water to cover. Cover and place in oven. Touch A8. Touch 3. Touch START. *(Oven cooks: 70, about 19 minutes; 50, about 30 minutes.)*

At Pause, turn roast over. Add water, if necessary, to cover roast. Cover. Touch START. *(Oven cooks: 30, 30 minutes.)*

Let stand 10 minutes. Strain broth; skim fat. Slice roast thinly. Season with salt, and serve with broth.

6 servings

Tenderloin of Beef Supreme

Total Cooking Time: 15 minutes

- 1 beef loin tenderloin roast (2 pounds)
- 3 tablespoons onion soup mix
- 1/2 pound fresh mushrooms, sliced

Place roast in shallow microproof baking dish. Pat soup mix over entire surface. Arrange mushrooms on top. Place in oven. Cover with waxed paper. Cook on HI, 5 minutes.

Turn roast over. Spoon juices and mushrooms over roast. Cover. Cook on HI, 5 minutes, then on 70, 5 minutes, or until desired doneness.

Let stand 5 minutes before serving.

4 servings

A8	3

Pot Roast in Sherry

Preset Cooking Time: about 1 hour 5 minutes

- 1 lean beef chuck roast (3 to 4 pounds)
- 1 envelope (1 1/2 ounces) onion soup mix
- 1/2 cup dry sherry
- 1/2 cup beef broth

Trim fat from roast. Sprinkle roast with soup mix. Cut a 1-inch strip from open end of cooking bag. Place roast in bag; place in shallow microproof baking dish. Pour sherry and broth over roast. Tie bag loosely with removed strip. Place in oven. Touch A8. Touch 3. Touch START. *(Oven cooks: 70, about 10 minutes; 50, about 30 minutes.)*

At Pause, carefully turn bag over to baste roast with drippings. Touch START. *(Oven cooks: 30, 25 minutes.)*

Squeeze sides of bag several times to baste roast with juices. Use drippings to make Easy Gravy (page 170), if desired.

6 to 8 servings

A4   1

Rib Roast, bone in (rare)

Preset Cooking Time: about 30 minutes

　1　envelope (1½ ounces) onion
　　　soup mix
　1　rib roast, bone in (5 pounds)
　1　pound mushrooms, sliced

　Rub soup mix all over roast. Place roast, fat-side down, on microwave roasting rack in shallow microproof baking dish. Sprinkle mushrooms over top and sides of roast. Insert temperature probe horizontally into densest part of roast without touching fat or bone. Place in oven. Plug in probe. Cover roast lightly with waxed paper. Touch A4. Touch 1. Touch START. *(Oven cooks: HI, to 90°F.)*

　At Pause, turn roast over, being careful not to remove temperature probe. Spoon juices and mushrooms over top. Cover. Touch START. *(Oven cooks: 70, to 120°F; stands: 0, 10 minutes.)* Internal temperature of roast will rise to approximately 135°F during preset standing time.

6 to 8 servings

Use A4-1 for any type of beef roast you'd like done rare. Use A4-2 for medium beef roast. Use A4-3 for well-done beef roast.

A4   2

Rib Roast, bone in (medium)

Preset Cooking Time: about 35 minutes

　1　envelope (1½ ounces) onion
　　　soup mix
　1　rib roast, bone in (5 pounds)
　1　pound mushrooms, sliced

　Rub soup mix all over roast. Place roast, fat-side down, on microwave roasting rack in shallow microproof baking dish. Sprinkle mushrooms over top and sides of roast. Insert temperature probe horizontally into densest part of roast without touching fat or bone. Place in oven. Plug in probe. Cover roast lightly with waxed paper. Touch A4. Touch 2. Touch START. *(Oven cooks: HI, to 90°F.)*

　At Pause, turn roast over, being careful not to remove temperature probe. Spoon juices and mushrooms over top. Cover. Touch START. *(Oven cooks: 70, to 130°F; stands: 0, 10 minutes.)* Internal temperature of roast will rise to approximately 145°F during preset standing time.

6 to 8 servings

If your family prefers well-done beef, touch A4, then touch 3. The size of the roast really doesn't matter. Like all automatic cooking with either the internal-temperature sensor or the surface-temperature sensor, you can vary weights and quantities to suit your needs.

Rare Rib Roast goes great with a green salad →

Pepper Steak

Total Cooking Time: 16¾ minutes

> 1 top round steak (1½ pounds),
>   ½ inch thick
> 1 tablespoon vegetable oil
> 1 clove garlic, minced
> 2 teaspoons cornstarch
> 2 tablespoons soy sauce
> 2 green peppers, cut into 1-inch
>   squares (2 cups)
> 1 cup thinly sliced onions
> 2 large stalks celery, sliced
> ½ cup water
> 1 jar (2 ounces) chopped pimiento,
>   drained
> 1 teaspoon instant beef bouillon
>   granules
> 1 teaspoon salt
> ¼ teaspoon pepper

Cut steak into ¼-inch wide strips; set aside. Pour oil into 2-quart microproof casserole. Place in oven.   Cook on HI, 45 seconds.

Add steak and garlic; stir to coat. Cook on 50, 7 minutes.

Cover. Cook on 50, 3 minutes.

Dissolve cornstarch in soy sauce. Stir into steak mixture. Blend in remaining ingredients. Cover. Cook on HI, 6 minutes.

Let stand 5 minutes before serving.

4 servings

Beef Roulade

Total Cooking Time: 49 minutes

> 1 top round steak (2 pounds),
>   ½ inch thick
> ½ cup chopped celery with leaves
> ¼ cup chopped onion
> 2 tablespoons butter or margarine
> 1 cup soft bread crumbs
> ¼ teaspoon rosemary
> ¼ teaspoon thyme
> ¼ teaspoon pepper
> 1 can (10¾ ounces) cream of
>   mushroom soup, undiluted

Pound steak with meat mallet. Cut into six 3-inch strips; set aside. Combine celery, onion, and butter in glass measure. Place in oven. Cook on HI, 4 minutes.

Blend in bread crumbs, rosemary, thyme, and pepper. Spread over steak strips. Roll strips around stuffing; fasten with wooden

toothpicks. Arrange in round or oval micro-proof baking dish. Spoon soup over beef rolls. Place in oven. Cook on 50, 20 minutes.

Turn beef rolls over and rearrange. Spoon soup over rolls. Cook on 50, 25 minutes. Let stand 5 minutes before serving.

6 servings

A8:0   LOWER

Oriental Beef

Preset Cooking Time: about 19 minutes

> ½ cup soy sauce
> ½ cup dry sherry
> ½ cup water
> 1 tablespoon sugar
> 1 clove garlic, minced
> 2 thin slices fresh ginger, minced
> 1 sirloin steak, boneless (1½ to
>   2 pounds), cut into
>   thin strips
> ½ medium bunch broccoli
> ½ pound bean sprouts
> 6 green onions, cut into 2-inch
>   pieces
> 1 can (5 ounces) sliced water
>   chestnuts, drained

Combine soy sauce, sherry, water, sugar, garlic, and ginger in 2-quart microproof casserole. Add steak and stir to coat. Cover and let stand at room temperature 2 hours, stirring occasionally. Cut broccoli stems diagonally into thin slices; break florets into individual pieces. Rinse bean sprouts in cool water and drain. Combine broccoli, bean sprouts, green onions, and water chestnuts. Push marinated steak to center of casserole. Arrange vegetables around steak. Cover and place in oven. Touch A8. Touch LOWER. Touch START. *(Oven cooks: HI, about 4 minutes.)*

At Pause, stir. Touch START. *(Oven cooks: 50, about 10 minutes; stands: 0, 5 minutes.)* Serve with hot rice.

4 to 6 servings

You can substitute 1 thawed package (10 ounces) frozen broccoli spears for fresh broccoli. If fresh bean sprouts are unavailable, substitute 2 cups drained canned bean sprouts.

A8 3

Tomato Swiss Steak

Preset Cooking Time: about 1 hour
10 minutes

- ¼ cup all-purpose flour
- 1 teaspoon salt
- ¼ teaspoon pepper
- 1 round or flank steak (1 pound),
  ½ inch thick
- 1 can (6 ounces) tomato paste
- 1 large onion, sliced
- ½ green pepper, seeded and cut
  into strips
- 1 cup beef broth, or 1 beef
  bouillon cube dissolved in
  1 cup water

Combine flour, salt, and pepper. Place steak on work surface. Pound half of the flour mixture into both sides of steak with meat mallet. Cut steak in half. Place in 8-inch round or oval microproof baking dish. Sprinkle with remaining flour mixture. Spread tomato paste over steak. Top with onion and green pepper. Add broth to cover. Double wrap with plastic wrap. Place in oven. Touch A8. Touch 3. Touch START. *(Oven cooks: 70, about 15 minutes; 50, about 25 minutes.)*

At Pause, turn steak over and spoon onion and green pepper over top. Double wrap with plastic wrap. Touch START. *(Oven cooks: 30, 30 minutes.)* Serve immediately.

2 servings

A4:0

Favorite Meatloaf

Preset Cooking Time: about 17 minutes

- 1 can (8 ounces) tomato sauce
- ¼ cup firmly packed brown sugar
- 1 teaspoon prepared mustard
- 2 pounds lean ground beef
- ¼ cup cracker crumbs
- 2 large eggs, lightly beaten
- 1 medium onion, minced
- 1 teaspoon salt
- ¼ teaspoon pepper

Combine tomato sauce, brown sugar, and mustard; set aside. Combine remaining ingredients. Blend in ½ cup tomato sauce mixture. Pat beef mixture into 8-cup microproof ring mold or 9 × 15-inch microproof loaf pan. Pour remaining tomato sauce mixture over top. Insert temperature probe into center of meatloaf. Place in oven. Plug in probe. Touch A4. Touch START. *(Oven cooks: HI, to 160°F; stands: 0, 10 minutes.)*

6 servings

Enchilada Casserole

Total Cooking Time: 15 minutes

- 1¾ pounds lean ground beef
- 1 large onion, chopped
- 2 cloves garlic, minced
- 1 can (16 ounces) tomato purée
- 1 envelope (1⅝ ounces) taco
  seasoning mix
- 6 corn tortillas
- 3 cups (12 ounces) shredded Cheddar
  cheese, divided

Crumble beef into 2-quart glass measure. Add onion and garlic; mix lightly. Place in oven. Cook on HI, 3 minutes.

Stir through several times. Cook on HI, 2 minutes.

Stir in purée and seasoning mix. Cook on HI, 3 minutes.

Layer tortillas, beef mixture, and 2½ cups cheese in 2-quart round microproof casserole. Cover and place in oven. Cook on HI, 7 minutes.

Sprinkle with remaining ½ cup cheese. Cut into wedges to serve.

4 to 6 servings

Beef Shanghai

Total Cooking Time: 9 minutes

    2 tablespoons vegetable oil
    1 top round or sirloin steak,
        boneless (1 pound), cut into
        thin strips
    1 can (16 ounces) whole tomatoes,
        broken up
    1 medium onion, finely chopped
    1 clove garlic, minced
    ½ teaspoon salt
    ⅛ teaspoon pepper
    2 large green peppers, seeded and
        cut into thin strips
    2 teaspoons cornstarch
    2 tablespoons soy sauce

Pour oil into 3-quart microproof casse-role. Add beef; stir to coat. Mix in tomatoes, onion, garlic, salt, and pepper. Cover and place in oven. Cook on HI, 2 minutes.
Stir; cover. Cook on HI, 2 minutes.
Add green peppers. Dissolve cornstarch in soy sauce. Stir into beef mixture. Cover. Cook on HI, 5 minutes.
Serve over hot rice. Top with chow mein noodles, if desired.

4 servings

Stuffed Green Peppers

Total Cooking Time: 15 minutes

    4 large green peppers
    1 pound lean ground beef
    1 small onion, finely chopped
    1 large clove garlic, minced
    2 tablespoons celery, chopped
    ½ cup cooked rice
    1 egg
    1 cup tomato sauce, divided
    3 tablespoons chopped parsley
    1 tablespoon Worcestershire
        sauce
    ¼ teaspoon salt
    ¼ teaspoon pepper

Wash green peppers. Remove tops and seeds. Set aside, upside down, on paper towel to drain.
Place beef, onion, garlic, and celery in 2-quart microproof bowl. Place in oven. Cook on HI, 3 minutes.
Stir. Cook on HI, 2 minutes.

Add rice, egg, ¾ cup tomato sauce, parsley, Worcestershire, salt, and pepper; blend well. Fill peppers with mixture, mounding on top. Arrange peppers in circle in round microproof baking dish just large enough to accommodate. Cover with plastic wrap. Place in oven. Cook on 70, 10 minutes.
Spread 1 tablespoon reserved tomato sauce on top of each pepper before serving.

4 servings

If you prefer your peppers cooked a bit more, continue to cook on 70, 2 to 4 minutes, or until done.

A8	3

Short Ribs of Beef

Preset Cooking Time: about 1 hour
                              10 minutes

    2 pounds meaty beef chuck short
        ribs
    1 medium onion, sliced
    4 medium potatoes, peeled and cut
        in half
    4 medium carrots, cut into 1-inch
        chunks
    1 clove garlic, minced
    ½ teaspoon salt
    ½ cup dry red wine
    1 tablespoon microwave browning
        sauce

Arrange ribs, bone-side up, in 3-quart microproof casserole. Arrange onion over ribs. Arrange potatoes and carrots around ribs. Sprinkle with garlic and salt. Combine wine and browning sauce; pour over ribs and vegetables. Cover and place in oven. Touch A8. Touch 3. Touch START. *(Oven cooks: 70, about 10 minutes; 50, about 30 minutes.)*
At Pause, rearrange vegetables and ribs. Touch START. *(Oven cooks: 30, about 30 minutes.)*

4 servings

*Stuffed Green Peppers, Spaghetti Squash →
(Guide, page 152)*

A8   2   LOWER

Hungarian Goulash

Preset Cooking Time: about 1 hour
30 minutes

  2 pounds beef for stew, cut
     into 1-inch cubes
  4 large tomatoes, peeled and cut
     into chunks
  1 medium onion, coarsely chopped
1½ tablespoons paprika
  ½ teaspoon salt
  ½ teaspoon pepper
  1 container (8 ounces) dairy
     sour cream

Combine beef, tomatoes, onion, paprika, salt, and pepper in 3-quart microproof casserole. Cover and place in oven. Touch A8. Touch 2. Touch LOWER. Touch START. *(Oven cooks: 70, about 27 minutes.)*

At Pause, stir. Touch START. *(Oven cooks: 50, about 1 hour 3 minutes.)*

Stir in sour cream. Serve over hot noodles.

4 to 6 servings

Zucchini Lasagna

Total Cooking Time: 31 minutes

  6 cups sliced zucchini
  ¼ cup water
  1 pound lean ground beef
  2 cans (8 ounces each) tomato
     sauce
  ¼ pound mushrooms, chopped
  1 small onion, minced
  1 clove garlic, minced
  1 teaspoon basil
  ½ teaspoon oregano
  ½ teaspoon thyme
  ½ teaspoon salt
  ¼ teaspoon pepper
  ¼ cup dry bread crumbs
 12 ounces low-fat cottage cheese,
     drained
  1 cup (4 ounces) shredded
     mozzarella cheese
  ⅓ cup grated Parmesan cheese

Place zucchini and water in 1½-quart microproof casserole. Cover and place in oven. Cook on HI, 7 minutes.

Drain zucchini and set aside. Crumble beef into 2-quart glass measure. Place in oven. Cook on HI, 4 minutes.

Stir to break up beef; drain. Add tomato sauce. Blend in mushrooms, onion, garlic, and seasonings. Place in oven. Cook on HI, 8 minutes.

Layer one-third of the zucchini in 11 × 7-inch microproof baking dish. Sprinkle with 1 tablespoon bread crumbs. Top with one-third of the beef mixture and half of the cottage cheese and mozzarella cheese. Repeat layers once. Top with remaining zucchini, beef mixture, and bread crumbs. Sprinkle with Parmesan cheese. Place in oven. Cover with waxed paper. Cook on HI, 12 minutes.

Let stand, covered, 5 minutes before serving.

8 to 10 servings

A1   6   LOWER   &   A2   2

Meatballs a la Russe

Preset Cooking Time: about 17 minutes

1½ pounds lean ground beef
  ½ cup milk
  1 envelope (1½ ounces) onion soup
     mix, divided
  3 tablespoons all-purpose flour
1½ cups water
  2 tablespoons chopped parsley
  ½ cup dairy sour cream, at room
     temperature

Combine beef, milk, and 2 tablespoons soup mix in bowl. Shape into 24 small balls. Place in 3-quart oval microproof baking dish. Place in oven. Touch A1. Touch 6. Touch LOWER. Touch START. *(Oven cooks: 80, about 8 minutes.)*

At Pause, turn meatballs over. Touch START. *(Oven cooks: 80, about 4 minutes.)*

Remove meatballs from dish with slotted spoon and set aside. Dissolve flour in water. Stir flour mixture, parsley, and remaining soup mix into drippings in baking dish. Place in oven. Touch A2. Touch 2. Touch START. *(Oven cooks: HI, about 3 minutes.)*

At Pause, stir in meatballs, coating well with sauce. Touch START. *(Oven cooks: HI, about 2 minutes.)*

Blend in sour cream. Let stand 5 minutes. Serve over hot rice or noodles.

6 servings

```
       A8    2
```

Beef Stew

Preset Cooking Time: about 2 hours

- 2 pounds beef for stew, trimmed and cut into 1½-inch cubes
- ¼ teaspoon salt
- 1 envelope (1½ ounces) brown gravy mix with mushrooms
- 1½ cups water
- 3 medium stalks celery, cut into 1-inch chunks
- 4 medium carrots, cut into chunks
- 4 medium potatoes, peeled and cut in half
- 1 large onion, sliced

Arrange beef in 3-quart microproof casserole. Sprinkle with salt. Blend gravy mix with water. Pour over beef. Cover and place in oven. Touch A8. Touch 2. Touch START. *(Oven cooks: 70, about 30 minutes.)*

At Pause, stir in vegetables, coating evenly with sauce. Cover. Touch START. *(Oven cooks: 50, about 1 hour 30 minutes.)*

4 to 6 servings

Beef Stew can be stored frozen in a covered shallow container. Defrost on 30, 10 minutes, stirring several times. Increase power to 70 and cook 20 minutes, or until heated through.

```
   A1   6   &   A1   6   HIGHER
```

Chili con Carne

Preset Cooking Time: about 19 minutes

- 1 pound lean ground beef
- ½ cup minced onions
- ½ cup chopped green pepper
- 1 clove garlic, minced
- 1 can (16 ounces) whole tomatoes, broken up
- 1 can (16 ounces) kidney beans
- 1 to 2 tablespoons chili powder, to taste
- 1 teaspoon salt

Crumble beef into 2-quart microproof casserole. Add onions, green pepper, and garlic. Place in oven. Touch A1. Touch 6. Touch START. *(Oven cooks: 80, about 6 minutes.)*

At Pause, stir. Touch START. *(Oven cooks: 80, about 4 minutes.)*

Remove from oven; drain. Add remaining ingredients; blend well. Cover and place in oven. Touch A1. Touch 6. Touch HIGHER. Touch START. *(Oven cooks: 80, about 5 minutes.)*

At Pause, stir. Cover. Touch START. *(Oven cooks: 80, about 4 minutes.)*

Let stand 5 minutes before serving.

4 servings

```
   A7   1   LOWER   &   A8:0
```

Stuffed Cabbage

Preset Cooking Time: about 31 minutes

- 1 head cabbage (about 1½ pounds), cored, blemished leaves discarded
- ¼ cup water
- 1 pound lean ground beef
- ½ pound ground pork
- ¾ cup cooked rice
- 1 large egg, lightly beaten
- 1 tablespoon chopped parsley
- 1 clove garlic, minced
- ½ teaspoon salt
- ¼ teaspoon pepper
- ½ teaspoon thyme
- ¼ cup butter or margarine
- 2 cans (8 ounces each) tomato sauce

Place cabbage and water in 3-quart microproof casserole. Cover and place in oven. Touch A7. Touch 1. Touch LOWER. Touch START. *(Oven cooks: HI, about 6 minutes.)*

Drain cabbage well; let cool slightly. Separate 6 to 8 large outside leaves, discarding tough centers. Combine beef, pork, rice, egg, parsley, garlic, salt, pepper, and thyme. Divide mixture evenly among large outside cabbage leaves, wrapping leaves tightly around mixture. Line bottom of 13×9-inch microproof baking dish with some of the remaining cabbage leaves. Top with stuffed cabbage rolls. Cover with remaining leaves. Dot with butter. Cover with tomato sauce. Cover with plastic wrap, and place in oven. Touch A8. Touch START. *(Oven cooks: HI, about 5 minutes.)*

At Pause, baste with pan juices. Touch START. *(Oven cooks: 50, about 15 minutes; stands: 0, 5 minutes.)*

Discard top leaves before serving.

4 servings

Veal Parmigiana

Total Cooking Time: 9 minutes

4 veal cutlets (¼ pound each)
1 medium egg
¼ teaspoon salt
⅓ cup grated Parmesan cheese
3 tablespoons cracker crumbs
2 tablespoons vegetable oil
¼ cup dry vermouth
1 medium onion, minced
1 cup (4 ounces) shredded
   mozzarella cheese
1 can (6 ounces) tomato paste
⅛ teaspoon pepper
⅛ teaspoon oregano

Place each veal cutlet between 2 sheets of waxed paper. Pound with smooth-surfaced meat mallet until veal is ¼ inch thick; set aside. Beat egg and salt in shallow dish. Combine Parmesan cheese and cracker crumbs on sheet of waxed paper. Dip veal in egg mixture, then in crumb mixture; set aside. Preheat microwave browning dish according to manufacturer's directions. Pour oil into browning dish. Place cutlets on browning dish in oven. Cover loosely with waxed paper. Cook on HI, 1½ minutes.

Turn cutlets over. Cook on HI, 1½ minutes.

Pour vermouth over veal. Sprinkle with onion. Top with mozzarella cheese and tomato paste. Sprinkle with pepper and oregano. Cook on 60, 6 minutes.

4 servings

A4 4

Veal Shoulder or Rump Roast, boneless

Preset Cooking Time: about 36 minutes

1 veal shoulder or rump roast,
   boneless (2 pounds)

Place roast, fat-side down, on microwave roasting rack in 11×7-inch microproof baking dish. Insert temperature probe horizontally into densest part of roast without touching fat. Place in oven. Cover roast lightly with waxed paper. Plug in probe. Touch A4. Touch 4. Touch START. *(Oven cooks: 70, to 90°F.)*

At Pause, turn over, being careful not to remove temperature probe. Cover. Touch START. *(Oven cooks: 70, to 145°F; stands: 0, 5 minutes.)*

Cover roast with aluminum foil and let stand an additional 5 minutes. During standing time, internal temperature of roast will rise to 160°F.

4 to 8 servings

All-American Meatballs

Total Cooking Time: 15 minutes

1 pound lean ground beef
1 medium potato, peeled and
   coarsely grated
2 tablespoons onion soup mix
1 tablespoon parsley flakes
1 egg, lightly beaten
2 cups beef broth
1 tablespoon Worcestershire sauce
2 tablespoons cornstarch
2 tablespoons water

Combine beef, potato, soup mix, parsley, and egg. Shape into twelve 1½-inch balls. Combine broth and Worcestershire in 2-quart microproof casserole. Add meatballs. Cover and place in oven. Cook on 70, 10 minutes.

Dissolve cornstarch in water. Stir into casserole. Cover. Cook on 70, 3 minutes.

Stir; cover. Cook on 70, 2 minutes.

Let stand 5 minutes before serving.

4 servings

Veal Cordon Bleu

Total Cooking Time: 4½ minutes

        2   veal cutlets (¼ pound each),
              ½ inch thick
        1   slice Swiss cheese, cut in half
        2   thin slices boiled ham
    1½   tablespoons all-purpose flour
        1   large egg
        1   tablespoon water
        ¼   cup dry bread crumbs
    1½   tablespoons butter or margarine
        1   tablespoon chopped parsley
        2   tablespoons dry vermouth

Cut veal cutlets in half. Place each piece between 2 sheets of waxed paper. Pound with smooth-surfaced meat mallet until veal is ⅛ inch thick; set aside. Fold each piece cheese in half. Place 1 piece cheese on each slice ham. Roll ham around cheese 3 times, being certain that finished roll is smaller than pieces of veal. Place 1 ham roll on 1 slice veal. Top with another slice veal. Press edges of veal together to seal. Repeat with remaining ham roll and veal. Place flour on sheet of waxed paper. Beat egg and water lightly. Place bread crumbs on separate sheet of waxed paper. Dip veal "sandwiches" in flour, then in egg mixture. Coat well with bread crumbs. Place butter and parsley in 8-inch round microproof baking dish. Place in oven. Cook on HI, 30 seconds.

Add veal to dish. Cook on HI, 2 minutes.

Turn veal over. Cook on HI, 2 minutes.

Transfer veal to serving platter. Mix vermouth into butter in baking dish. Pour over veal and serve.

2 servings

A7	1	LOWER

Shish Kabobs

Preset Cooking Time: about 6 minutes

        ½   cup wine vinegar
        ½   cup vegetable oil
        ½   cup water
        ¼   cup soy sauce
        1   teaspoon onion salt
        1   teaspoon oregano
        1   clove garlic, cut in half
        1   sirloin steak or lamb shoulder
              roast, boneless (2 pounds),
              cut into 1-inch cubes
        ½   pound small mushrooms
       12   very firm cherry tomatoes
        1   green pepper, seeded and cut
              into 1-inch squares

Combine vinegar, oil, water, soy sauce, onion salt, oregano, and garlic. Add meat. Refrigerate 5 to 6 hours, stirring occasionally. Thread meat cubes and vegetables alternately on 6 long wooden skewers. Arrange on microwave roasting rack, or microproof plate, spoke fashion. Brush with marinade. Place in oven with 1 kabob over circle on glass tray. Touch A7. Touch 1. Touch LOWER. Touch START. *(Oven cooks: HI, about 6 minutes.)* Brush with marinade before serving.

6 servings

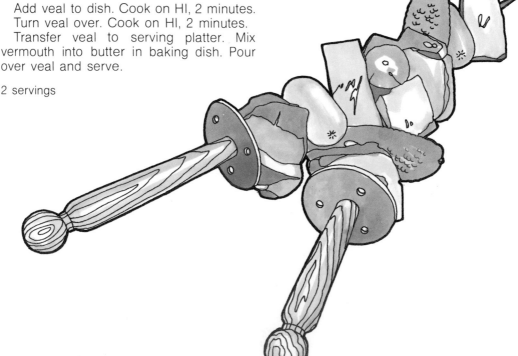

Lamb Ragout

Total Cooking Time: 40 minutes

- 1 pound lamb for stew, cut into 1-inch cubes
- 1 envelope (⅝ ounce) brown gravy mix
- 3 medium carrots, cut into chunks
- 2 medium stalks celery, cut into chunks
- 2 medium potatoes, peeled and cut into cubes
- 1 cup water
- ¼ cup dry red wine
- 2 tablespoons all-purpose flour
- 1 teaspoon salt
- ½ teaspoon Worcestershire sauce
- ⅛ teaspoon pepper
- 1 clove garlic, minced

Combine lamb and gravy mix in 3-quart microproof casserole. Place in oven. Cook on 50, 5 minutes.

Stir. Cook on 50, 5 minutes.

Add remaining ingredients; blend well. Cover. Cook on 50, 15 minutes.

Stir. Cover. Cook on 50, 15 minutes.

Let stand 3 to 4 minutes before serving.

4 servings

A4 4

Herbed Leg of Lamb (medium)

Preset Cooking Time: about 50 minutes

- 2 cloves garlic
- 1 boneless leg of lamb (4 pounds), butterflied
- 1½ tablespoons soy sauce
- 1 tablespoon dry mustard
- 1 teaspoon salt
- 1 teaspoon lemon juice
- ½ teaspoon thyme
- ¼ teaspoon rosemary
- ⅛ teaspoon pepper

Cut 1 clove garlic in half and rub all over lamb. Cut both cloves garlic into slivers. Slit outside of lamb at intervals and insert garlic slivers. Combine remaining ingredients. Spread all over lamb. Roll roast up and tie at intervals with string. Place on microwave roasting rack in shallow microproof baking dish. Insert temperature probe horizontally into densest part of meat. Place in oven. Plug in probe. Cover lamb lightly with waxed paper. Touch A4. Touch 4. Touch START. (Oven cooks: 70, to 90°F.)

At Pause, turn lamb over, being careful not to remove temperature probe. Cover. Touch START. (Oven cooks: 70, to 145°F; stands: 0, 5 minutes.)

6 to 8 servings

A4 5

Herbed Leg of Lamb (well done)

Preset Cooking Time: about 1 hour

Follow directions for preparing Herbed Leg of Lamb (medium). Place lamb on microwave roasting rack in shallow microproof baking dish. Insert temperature probe horizontally into densest part of meat. Place in oven. Plug in probe. Cover lamb lightly with waxed paper. Touch A4. Touch 5. Touch START. (Oven cooks: 70, to 90°F.)

At Pause, turn lamb over, being careful not to remove temperature probe. Cover. Touch START. (Oven cooks: 70, to 165°F; stands: 0, 10 minutes.)

6 to 8 servings

A8:0 HIGHER

Zesty Lamb Chops

Preset Cooking Time: about 32 minutes

- ½ cup catsup
- 2 tablespoons Worcestershire sauce
- 1 tablespoon prepared mustard
- 4 shoulder lamb chops (1¾ pounds)
- ½ cup coarsely chopped onions
- 1 clove garlic, minced

Combine catsup, Worcestershire, and mustard; set aside. Arrange chops in single layer in microproof baking dish. Sprinkle with onions and garlic. Place in oven with 1 chop over circle on glass tray. Touch A8. Touch HIGHER. Touch START (Oven cooks: HI, about 8 minutes.)

At Pause, spread catsup mixture over chops. Touch START. (Oven cooks: 50, about 19 minutes; stands: 0, 5 minutes.)

4 servings

A4	4

Lamb Leg or Shoulder Roast, bone in (medium)

Preset Cooking Time: about 32 minutes

> 1 lamb leg or shoulder roast,
> bone in (4 pounds)

Place roast, fat-side down, on microwave roasting rack in 11×7-inch microproof baking dish. Insert temperature probe horizontally into densest part of roast without touching fat or bone. Place in oven. Plug in probe. Cover roast lightly with waxed paper. Touch A4. Touch 4. Touch START. *(Oven cooks: 70, to 90°F.)*

At Pause, turn roast over, being careful not to remove temperature probe. Cover end of leg bone with aluminum foil, keeping foil at least 1 inch from oven wall. Cover roast with waxed paper. Touch START. *(Oven cooks: 70, to 145°F; stands: 0, 5 minutes.)*

8 to 10 servings

A4	5

Lamb Leg or Shoulder Roast, bone in (well done)

Preset Cooking Time: about 40 minutes

> 1 lamb leg or shoulder roast,
> bone in (4 pounds)

Place roast, fat-side down, on microwave roasting rack in 11×7-inch microproof baking dish. Insert temperature probe horizontally into densest part of roast without touching fat or bone. Place in oven. Plug in probe. Cover roast lightly with waxed paper. Touch A4. Touch. 5 Touch START. *(Oven cooks: 70, to 90°F.)*

At Pause, turn roast over, being careful not to remove temperature probe. Cover end of leg bone with aluminum foil, keeping foil at least 1 inch from oven wall. Cover roast with waxed paper. Touch START. *(Oven cooks: 70, to 165°F; stands: 0, 10 minutes.)*

8 to 10 servings

Eggplant Parthenon

Total Cooking Time: 23 minutes

> 2 eggplants (1 pound each)
> 1 pound ground lamb
> 2 medium onions, chopped
> 2 cloves garlic, minced
> 1 beef bouillon cube
> ½ cup hot water
> 1 can (8 ounces) tomato sauce, divided
> 2 tablespoons chopped parsley
> 1 teaspoon oregano
> ½ teaspoon salt
> ¼ teaspoon pepper
> ¼ teaspoon cinnamon
> ½ cup dry bread crumbs

Wash eggplants; cut in half lengthwise. Pierce skin in several places. Place, cut-sides down, on microwave roasting rack. Place in oven. Cook on HI, 5 minutes.

Remove from oven. Scoop out centers, leaving 1-inch thick shells. Chop pulp; set aside shells and pulp.

Crumble lamb into 2-quart glass measure. Add onions and garlic. Place in oven. Cook on HI, 5 minutes.

Stir to break up lamb; drain. Dissolve bouillon in hot water; stir into lamb mixture. Add ½ cup tomato sauce and eggplant pulp. Place in oven. Cook on 80, 8 minutes.

Stir in parsley, oregano, salt, pepper, and cinnamon. Place eggplant shells in shallow microproof baking dish just large enough to accommodate shells. Fill shells with lamb mixture. Sprinkle with bread crumbs. Drizzle remaining tomato sauce over crumbs. Place in oven. Cook on 80, 5 minutes.

4 servings

A2	4

Bacon

Preset Cooking Time: about 5 minutes

> 5 slices bacon

Place bacon on paper towel on microproof plate. Place in oven. Cover with another paper towel. Touch A2. Touch 4. Touch START. *(Oven cooks: HI, about 5 minutes.)*

1 serving

`A1  3  HIGHER  &  A1  6  HIGHER`

Stuffed Pork Chops

Preset Cooking Time: about 13 minutes

- 2 tablespoons butter or margarine
- 1 cup coarse dry bread crumbs
- ½ cup chopped apple
- 2 tablespoons chopped raisins
- 2 tablespoons sugar
- 2 tablespoons minced onion
- ½ teaspoon salt
- ¼ teaspoon pepper
  Pinch sage
- 2 tablespoons hot water
- 8 thin pork loin chops (1 pound), trimmed
- ½ envelope (⅜ ounce) brown gravy mix

Place butter in 1-quart microproof bowl. Place in oven. Touch A1. Touch 3. Touch HIGHER. Touch START. *(Oven cooks: 80, about 1 minute.)*

Add bread crumbs, apple, raisins, sugar, onion, salt, pepper, and sage; stir lightly. Add hot water and stir just until moistened. Place 4 chops in microproof baking dish. Divide stuffing evenly over chops. Cover with remaining 4 chops. Press together lightly. Sprinkle with gravy mix. Place in oven. Cover with waxed paper. Touch A1. Touch 6. Touch HIGHER. Touch START. *(Oven cooks: 80, about 7 minutes.)*

At Pause, baste chops with pan juices. Cover. Touch START. *(Oven cooks: 80, about 5 minutes.)*

4 servings

Orange Ginger Pork Chops

Total Cooking Time: 16 minutes

- 6 lean pork loin chops (1½ pounds), trimmed
- ¼ cup orange juice
- 2 teaspoons ginger
- ½ teaspoon salt
- ½ teaspoon garlic powder
- 6 strips orange peel
- ½ cup dairy sour cream

Place pork chops in rectangular microproof baking dish. Pour juice over chops. Place in oven. Cover with waxed paper. Cook on 80, 4 minutes.

Turn chops over. Cover. Cook on 80, 2 minutes.

Sprinkle with ginger, salt, and garlic powder. Place 1 strip orange peel on each chop. Cover. Cook on HI, 10 minutes.

Discard orange peel. Top each chop with dollop of sour cream. Cover and let stand 5 minutes before serving.

6 servings

Sausage

Total Cooking Time: 5 minutes

- 1 package (1 pound) bulk pork sausage

Crumble sausage into 1½-quart microproof casserole. Cover and place in oven. Cook on HI, 3 minutes.

Stir to break up sausage. Cover. Cook on HI, 2 minutes.

Drain before serving.

2 servings

`A8  3`

Country Style Ribs

Preset Cooking Time: about 1 hour 10 minutes

- 3 pounds meaty country style pork ribs
- ½ cup barbecue sauce
- 3 tablespoons olive oil
- 1 tablespoon wine vinegar
- 1 tablespoon chopped onion
- 1 teaspoon chopped parsley
- ½ teaspoon salt
- ⅛ teaspoon pepper
- 1 clove garlic, minced

Cut 1-inch strip from open end of cooking bag. Arrange ribs in bag in large microproof baking dish. Tie bag with removed strip. Place in oven. Touch A8. Touch 3. Touch START. *(Oven cooks: 70, about 10 minutes; 50, about 30 minutes.)*

At Pause, open bag and turn ribs over; drain. Combine remaining ingredients; blend well. Pour over ribs in bag. Close bag. Place in oven. Touch START. *(Oven cooks: 30, about 30 minutes.)*.

4 to 6 servings

You can substitute ½ cup Spicy Barbecue Sauce (page 171) for ready-made sauce, if desired.

Sweet and Sour Pork

Total Cooking Time: 29 minutes

- 4 medium carrots, thinly sliced
- ¼ cup vegetable oil
- 2 pounds lean boneless pork, cut into ¾-inch cubes
- 2 medium green peppers, seeded and sliced
- 1 medium onion, sliced
- ¼ cup cornstarch
- 1 can (16 ounces) pineapple chunks, drained, ½ cup juice reserved
- ½ cup firmly packed brown sugar
- ½ cup soy sauce
- ¼ cup wine vinegar
- 1 tablespoon Worcestershire sauce
- ½ teaspoon pepper
- ¼ teaspoon hot pepper sauce

Mix carrots and oil in 3-quart microproof casserole. Cover and place in oven. Cook on HI, 4 minutes.

Mix in pork, green peppers, and onion. Cover. Cook on HI, 5 minutes.

Dissolve cornstarch in reserved pineapple juice. Stir in remaining ingredients except pineapple. Blend into pork mixture. Stir in pineapple. Cover. Cook on 50, 10 minutes.

Stir through several times. Cover. Cook on 50, 10 minutes.

Serve immediately over hot rice.

8 servings

A4	6

Smoked Ham Shank

Preset Cooking Time: about 20 minutes

- 1 smoked ham shank (2 pounds)

Place ham, fat-side down, on microwave roasting rack in 11 × 7-inch microproof baking dish. Insert temperature probe horizontally into densest part of ham without touching fat or bone. Place in oven. Plug in probe. Cover ham lightly with waxed paper. Touch A4. Touch 6. Touch START. *(Oven cooks: HI, to 120°F.)*

At Pause, turn ham over, being careful not to remove temperature probe. Cover. Touch START. *(Oven cooks: 70, to 165°F; stands: 0, 10 minutes.)*

4 servings

A8	3	LOWER

Barbecued Spareribs

Preset Cooking Time: about 54 minutes

- 2½ pounds pork spareribs, cut into individual ribs
- 1 can (8 ounces) tomato sauce
- 2 tablespoons onion flakes
- 1 tablespoon brown sugar
- 1 tablespoon lemon juice
- 1 teaspoon Worcestershire sauce
- 1 teaspoon prepared mustard
- ½ teaspoon salt
- ¼ teaspoon pepper
- ¼ teaspoon hot pepper sauce

Cut 1-inch strip from open end of cooking bag. Arrange ribs in bag in large microproof baking dish. Tie bag with removed strip. Place in oven. Touch A8. Touch 3. Touch LOWER. Touch START. *(Oven cooks: 70, about 7 minutes; 50 about 26 minutes.)*

At Pause, open bag and turn ribs over; drain. Combine remaining ingredients; blend well. Pour over ribs in bag. Close bag. Place in oven. Touch START. *(Oven cooks: 30, about 21 minutes.)* Let stand 10 minutes before serving.

4 servings

NOTE: Automatic cooking functions identified in charts and on oven control panel are representative. Some programs may be used to cook foods other than those listed. Follow recipe instructions.

All Seasons Rice (page 148), →
Sweet and Sour Pork

A4 6

Honey-Glazed Pork Roast

Preset Cooking Time: about 30 minutes

- ¼ cup honey
- 2 tablespoons orange juice
- ¾ teaspoon cinnamon
- 1 pork loin roast, boneless
  (3 pounds)

Combine honey, juice, and cinnamon; set aside. Place roast, fat-side down, on microwave roasting rack in shallow microproof baking dish. Insert temperature probe horizontally into densest part of roast. Brush roast with half of the glaze. Place in oven. Plug in probe. Cover roast lightly with waxed paper. Touch A4. Touch 6. Touch START. *(Oven cooks: HI, to 120°F.)*

At Pause, turn roast over, being careful not to remove temperature probe. Brush with remaining glaze. Touch START. *(Oven cooks: 70, to 165°F; stands: 0, 10 minutes.)*

6 to 8 servings

A4 7

Precooked Ham

Preset Cooking Time: about 35 minutes

- 1 precooked ham (3 pounds)

Place ham on microwave roasting rack in 11 × 7-inch microproof baking dish. Insert temperature probe horizontally into center of ham, without touching fat or bone. Place in oven. Plug in probe. Cover lightly with waxed paper. Touch A4. Touch 7. Touch START. *(Oven cooks: 70, to 90°F.)*

At Pause, turn ham over, being careful not to remove probe. Touch START. *(Oven cooks: 70, to 120°F; stands: 0, 5 minutes.)*

6 to 10 servings

A4 6

Pork Loin Roast, boneless

Preset Cooking Time: about 46 minutes

- 1 pork loin roast, boneless
  (3 pounds)

Place roast, fat-side down, on microwave roasting rack in 11 × 7-inch microproof baking dish. Insert temperature probe horizontally into densest part of roast without touching fat. Place in oven. Plug in probe. Cover roast lightly with waxed paper. Touch A4. Touch 6. Touch START. *(Oven cooks: HI, to 120°F.)*

At Pause, turn roast over, being careful not to remove temperature probe. Touch START. *(Oven cooks: 70, to 165°F; stands: 0, 10 minutes.)*

6 servings

Honey-Glazed Pork Roast →

Cherry-Glazed Ham Slice

Total Cooking Time: about 15 minutes

> ¼ cup cherry jelly
> 6 maraschino cherries, chopped
> 1 tablespoon brown sugar
> ½ teaspoon dry mustard
> 1 center cut ham slice (1 pound)

Combine jelly, cherries, brown sugar, and mustard in 1-cup glass measure. Place in oven. Cook on 80, 1 minute. Stir.

Place ham in 11×7-inch microproof baking dish. Spread half of the glaze on top of ham. Insert temperature probe horizontally into center of ham without touching fat or bone. Place in oven. Plug in probe. Cook on 70, with probe set at 90°F.

Turn ham over, being careful not to remove temperature probe. Spread with remaining glaze. Cook on 70, with probe set at 120°F. Let stand 5 minutes before serving. Spoon glaze and drippings over ham on serving platter.

2 servings

A4 7

Baked Ham with Pineapple

Preset Cooking Time: about 27 minutes

> 1 precooked ham (3 pounds)
> ¼ cup firmly packed brown sugar
> 1 can (4 ounces) pineapple slices, drained, 2 teaspoons juice reserved
> Whole cloves

Place ham, fat-side down, in shallow microproof baking dish. Insert temperature probe into center of ham without touching fat or bone. Place in oven. Plug in probe. Touch A4. Touch 7. Touch START. *(Oven cooks: 70, to 90°F.)*

At Pause, turn ham over, being careful not to remove temperature probe. Mix brown sugar and reserved pineapple juice to make paste. Spread over top of ham. Arrange pineapple slices on top, attaching with wooden toothpicks, if necessary. Stud ham with cloves. Touch START. *(Oven cooks: 70, to 120°F; stands: 0, 5 minutes.)*

Cover with aluminum foil and let stand an additional 10 minutes before slicing.

8 to 10 servings

Liver Venetian Style

Total Cooking Time: 18 minutes

> 4 slices bacon
> 2 medium onions, thinly sliced
> 1 pound sliced calves liver
> Salt and pepper

Place bacon in 2-quart microproof casserole. Cover and place in oven. Cook on HI, 4 minutes.

Remove bacon from casserole and drain on paper towels; reserve drippings in casserole. Add onions to drippings and stir to coat. Cover. Cook on HI, 5 minutes.

Push onions to side of casserole. Add liver; turn to coat both sides. Cover. Cook on 50, 5 minutes.

Turn liver over. Cover. Cook on 50, 4 minutes.

Season liver with salt and pepper. Top with onions and crumbled bacon.

4 servings

Prime Time Poultry

Chicken, turkey, duck, and Cornish hen are especially juicy, tender, and flavorful when cooked in a microwave oven. Because they require less attention than other meats, they are great favorites for microwave cooks on those days when too many things seem to be happening at once. Poultry turns out golden brown but not crisp. If you have crisp-skin lovers at your table, you can satisfy them by crisping the skin in a conventional oven at 450°F, after the microwave cooking. You can also avoid the frustrations of long barbecue cooking by partially cooking poultry in the microwave oven, then finishing it off on the charcoal grill. Try the tasty recipes suggested here and then adapt your own. You'll even want to experiment with new recipes when you discover how much easier it is to cook poultry in your microwave oven than in the conventional oven. The nicest thing of all is that just about all poultry recipes cook automatically. The surface-temperature sensor and the internal-temperature sensor share the honors.

Plain, crumb-coated, soy brushed, barbecue-sauced, and honey-glazed chicken breasts all demonstrate appetizing color (above left). The best arrangement for chicken parts places thickest portions toward outside of dish. Surface-temperature sensor cooking or defrosting requires that dish be placed with thigh, not center of dish, over circle on glass tray (above). Turning Micro-Fried Chicken (page 111) in a browning dish (left).

Adapting Your Recipes

Conventional one-dish poultry recipes that call for cut-up pieces are easy to adapt to the microwave. The temperature probe can help achieve accurate doneness in whole-chicken recipes as well as in casseroles. Refer to the comparative chicken recipes on page 36 to guide you in converting your favorite dishes. Here are some good tips to follow:

☐ To obtain uniform doneness and flavor, cook poultry weighing no more than 14 pounds in the microwave oven. Poultry over 14 pounds should be cooked conventionally.

☐ Butter- or oil-injected turkeys often have uneven concentrations of fat and thus cook unevenly. For best results, use uninjected turkeys.

☐ Conventional pop-up indicators for doneness do not work correctly in the microwave oven.

☐ The temperature probe may be used in cooking whole poultry. Insert the probe in the fleshy part of the inside thigh muscle without touching the bone.

☐ The automatic A5 program offers cooking of most poultry with built-in pauses and standing time. The internal-temperature sensor, the temperature probe, is used. See the *Guides* on pages 31 and 108 for the several variations available.

☐ Poultry pieces prepared in a cream sauce should be cooked on 70 to prevent the cream from separating or curdling.

☐ Chicken coated with a crumb mixture cooks to crispness more easily if left uncovered.

☐ Less tender game birds should be cooked on 70 on a microwave roasting rack. Pour off fat as necessary. For best results, marinate game birds before cooking.

☐ Standing time is essential to complete cooking. Allow up to 15 minutes standing time for whole poultry depending upon size. The internal temperature will rise approximately 15°F during 15 minutes standing time. Chicken pieces and casseroles need only 5 minutes standing time.

Using the Automatic Defrosting Guide

1. Remove poultry from original paper or plastic wrappings. Metal leg clamps of frozen turkey need not be removed until after thawing. Keep metal at least 1 inch from oven walls.

2. Defrost only as long as necessary. Poultry should be cool in center.

3. If you wish to use the oven, remove poultry during standing time. Poultry may then be placed in a cold-water bath.

4. Separate cut-up chicken pieces as soon as partially thawed.

5. Wing and leg tips and area near breastbone may need to be shielded to prevent cooking. As soon as they appear thawed, cover with small strips of foil, keeping at least 1 inch from oven walls.

6. Turn all poultry over at Pause.

AUTOMATIC DEFROSTING GUIDE — POULTRY

Food	Amount	Approximate Time Per Pound*	Automatic Sensor Method
Capon	6 - 8 lbs.	2 minutes	A0-4 Higher
Chicken, cut-up	under 2 lbs. 2 - 4 lbs.	5 minutes 5 minutes	A0-4 Lower A0-4
Chicken, whole	3 - 4 lbs.	7 minutes	A0-4
Cornish hens	1 - 1½ lbs.	7 minutes	A0-4
Duckling	4 - 5 lbs.	7 minutes	A0-4 Higher
Turkey	8 - 14 lbs.	9 minutes	A0-5 Higher
Turkey breast	3 - 6 lbs.	6 minutes	A0-4
Turkey parts	1 - 2 lbs.	4 minutes	A0-4 Higher
Turkey roast, boneless	2 - 4 lbs.	4 minutes	A0-4 Higher

* Not including recommended standing time. Due to relatively-long standing time for most poultry to finish thawing, it is not programmed as part of the automatic defrost feature. Let poultry stand, in or outside the oven: 10 to 20 minutes for small poultry; 30 to 60 minutes for whole chicken, capon, or turkey.

Using the Cooking Guide

1. Defrost frozen poultry completely before cooking.

2. Remove the giblets, rinse poultry in cool water, and pat dry.

3. Brush poultry with browning sauce before cooking, if desired.

4. When cooking whole birds, place on a microwave roasting rack in a glass baking dish large enough to catch drippings.

5. Turn over, as directed in Guide, or when Pause appears in Display Window. Baste if you wish.

6. Cook whole poultry covered loosely with a waxed paper tent to prevent splattering. Toward end of cooking time, small pieces of aluminum foil may be used for shielding to cover legs, wing tips, or breastbone area to prevent overcooking. Foil should be at least 1 inch from oven walls.

7. Cover poultry pieces with either glass casserole lid or plastic wrap during cooking and standing time.

8. Use temperature probe inserted in thickest part of thigh, set at 180°F for whole poultry, and at 170°F for parts, including turkey breasts.

9. Standing time completes the cooking of poultry. Cooked whole birds may be covered with aluminum foil during standing time.

COOKING GUIDE — POULTRY

Food	First Cook Control Setting and Time (in minutes)	Second Cook Control Setting and Time (in minutes)	or	Automatic Sensor Method	Standing Time Method	Special Notes
Chicken, whole, 2 - 3 pounds	HI (max. power) 3 - 4 per pound	Turn over. HI (max. power) 4 per pound	or	A5-0	5 (covered with foil)	Shallow baking dish, roasting rack, breast up.
3 - 5 pounds	HI (max. power) 4 per pound	Turn over. HI (max. power) 4 - 5 per pound	or	A5-0	5	12 × 7-inch baking dish, roasting rack, breast up.
Chicken, cut up 2½-3½ pounds	HI (max. power) 10	Turn over. HI (max. power) 8 - 12	or	A7-3 Higher	5	12 × 7-inch baking dish. Cover.
Chicken, quartered	HI (max. power) 3 - 4 per pound	Turn over. HI (max. power) 3 - 4 per pound	or	A5-1	5	Shallow baking dish, skin side down.
Cornish hens 1½ - 2 pounds	HI (max. power) 4 per pound	HI (max. power) 3 per pound	or	A5-3	5	Shallow baking dish, breast down. Cover.
Duckling 4 - 5 pounds	70 (roast) 4 per pound	Turn over. Drain excess fat. 70 (roast) 4 per pound	or	A5-0	8 - 10	Shallow baking dish, roasting rack. Cover.
Turkey, whole, 8 - 14 pounds	HI (max. power) 5 per pound	Turn over. 70 (roast) 4 per pound	or	A5-2	10 - 15 (covered with foil)	Shallow baking dish, 13 × 9-inch, roasting rack, breast up.
Turkey breast, 3 - 4 pounds	HI (max. power) 7 per pound	Turn over. 70 (roast) 5 per pound	or	A5-3		Shallow baking dish, roasting rack.
Turkey roast, boneless 2 - 4 pounds	70 (roast) 10 per pound	Turn over. 70 (roast) 9 per pound	or	A5-2	10 - 15	Loaf pan. Cover with plastic wrap.
Turkey parts, 2 - 3 pounds	70 (roast) 7 - 8 per pound	Turn over. 70 (roast) 7 - 8 per pound	or	A5-3 (use time if wings)	5	Shallow baking dish with roasting rack.

A7	3	HIGHER

Chicken, Cut Up

Preset Cooking Time: about 28 minutes

    1 broiler-fryer chicken (3½ pounds),
         cut up
       Microwave browning sauce

Rinse chicken in cool water and pat dry. Arrange chicken in shallow round or oval microproof baking dish, skin-side down, with thickest parts toward outside of dish. Brush chicken with browning sauce. Place in oven with chicken thigh over circle on glass tray. Cover lightly with waxed paper. Touch A7. Touch 3. Touch HIGHER. Touch START. (Oven cooks: HI, about 8 minutes.)

At Pause, turn chicken over. Brush with pan juices. Touch START. (Oven cooks: HI, about 20 minutes.)

4 servings

| A2 | 2 | HIGHER | & | A7 | 1 | HIGHER |

Chicken Veronique

Preset Cooking Time: about 7 minutes

- 3 cups cooked rice
- 2 cups coarsely cut up cooked chicken
- 1 cup halved seedless green or white grapes
- ½ cup diced celery
- ¾ cup milk
- ¼ cup white wine
- 2 tablespoons butter or margarine
- 2 tablespoons all-purpose flour
- ½ teaspoon chervil
- ½ teaspoon parsley flakes
- ¼ teaspoon tarragon
  Dash white pepper

Combine rice, chicken, grapes, and celery in 1½-quart microproof casserole; set aside. Pour milk and wine into 2-cup glass measure; set aside. Place butter and flour in separate 2-cup glass measure. Place in oven. Touch A2. Touch 2. Touch HIGHER. Touch START. *(Oven cooks: HI, about 1 minute.)*

At Pause, stir in milk mixture. Touch START. *(Oven cooks: HI, about 1 minute.)*

Remove from oven and whisk until smooth. Stir in seasonings. Pour over chicken mixture. Cover and place in oven. Touch A7. Touch 1. Touch HIGHER. Touch START. *(Oven cooks: HI, about 5 minutes.)*

Let stand 2 minutes before serving.

4 to 6 servings

Swiss Coated Chicken

Total Cooking Time: 5½ minutes

- 1 whole chicken breast (1 pound), split, skinned, and boned
- 1 teaspoon cornstarch
- ¼ teaspoon paprika
- ¼ teaspoon white pepper
- ⅓ cup half-and-half
- 2 tablespoons apple juice
- ½ cup (2 ounces) shredded Swiss cheese
- 1 tablespoon chopped parsley

Place chicken in shallow microproof baking dish. Combine cornstarch, paprika, and pepper in small bowl. Add half-and-half

and apple juice, and stir until cornstarch is dissolved. Pour over chicken. Cover and place in oven. Cook on HI, 1 minute.

Turn chicken over. Stir sauce and baste chicken. Cover. Cook on HI, 3 minutes.

Stir sauce and baste chicken. Sprinkle with cheese. Cook on HI, uncovered, 1½ minutes, or until chicken is cooked through. Sprinkle with parsley and serve.

2 servings

| A5 | 1 |

Tarragon Grilled Chicken

Preset Cooking Time: about 26 minutes

- ¼ cup olive oil
- ¼ cup dry sherry or chicken broth
- 1 tablespoon onion flakes
- 1 clove garlic, minced
- ½ teaspoon salt
- ½ teaspoon tarragon
- ⅛ teaspoon white pepper
- 1 broiler-fryer chicken (3 pounds), quartered

Combine all ingredients except chicken. Arrange chicken, skin-side down, in shallow oval microproof baking dish, with thickest parts toward outside of dish. Insert temperature probe into fleshy part of inside thigh muscle without touching bone. Brush chicken with half of the oil mixture. Place in oven. Plug in probe. Cover chicken with waxed paper. Touch A5. Touch 1. Touch START. *(Oven cooks: HI, to 120°F.)*

At Pause, turn chicken over, being careful not to remove temperature probe. Brush with remaining oil mixture. Cover. Touch START. *(Oven cooks: HI, to 170°F; 20, 5 minutes.)*

4 servings

This chicken dish is delicious when finished on a charcoal grill. Prepare and cook chicken as directed above. Reserve pan juices. Barbecue about 4 inches above hot coals 10 to 12 minutes, or until golden brown. Turn occasionally and brush with reserved juices.

Micro-Fried Chicken

Total Cooking Time: 9 minutes

- ½ cup all-purpose flour
- ½ teaspoon salt
- ¼ teaspoon pepper
- ⅛ teaspoon dry mustard
- 1 broiler-fryer chicken (2½ pounds), cut up, backbone and wing tips removed
- 2 tablespoons lemon juice
- 2 tablespoons vegetable oil
- 2 tablespoons butter
  Paprika

Combine flour, salt, pepper, and mustard in paper bag. Brush chicken with lemon juice. Add chicken to seasoned flour in batches and shake to coat well, shaking off excess. Preheat large microwave browning dish according to manufacturer's directions. Add oil and butter to dish. Arrange chicken, skin-side down, on browning dish; do not crowd. Cover lightly with waxed paper. Cook on HI, 4 minutes.

Turn chicken over. Sprinkle with paprika. Cover. Cook on HI, 5 minutes.

4 servings

A7:0 & A5:0

Chicken with Cornbread Stuffing

Preset Cooking Time: about 30 minutes

- ½ cup diced onions
- ½ cup diced celery
- 2 tablespoons butter or margarine
- 1 cup diced mushrooms
- ¾ cup chicken stock or bouillon, divided
- 1 package (6 ounces) cornbread stuffing mix
- 1 broiler-fryer chicken (3½ pounds), giblets removed
- 1 slice bread
  Vegetable oil
  Paprika

Combine onions, celery, and butter in 2-quart microproof bowl. Place in oven. Touch A7. Touch START. *(Oven cooks: HI, about 3 minutes.)*

At Pause, add mushrooms, ½ cup stock, and stuffing mix. Blend lightly, adding remaining ¼ cup stock if mixture seems too dry. Spoon stuffing into chicken cavity. Tuck bread into cavity to secure stuffing. Place chicken, breast-side up, on microwave roasting rack in shallow microproof baking dish. Tuck wings under chicken. Insert temperature probe into fleshy part of inside thigh muscle without touching bone. Rub outside of chicken with oil and sprinkle with paprika. Place in oven. Plug in probe. Cover chicken with waxed paper. Touch A5. Touch START. *(Oven cooks: HI, to 120°F.)*

At Pause, turn chicken breast-side down, being careful not to remove temperature probe. Cover. Touch START. *(Oven cooks: HI, to 180°F; 30, 5 minutes.)*

Let stand, covered with aluminum foil, 10 to 15 minutes before serving.

4 servings

We recommend cooking poultry in the French manner, beginning breast-side up and finishing breast-side down. Try it. You'll be pleased with the especially tender and juicy meat.

← *Micro-Fried Chicken*

A5:0

Whole Roast Chicken

Preset Cooking Time: about 30 minutes

> 1 broiler-fryer chicken (3 pounds),
> giblets removed
> Salt and pepper
> 2 medium stalks celery, cut
> into 1-inch chunks
> 1 small onion, cut into
> quarters
> 2 tablespoons butter or margarine,
> softened
> teaspoon thyme

Rinse chicken in cool water and pat dry. Sprinkle cavity with salt and pepper. Place celery and onion inside cavity. Place chicken, breast-side up, on microwave roasting rack in shallow microproof baking dish. Tuck wings under chicken. Spread butter over chicken. Sprinkle with thyme. Insert temperature probe horizontally into fleshy part of inside thigh muscle without touching bone. Place in oven. Plug in probe. Cover chicken with waxed paper. Touch A5. Touch START. *(Oven cooks: HI, to 120°F.)*

At Pause, turn chicken over, being careful not to remove temperature probe. Touch START. *(Oven cooks: HI, to 180°F; 30, 5 minutes.)*

Let stand 10 to 15 minutes before serving.

4 servings

It is perfectly fine to cover chicken with an aluminum foil tent during standing time. In fact, it's recommended.

A5:0

Soy Sherry Chicken

Preset Cooking Time: about 40 minutes

> 1 broiler-fryer chicken (3 pounds),
> giblets removed
> ¼ cup soy sauce
> ¼ cup dry sherry
> 1 small onion, sliced
> 3 slices fresh ginger (⅛ inch
> thick)

Cut 1-inch strip from open end of cooking bag. Rinse chicken in cool water and pat dry. Brush generously with soy sauce. Place chicken, breast-side up, in cooking bag in microproof baking dish. Add sherry, any

remaining soy sauce, onion, and ginger to bag. Insert temperature probe horizontally into fleshy part of inside thigh muscle without touching bone. Place in oven. Plug in probe. Tie bag loosely with removed strip. Touch A5. Touch START. *(Oven cooks: HI, to 120°F.)*

At Pause, turn bag over, being careful not to remove temperature probe. Touch START. *(Oven cooks: HI to 180°F; 30, 5 minutes.)*

Remove chicken from bag. Discard ginger. Pour cooking juices and onion over chicken and serve.

4 servings

Garlic Chicken Italiano

Total Cooking Time: 21 minutes

> ⅓ cup olive oil
> 24 large cloves garlic
> 1 medium stalk celery, thinly
> sliced
> 2 tablespoons chopped parsley
> 1 teaspoon salt
> ½ teaspoon pepper
> ½ teaspoon oregano
> Pinch nutmeg
> 4 chicken legs (¼ pound each)
> 4 chicken thighs (¼ pound each)

Combine all ingredients except chicken in shallow microproof baking dish. Add chicken, turning to coat all sides with marinade. Cover and refrigerate at least 3 hours, turning several times. Cover and place in oven. Cook on HI, 8 minutes.

Turn chicken over. Baste with pan juices. Cover. Cook on HI, 8 minutes; then on 10, 5 minutes.

4 servings

```
         A5    1    HIGHER
```

Honey-Glazed Chicken

Preset Cooking Time: about 26 minutes

  1 broiler-fryer chicken (3 pounds),
      split in half
¼ teaspoon paprika
¼ cup honey, divided

Arrange chicken in microproof baking dish, skin-side up, with thickest parts toward outside of dish. Insert temperature probe horizontally into fleshy part of inside thigh muscle without touching bone. Sprinkle chicken with paprika. Brush with half of the honey. Place in oven. Plug in probe. Cover chicken with waxed paper. Touch A5. Touch 1. Touch HIGHER. Touch START. (Oven cooks: HI, to 120°F.)

At Pause, turn chicken over, being careful not to remove temperature probe. Brush with remaining honey. Cover. Touch START. (Oven cooks: HI, to 170°F; 20, 5 minutes.)

Let stand, covered, 5 minutes before serving.

2 servings

Chicken Supreme

Total Cooking Time: 55 minutes

  5 slices bacon
  1 can (10¾ ounces) cream of onion
      soup, undiluted
½ cup dry red wine or dry sherry
½ cup chopped onions
  1 clove garlic, minced
  1 tablespoon minced parsley
1½ teaspoons chicken bouillon
      granules
½ teaspoon salt
¼ teaspoon pepper
¼ teaspoon thyme
  6 small potatoes, peeled and cut
      in half
  2 medium carrots, thinly sliced
  1 broiler-fryer chicken
      (2½ pounds), cut up
½ pound mushrooms, sliced

Arrange bacon on paper towel on microproof plate. Place in oven. Cover with another paper towel. Cook on HI, 5 minutes.

Crumble bacon and set aside. Mix soup, wine, onions, garlic, parsley, bouillon, and seasonings; set aside. Place potatoes and carrots in 3-quart microproof casserole. Arrange chicken on top, skin-side down, with thickest parts toward outside of casserole. Pour soup mixture over top. Cover and place in oven. Cook on HI, 30 minutes.

Rearrange chicken, bringing bottom pieces to top, skin-side up. Sprinkle with bacon and mushrooms. Cover. Cook on 70, 15 minutes; then on 10, 5 minutes.

4 to 6 servings

Chicken Milano

Total Cooking Time: 11 minutes

¼ cup olive oil
  1 teaspoon salt
½ teaspoon pepper
¼ teaspoon oregano
¼ teaspoon basil
  4 chicken thighs (¼ pound each)
  1 cup dry bread crumbs
½ teaspoon paprika
  2 medium potatoes, peeled and cut
      into quarters

Combine oil, salt, pepper, oregano, and basil. Add chicken and turn to coat all sides. Cover and refrigerate 2 hours. Combine bread crumbs and paprika. Remove 1 piece chicken from marinade and drain. Roll in crumb mixture to coat. Repeat with remaining chicken. Set remaining marinade and crumb mixture aside. Arrange chicken, skin-side down, in 9-inch round microproof baking dish, with thickest parts toward outside of dish. Cut ends from potatoes to make quarters even; pat dry. Roll potatoes in remaining marinade to coat, adding more oil to marinade if necessary. Arrange potatoes around chicken. Place in oven. Cover with waxed paper. Cook on HI, 6 minutes.

Turn chicken and potatoes over. Sprinkle with remaining crumb mixture. Cook on HI, 5 minutes. Let stand 5 minutes before serving.

2 servings

```
   A7:0   &   A8:0    HIGHER
```

Chicken Cacciatore

Preset Cooking Time: about 38 minutes

- 1 medium onion, chopped
- 1 medium green pepper, seeded and thinly sliced
- 1 tablespoon butter or margarine
- 1 can (28 ounces) whole tomatoes, broken up
- 1/4 cup all-purpose flour
- 1/2 cup dry red wine or water
- 1 tablespoon parsley flakes
- 1 teaspoon salt
- 1 teaspoon paprika
- 1/2 teaspoon oregano
- 1/4 teaspoon pepper
- 1/4 teaspoon basil
- 1 bay leaf
- 1 clove garlic, minced
- 1 broiler-fryer chicken (3 pounds), cut up

Combine onion, green pepper, and butter in 3-quart microproof casserole. Place in oven. Touch A7. Touch START. *(Oven cooks: HI, about 5 minutes.)*

Add tomatoes and flour; stir until smooth. Stir in the remaining ingredients and top with chicken, placing thickest parts of chicken toward outside of casserole and breast in center. Cover and place in oven. Touch A8. Touch HIGHER. Touch START. *(Oven cooks: HI, about 8 minutes.)*

At Pause, rearrange chicken and spoon sauce over. Cover. Touch START. *(Oven cooks: 50, about 20 minutes; stands: 0, 5 minutes.)*

Discard bay leaf. Serve with hot spaghetti or rice.

4 to 6 servings

```
              A5      1
```

Barbecued Chicken

Preset Cooking Time: about 25 minutes

- 1 broiler-fryer chicken (2 1/2 pounds), quartered
- 1/2 cup barbecue sauce
- 1 tablespoon parsley flakes
- 1 tablespoon onion flakes

Arrange chicken in round or oval microproof baking dish, skin-side down, with thickest parts toward outside of dish. Insert temperature probe horizontally into densest part of chicken without touching bone. Combine remaining ingredients; brush half of the sauce mixture over chicken. Place in oven. Plug in probe. Cover chicken with waxed paper. Touch A5. Touch 1. Touch START. *(Oven cooks: HI, to 120°F.)*

At Pause, turn chicken over, being careful not to remove temperature probe. Brush with remaining sauce mixture. Cover. Touch START. *(Oven cooks: HI, to 170°F; 20, 5 minutes.)*

4 servings

Chicken Sukiyaki

Total Cooking Time: 10 minutes

- 1/2 cup soy sauce
- 1/2 cup chicken broth
- 1/4 cup dry sherry
- 2 tablespoons sugar
- 2 chicken breasts (1/2 pound each), skinned, boned, and cut into 1/2-inch slices
- 1 pound spinach, stems removed
- 1/2 pound bean sprouts
- 1/4 pound pea pods
- 1/2 cup sliced celery
- 1 medium onion, thinly sliced
- 1 medium bunch green onions, cut into 3-inch strips
- 6 small mushrooms, sliced

Combine soy sauce, broth, sherry, and sugar in 2-cup glass measure; stir until sugar is dissolved. Place in oven. Cook on HI, 2 minutes.

Combine remaining ingredients in 3-quart microproof casserole. Pour sauce mixture over chicken mixture. Cover and place in oven. Cook on HI, 3 minutes.

Stir. Cover. Cook on HI, 2 minutes. Stir again. Cover. Cook on HI, 3 minutes. Pass additional soy sauce at table.

4 servings

Chicken Cacciatore →

```
A8    3 LOWER
```

Chicken Marengo

Preset Cooking Time: about 57 minutes

- 1 broiler-fryer chicken (3½ pounds), cut up
- ¼ cup vegetable oil
- 2 cups soft bread crumbs
- 1 package (3 ounces) spaghetti sauce mix
- 2 cups sliced mushrooms
- 1 can (16 ounces) whole tomatoes, broken up
- 1 cup dry white wine

Rinse chicken in cool water and pat dry. Brush with oil. Combine bread crumbs and sauce mix in plastic bag. Shake chicken, 1 piece at a time, in bag to coat well. Arrange chicken in 3-quart round or oval microproof casserole with thickest parts toward outside of casserole. Place in oven with thigh over circle on glass tray. Touch A8. Touch 3. Touch LOWER. Touch START. *(Oven cooks: 70, about 21 minutes; 50, about 15 minutes.)*

At Pause, add remaining ingredients. Cover. Touch START. *(Oven cooks: 30, about 21 minutes.)*

4 to 6 servings

Chicken and Vegetables

Total Cooking Time: 20 minutes

- 2 medium carrots
- 2 medium stalks celery
- 2 small parsnips, peeled
- 2 small potatoes, peeled
- 1 medium onion
- 2 tablespoons butter or margarine
- 2 tablespoons minced parsley
- ½ teaspoon salt
  Dash pepper
- ⅛ teaspoon paprika
- 2 whole chicken breasts (1 pound each), split, skinned, and boned

Cut all vegetables into 1½ × ¼-inch strips (about 4 cups total). Place in shallow round or oval microproof baking dish. Dot with butter. Season with parsley, salt, pepper, and paprika. Cover with plastic wrap. Place in oven. Cook on HI, 5 minutes.

Stir through several times. Cover. Cook on HI, 5 minutes.

Arrange chicken on vegetables around outside of dish. Sprinkle with additional paprika. Cover with plastic wrap. Cook on HI, 10 minutes.

Let stand 5 minutes. Spoon vegetables over chicken. Sprinkle with additional parsley before serving.

4 servings

```
A3    2    &    A5    3
```

Cornish Hens with Wild Rice

Preset Cooking Time: about 42 minutes

- 2 Cornish hens (1½ pounds each)
- 1 package (10 ounces) frozen wild rice
- 2 tablespoons butter or margarine
- ½ cup currant jelly
- 2 teaspoons dry sherry

Rinse Cornish hens in cool water and pat dry; set aside. Place rice and butter in 3-quart microproof casserole. Cover and place in oven. Touch A3. Touch 2. Touch START. *(Oven cooks: 80, about 4 minutes.)*

At Pause, stir. Touch START. *(Oven cooks: 80, about 3 minutes.)*

Remove rice from oven and let stand until cool. Combine jelly and sherry; set aside. Spoon cooled rice into hen cavities and secure with wooden toothpicks; set any extra rice aside. Place hens, breast-side down, in oval microproof baking dish with thickest parts toward outside of dish. Insert temperature probe horizontally into fleshy part of inside thigh muscle without touching bone. Brush hens evenly with half of the sherry glaze. Place in oven. Plug in probe. Touch A5. Touch 3. Touch START. *(Oven cooks: HI to 120°F.)*

At Pause, turn hens breast-side up, being careful not to remove temperature probe. Brush with remaining sherry glaze. Arrange reserved rice around hens. Place in oven. Touch START. *(Oven cooks: HI, to 170°F; 20, 5 minutes.)*

4 servings

There's no need to worry if your Cornish hens aren't exactly the 1½ pounds called for in the recipe. The oven's internal-temperature sensor will automatically adjust the cooking time.

A8:0	&	A3	5

Chicken Liver Chow Mein

Preset Cooking Time: about 24½ minutes

- ½ pound chicken livers, rinsed and drained
- ½ cup sliced celery
- ¼ cup chopped onion
- 3 tablespoons butter or margarine, divided
- 1 envelope (1¾ ounces) mushroom gravy mix
- 1 can (16 ounces) Chinese vegetables
- 1 can (8 ounces) sliced water chestnuts, drained
- 1 tablespoon soy sauce

Cut livers into bite-size pieces; discard membranes. Combine celery, onion, and 1 tablespoon butter in 3-quart microproof casserole. Cover and place in oven. Touch A8. Touch START. *(Oven cooks: HI, about 3 minutes.)*

At Pause, stir in gravy mix. Add Chinese vegetables, water chestnuts, and soy sauce, and stir until gravy mix is dissolved. Cover. Touch START. *(Oven cooks: 50, about 15 minutes; stands: 0, 5 minutes.)*

Remove from oven and set aside. Place liver and remaining 2 tablespoons butter in 4-cup glass measure. Place in oven. Cover with waxed paper. Touch A3. Touch 5. Touch START. *(Oven cooks: 80, about 1 minute.)*

At Pause, stir. Touch START. *(Oven cooks: 80, about 30 seconds.)*

Drain livers well. Stir into vegetable mixture. Let stand, covered, 2 minutes before serving. Serve over hot rice, and top with chow mein noodles, if desired.

4 to 6 servings

A2   1   &   A5:0

Roast Orange Duckling

Total Cooking Time: 45½ minutes

- 1 duckling (4 pounds), giblets removed
- 1 medium orange, peeled and cut into chunks
- 1 medium onion, cut into quarters
- ½ cup orange marmalade
  - Orange Sauce (page 174)

Rinse duckling in cool water and pat dry. Place orange and onion in cavity. Secure neck skin with wooden toothpicks or skewers. Tie legs together with string; tie wings to body. Pierce skin all over to allow fat to drain. Place duckling, breast-side up, on microwave roasting rack in 11 × 7-inch microproof baking dish; set aside. Place marmalade in 1-cup glass measure. Place in oven over circle on glass tray. Touch A2. Touch 1. Touch START. (Oven cooks: 70, about 1 minute.)

Insert temperature probe into fleshy part of inside thigh muscle without touching bone. Spread half of the marmalade over duckling. Place duckling in oven. Plug in probe. Cover duckling loosely with waxed paper. Touch A5. Touch START. (Oven cooks: HI, to 120°F.)

At Pause, turn duckling over, being careful not to remove probe. Brush with remaining marmalade. Cover with waxed paper. Touch START. (Oven cooks: HI, to 180°F; 30, 5 minutes.) Serve immediately with Orange Sauce, if desired.

2 servings

If you like duckling with crispy skin, place cooked duckling in conventional oven pre-heated to 350°F. Bake 10 minutes or until desired crispness is reached.

A5:0

Duckling

Preset Cooking Time: about 45 minutes

- 1 duckling (4 pounds), giblets removed
  - Salt and pepper

Rinse duckling in cool water and pat dry. Pierce skin all over to allow fat to drain. Place duckling, breast-side up, on microwave roasting rack in 11 × 7-inch microproof baking dish. Insert temperature probe into fleshy part of inside thigh muscle without touching bone. Sprinkle duckling with salt and pepper. Place in oven. Plug in probe. Cover duckling with waxed paper. Touch A5. Touch START. (Oven cooks: HI, to 120° F.)

At Pause, turn duckling over, being careful not to remove temperature probe. Drain. Brush duckling with pan juices. Cover. Touch START. (Oven cooks: HI to 180°F; 30, 5 minutes.)

2 servings

Roast Orange Duckling →

A7:0	&	A5	2

Turkey with Nut Stuffing

Preset Cooking Time: about 1 hour
45 minutes

1	turkey (12 pounds), neck and giblets removed
1	cup chicken broth
½	cup butter or margarine
2	medium stalks celery, thinly sliced
1	large onion, chopped
10	cups day-old bread crumbs or ½-inch cubes
1	cup coarsely chopped walnuts or pecans
¼	cup chopped parsley
1	teaspoon poultry seasoning
½	teaspoon salt
1	tablespoon bottled brown sauce

Rinse turkey in cool water and pat dry; set aside. Place broth and butter in 3-quart microproof casserole. Add celery and onion. Cover and place in oven. Touch A7. Touch START. *(Oven cooks: HI, about 5 minutes.)*

Remove from oven. Add bread crumbs, nuts, parsley, poultry seasoning, and salt; stir lightly. Stuff neck opening of turkey with part of the stuffing. Secure neck skin with strong wooden toothpicks or skewers. Stuff cavity with remaining stuffing. Tie legs together with strong string; tie wings to body. Place turkey, breast-side up, on microwave roasting rack in large microproof baking dish. Insert temperature probe into fleshy part of inside thigh muscle without touching bone. Place in oven. Plug in probe. Cover turkey with waxed paper. Touch A5. Touch 2. Touch START. *(Oven cooks: HI, to 120°F.)*

At Pause, turn turkey over, being careful not to remove temperature probe. Baste with pan juices and brown sauce. Cover with waxed-paper tent. Touch START. *(Oven cooks: HI to 180°F; 30, 5 minutes.)*

Remove from oven. Cover with aluminum foil and let stand 20 minutes before carving.

6 to 8 servings

If you like turkey with extra-crisp skin, place cooked turkey in conventional oven preheated to 450°F. Bake 10 to 15 minutes, or until desired crispness is reached.

A7	1	&	A5	3

Breast of Turkey Jardiniere

Preset Cooking Time: about 47 minutes

2	medium carrots, cut into 2-inch strips
2	medium stalks celery, cut into 2-inch strips
1	medium potato, peeled and cut into 2-inch strips
1	small onion, cut into 2-inch strips
2	tablespoons minced parsley
3	tablespoons butter or margarine
	Salt and pepper
½	turkey breast (3 pounds), skinned and boned, if desired
2	tablespoons vegetable oil
¾	teaspoon paprika

Arrange vegetables and parsley in center of oval microproof baking dish. Dot with butter and sprinkle with salt and pepper. Cover with plastic wrap. Place in oven. Touch A7. Touch 1. Touch START. *(Oven cooks: HI, about 7 minutes.)*

Stir vegetables. Place turkey over vegetables. Insert temperature probe horizontally into densest part of turkey without touching bone. Combine oil and paprika; brush over turkey. Place in oven. Plug in probe. Cover with waxed paper. Touch A5. Touch 3. Touch START. *(Oven cooks: HI, to 120°F.)*

At Pause, turn turkey over, being careful not to remove temperature probe. Touch START. *(Oven cooks: HI, to 170°F; 20, 5 minutes.)*

Let stand 5 minutes before serving.

4 servings

This is one of several recipes that combine the benefits of two automatic cooking programs within one recipe. Simply follow the sequence given in the recipe for excellent results.

Catch of the Day

Poaching and steaming have always been the most classic methods of cooking fish. Now, discover the newest "classic" — fish and shellfish microwave-style! So moist, tender, and delicious that you'll never want to cook seafood any other way. And all this with no elaborate procedures: No need to tie the fish in cheesecloth or use a special fish poacher. Shellfish steam to a succulent tenderness with very little water. If you think your microwave oven cooks chicken and meat fast, you'll be amazed at its speed with fish! For best results, fish should be prepared at the last minute. Even standing time is short. So, when planning a fish dinner, have everything ready. *Then* start to cook.

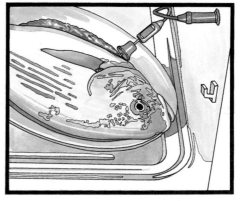

Poached Salmon (page 125) is best prepared in an oval baking dish (top left). Oysters and other bivalves should be arranged in a circle with one in center for thawing or cooking (top right). Rolled fish fillets are arranged in circular microwave pattern. Position one fillet, not center of dish, over circle on glass tray for surface-temperature sensor cooking (above left). Stuffed Bass (page 130) cooks perfectly using the temperature probe (above right).

Adapting Your Recipes

If your family likes seafood only when it is fried crackly-crisp, surprise them with a new taste delight when you try traditional fish recipes cooked in the microwave oven. They'll swear fish has been pampered and poached by the most famous French chef. Use the cooking charts and the preset recipes as guides for adapting your own dishes. If you don't find a recipe that matches or comes close to the conventional recipe you want to adapt, follow this general rule of thumb: Begin cooking at 70 or at HI for one-fifth of the time the conventional recipe recommends. Observe, and if it appears to be done earlier, open door and check. If the dish is not done, continue cooking 30 seconds at a time. As in conventional cooking, the secret to seafood is to watch it carefully, since fish can overcook in seconds. It's best to remove it when barely done and allow standing time to finish the cooking. If you follow these simple tips, you'll have excellent results:

☐ Most recipes that specify a particular variety of fish will work when any white fish is substituted. When a recipe calls for fresh or thawed frozen fish fillets, use sole, flounder, bluefish, cod, scrod, or any similar fish.

☐ Cook fish covered unless it is coated with crumbs, which seal in the juices.

☐ When cooking whole fish, the dish should be rotated one-quarter turn twice during the cooking process to help provide even cooking. The odd shape of the fish requires this procedure.

☐ Fish is done when the flesh becomes opaque and barely flakes with a fork.

☐ Shellfish is done when flesh is opaque and just firm.

☐ Shellfish come in their own cooking containers which respond well to microwaves. Clam and mussel shells open before your eyes. Shrimp, crab, and lobster shells turn pink.

☐ You can use the browning dish for fillets or fish patties. Preheat, add butter or oil, and brown on one side for best results.

☐ To remove seafood odors from the oven, combine 1 cup water with lemon juice and a few cloves in a small bowl. Cook on HI, 3 to 5 minutes.

Using the Defrosting Guide

1. Remove seafood from its original wrapper.
2. Place seafood in microproof dish.
3. One pound of frozen seafood takes 4 to 6 minutes to nearly thaw on 30 (defrost).
4. To prevent the outer edges from drying out or beginning to cook, it is best to remove seafood from the oven before it has completely thawed. By touching, you can judge whether it is becoming warm. It should then be removed. This is true even if the surface-temperature sensor has not yet turned the oven off automatically. Seafood is so delicate that you must be the final judge.
5. Finish defrosting under cold running water, separating fillets.
6. All seafood profits from 5 minutes standing time. This is automatically included in surface-temperature defrosting.
7. Cover head of whole fish with aluminum foil during thawing.
8. Feel free to turn seafood over or rearrange during defrosting. Simply open door. Touch START to resume thawing.

DEFROSTING GUIDE — SEAFOOD

Food	Amount	Cook Control Setting	Time (in minutes)	or	Automatic Sensor Method	Special Notes
Fish Fillets	1 lb. 2 lbs.	30 (defrost) 30 (defrost)	4 - 6 5 - 7	or	A0-7	Carefully separate fillets under cold water. Turn once.
Fish steaks	1 lb.	30 (defrost)	4 - 6	or	A0-6	Carefully separate steaks under cold running water.
Whole fish	8 - 10 oz. 1½ - 2 lbs.	30 (defrost) 30 (defrost)	4 - 6 5 - 7	or	A0-6	Shallow dish; shape of fish determines size. Should be icy when removed. Finish at room temperature. Cover head with aluminum foil. Turn once.
Lobster tails	8 oz. package	30 (defrost)	5 - 7	or	A0-7	Remove from package to baking dish.
Crab legs	8 - 10 oz.	30 (defrost)	5 - 7	or	A0-7	Glass baking dish. Break apart and turn once.
Crabmeat	6 oz.	30 (defrost)	4 - 5	or	A0-7	Break apart. Turn once.
Shrimp	1 lb.	30 (defrost)	3 - 4	or	A0-7	Remove from package to dish. Spread loosely in baking dish and rearrange during thawing as necessary.
Scallops	1 lb.	30 (defrost)	8 - 10	or	A0-7	Defrost in package if in block; spread out on baking dish if in pieces. Turn over and rearrange during thawing as necessary.
Oysters	12 oz.	30 (defrost)	3 - 4	or	A0-7	Remove from package to dish. Turn over and rearrange during thawing as necessary.

Using the Cooking Guide

1. Defrost seafood fully; then cook.
2. Remove original wrapping. Rinse under cold running water.
3. Place seafood in microproof baking dish with thick edges of fillets and steaks and thick ends of shellfish toward the outer edge of the dish.
4. Cover dish with plastic wrap or waxed paper.
5. Test often during the cooking period to avoid overcooking.
6. Method and time are the same for seafood in the shell or without the shell.

COOKING/DEFROSTING GUIDE — CONVENIENCE SEAFOOD
For Automatic Cooking, see Guide on page 29

Food	Amount	Cook Control Setting	Time (in minutes)	Special Notes
Shrimp croquettes	12 oz. package	80 (reheat)	6 - 8	Pierce sauce pouch, place on serving plate with croquettes. Cover, turn halfway through cooking time.
Fish sticks, frozen	4 oz. 8 oz.	80 (reheat) 80 (reheat)	2 - 3 3½ - 4½	Will not crisp. Cook on serving plate.
Tuna casserole, frozen	11 oz. package	HI (max. power)	4 - 6	Remove from package to 1-quart casserole. Stir once during cooking and before serving.
Shrimp or crab newburg, frozen pouch	6½ oz.	HI (max. power)	4 - 6	Place pouch on plate. Pierce pouch. Flex pouch to mix halfway through cooking time. Stir before serving.

COOKING GUIDE — SEAFOOD AND FISH

Food	Cook Control Setting	Time (in Minutes)	or	Automatic Sensor Method	Standing Time (in minutes)	Special Notes
Fish fillets, 1 lb. ½ inch thick,	HI (max. power)	4 - 5	or	A6-1	4 - 5	12 × 7-inch dish, covered.
2 lbs.	HI (max. power)	7 - 8	or	A6-1	4 - 5	
Fish steaks, 1 inch thick, 1 lb.	HI (max. power)	5 - 6	or	A6-1	5 - 6	12 × 7-inch dish, covered.
Whole fish 8 - 10 oz.	HI (max. power)	2½ - 3	or	A6-0	3 - 4	Appropriate shallow dish.
1½ - 2 lbs.	HI (max. power)	5 - 7	or	A6-0	5	
Crab legs 8 - 10 oz.	HI (max. power)	3 - 4	or	A6-2	5	Appropriate shallow dish. Rearrange at pause.
16 - 20 oz.	HI (max. power)	5 - 6		A6-2	5	
Shrimp, scallops 8 oz.	70 (roast)	3 - 4	or	A6-2		Appropriate shallow dish. At pause, remove cooked pieces. Rearrange.
1 lb.	70 (roast)	5 - 7	or	A6-2		
Snails, clams, oysters, 12 oz.	70 (roast)	3 - 4		not applicable		Shallow dish, covered. Rearrange halfway.
Lobster tails 1: 8 oz.	HI (max. power)	3 - 4	or	A6-3	5	Shallow dish. Split shell to reduce curling.
2: 8 oz. each	HI (max. power)	5 - 6	or	A6-3	5	
4: 8 oz. each	HI (max. power)	9 - 11	or	A6-3	5	

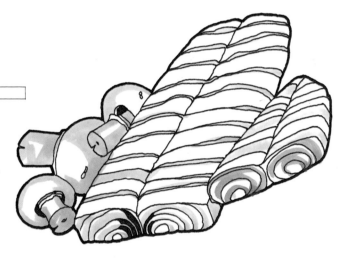

| A6 | 1 |

Fish Fillets with Mushrooms

Preset Cooking Time: about 4 minutes

- 1 pound fish fillets
- 2 tablespoons butter or margarine
- 2 tablespoons dry white wine
- ½ teaspoon lemon juice
- 1 medium tomato, peeled and cut into cubes
- 2 green onions, thinly sliced
- ½ cup sliced mushrooms
- ¼ teaspoon salt

Arrange fillets in 8-inch round or oval microproof baking dish with thickest parts toward outside of dish. Dot with butter. Combine wine and lemon juice. Pour over fillets. Top with remaining ingredients. Place in oven with 1 fillet over circle on glass tray. Cover with waxed paper. Touch A6. Touch 1. Touch START. *(Oven cooks: HI, about 4 minutes.)* Let stand 3 minutes before serving.

2 servings

| A6 | 1 |

Fish Fillets

Preset Cooking Time: about 4 minutes

1 pound fish fillets, ½ inch thick

Arrange fillets in round or oval microproof baking dish with thickest parts toward outside of dish. Place in oven with 1 fillet over circle on glass tray. Cover with waxed paper. Touch A6. Touch 1. Touch START. *(Oven cooks: HI, about 4 minutes.)* Let stand 3 minutes before serving.

2 servings

```
A6    1
```

Fish Steaks

Preset Cooking Time: about 6 minutes

- 2 halibut, salmon, swordfish, or
   shark steaks (1/2 pound each),
   1 inch thick
- 2 tablespoons butter, melted
- 2 teaspoons lemon juice
- 1/2 teaspoon dillweed (optional)

Arrange fish in round or oval microproof baking dish with thickest parts toward outside of dish. Combine butter and lemon juice. Brush over fish. Sprinkle with dillweed. Place in oven with 1 steak over circle on glass tray. Cover with waxed paper. Touch A6. Touch 1. Touch START. *(Oven cooks: HI, about 6 minutes.)* Let stand 3 minutes before serving.

2 servings

```
A7:0   HIGHER   &   A6   1   HIGHER
```

Poached Salmon

Preset Cooking Time: about 11 minutes

- 2 cups water
- 1 medium stalk celery, cut into
   chunks
- 1/2 medium lemon, sliced
- 1/2 medium onion, sliced
- 3 tablespoons vinegar
- 2 tablespoons lemon juice
- 1 1/2 teaspoons salt
- 6 whole cloves
- 1 bay leaf
- 4 salmon, swordfish, halibut, or
   other fish steaks (5 to 6
   ounces each)
   Parsley sprigs

Combine all ingredients except fish and parsley in 2-quart microproof casserole. Cover and place in oven. Touch A7. Touch HIGHER. Touch START. *(Oven cooks: HI, about 7 minutes.)*

At Pause, add fish; spoon liquid over top. Do not cover. Touch A6. Touch 1. Touch HIGHER. Touch START. *(Oven cooks: HI, about 4 minutes.)*

Carefully turn fish over. Cover and let stand 5 minutes. Transfer to serving platter and garnish with parsley. Serve hot or chilled.

4 servings

Grilled Swordfish Steaks

Total Cooking Time: 3 minutes

- 2 swordfish or salmon steaks
   (1/2 pound each)
- 1 tablespoon vegetable oil
   Lemon pepper
   Paprika

Brush fish on 1 side with oil. Sprinkle with lemon pepper and paprika; set aside. Preheat 9-inch microwave browning dish according to manufacturer's directions. Arrange fish on preheated dish, seasoned-side down, with thickest parts toward outside of dish. Place in oven. Cover loosely with waxed paper. Cook on HI, 2 minutes.

Turn fish over. Cover. Cook on HI, 1 minute. Let stand 2 minutes before serving.

2 servings

Tuna-Mushroom Patties

Total Cooking Time: 9 1/2 minutes

- 2 tablespoons milk
- 1 can (10 3/4 ounces) cream of celery
   soup, undiluted, divided
- 2 cans (6 1/2 ounces each) tuna,
   drained
- 1/2 cup dry bread crumbs
- 1/2 cup chopped mushrooms
- 1 large egg, beaten
- 2 tablespoons instant minced onion
- 1/4 teaspoon white pepper
- 2 tablespoons minced parsley

Combine milk and half of the soup in 2-cup glass measure; set aside. Blend remaining soup, tuna, bread crumbs, mushrooms, egg, onion, and pepper. Shape into 6 patties, using about 1/2 cup mixture for each. Place in shallow microproof baking dish. Place in oven. Cover with waxed paper. Cook on HI, 8 minutes.

Remove from oven. Place milk mixture in oven. Cook on HI, 1 1/2 minutes.

Stir sauce several times. Pour over tuna patties. Sprinkle with parsley and serve.

6 servings

```
       A2    2    &   A6    1
```

Fillet of Fish Amandine

Preset Cooking Time: about 7 minutes

- ½ cup slivered almonds
- ½ cup butter or margarine
- 1 pound fish fillets
- 1 tablespoon lemon juice
- 1 teaspoon chopped parsley
- ½ teaspoon salt
- ¼ teaspoon dillweed
- ⅛ teaspoon pepper

Place almonds and butter in 8-inch microproof baking dish. Place in oven. Touch A2. Touch 2. Touch START. *(Oven cooks: HI, about 2 minutes.)*

At Pause, stir. Touch START. *(Oven cooks: HI, about 1 minute.)*

Remove almonds from dish with slotted spoon; set aside. Add fillets; turn to coat both sides with butter. Sprinkle with lemon juice, parsley, salt, dillweed, and pepper. Roll up fillets in dish. Place in oven with 1 fillet over circle on glass tray. Cover with waxed paper. Touch A6. Touch 1. Touch START. *(Oven cooks: HI, about 4 minutes.)*

Sprinkle with almonds. Cover and let stand 4 minutes. Serve garnished with lemon wedges, parsley sprigs, or paprika.

2 to 3 servings

This is one of several recipes that combine the benefits of two automatic cooking programs with one recipe. Simply follow the sequence given in the recipe for excellent results.

← *Fillet of Fish Amandine*

Scallops Vermouth

Total Cooking Time: 11 minutes

- ¼ cup butter or margarine
- 1 tablespoon minced onion
- 2 tablespoons all-purpose flour
- 1 pound bay scallops
- ½ cup sliced mushrooms
- ¼ cup dry vermouth
- 2 teaspoons lemon juice
- ½ teaspoon salt
- ⅛ teaspoon pepper
- 1 bay leaf
- ½ cup half-and-half
- 1 egg yolk
- ½ teaspoon hot pepper sauce (optional)
- 1 tablespoon chopped parsley

Combine butter and onion in 2-quart microproof casserole. Place in oven. Cook on HI, 2 minutes.

Stir in flour. Add scallops, mushrooms, vermouth, lemon juice, salt, pepper, and bay leaf; stir carefully. Cover. Cook on 80, 4 minutes.

Discard bay leaf. Whisk half-and-half with egg yolk. Whisk small amount of hot liquid into yolk mixture; whisk mixture back into casserole. Stir in hot pepper sauce. Cover. Cook on 60, 3 minutes.

Stir. Cover. Cook on 60, 2 minutes.

Sprinkle with parsley and serve.

4 servings

Simple Salmon Ring

Total Cooking Time: 35 minutes

- 2 cans (16 ounces each) red salmon, drained, skin and bones discarded
- 3 slices soft bread, cut into cubes
- ½ cup milk
- ¼ cup butter, melted
- 1 large egg, lightly beaten
- ½ teaspoon salt

Grease 10-cup microproof ring mold. Combine all ingredients. Turn into prepared mold, packing firmly. Place in oven. Cover with waxed paper. Cook on 70, 30 minutes, then on 10, 5 minutes.

Unmold onto serving platter. Serve with Lemon Butter Sauce (page 174) or Hot Lemony Dill Sauce (page 175) in center of ring, if desired.

6 to 8 servings

Salmon Ring

Total Cooking Time: 12 minutes

            Paprika
  1   can (16 ounces) red salmon,
          undrained
  1   cup soft bread crumbs
  ¾   cup finely chopped celery
  2   large eggs, lightly beaten
  3   tablespoons minced green onion
  2   tablespoons mayonnaise
      Pinch dillweed
      Minced parsley

Butter 6-cup microproof ring mold. Sprinkle with paprika and set aside. Combine remaining ingredients except parsley. Turn into prepared mold, spreading evenly. Place in oven. Cook on HI, 7 minutes, then on 20, 5 minutes. Unmold onto serving platter. Garnish with parsley and serve.

4 to 6 servings

Scampi

Total Cooking Time: 4 minutes

  3   tablespoons vegetable oil
  2   large cloves garlic, minced
  3   tablespoons minced parsley
  2   tablespoons dry white wine
  ⅛   teaspoon paprika
  ¾   pound large shrimp, shelled,
          deveined, and butterflied,
          tails intact
      Juice of ½ medium lemon
      Salt and pepper
      Chopped parsley

Combine oil and garlic in oval microproof baking dish just large enough to hold all ingredients. Place in oven. Cook on HI, 1 minute.
Stir in minced parsley, wine, and paprika. Cook on HI, 1 minute.
Add shrimp. Sprinkle with lemon juice, salt, and pepper, and stir to coat well. Arrange shrimp with tails toward center of dish. Cover with waxed paper. Cook on HI, 1 minute.
Stir; cover. Cook on HI, 1 minute.
Garnish with parsley and serve.

2 servings

Shrimp Creole

Total Cooking Time: 15 minutes

  4   green onions, thinly sliced
  ½   cup chopped green pepper
  ¼   cup chopped celery
  1   clove garlic, minced
  2   tablespoons butter or margarine
  1   can (16 ounces) whole tomatoes,
          drained and chopped
  1   can (6 ounces) tomato paste
  2   teaspoons parsley flakes
  ½   teaspoon salt
  ¼   teaspoon cayenne
  1   package (10 ounces) frozen cooked
          shrimp, thawed

Combine green onions, green pepper, celery, garlic, and butter in 2-quart microproof casserole. Cover and place in oven. Cook on HI, 3 minutes.
Stir in remaining ingredients except shrimp. Cover. Cook on 80, 5 minutes.
Blend in shrimp. Cover. Cook on 80, 3 minutes.
Stir; cover. Cook on 80, 4 minutes.
Stir through several times. Serve over hot rice.

4 to 6 servings

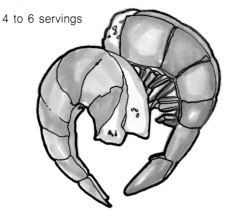

Broccoli (Guide, page 151), →
Salmon Ring and Parsley New Potatoes (page 160)

```
A6:0    HIGHER
```

Stuffed Mountain Trout

Preset Cooking Time: about 4 minutes

- 2 trout (8 ounces each), or one 1-pound trout
- ¼ cup butter or margarine, melted
- ¼ cup instant minced onion
- ¼ cup slivered almonds
- 4 teaspoons minced parsley
- 4 to 5 medium mushrooms, sliced (optional)

Rinse trout in cool water and pat dry. Place in shallow microproof baking dish. Brush cavities with some of the butter. Stuff with some of the onion, almonds, parsley, and mushrooms. Pour remaining butter over trout. Sprinkle with remaining onion, almonds, and parsley; arrange remaining mushrooms around trout. Place in oven. Cover with waxed paper. Touch A6. Touch HIGHER. Touch START. *(Oven cooks: HI, about 4 minutes.)*

2 servings

You can save some clean-up time by preparing and cooking the trout right on a microproof serving platter.

Stuffed Bass

Total Cooking Time: about 14½ minutes

- 1 whole bass (2 pounds), cleaned
- ¼ cup chopped onion
- 2 tablespoons butter or margarine
- ¾ cup dry bread crumbs
- ½ cup chopped mushrooms
- 2 tablespoons minced parsley
- 1 large egg, beaten
- 1 tablespoon lemon juice
- ½ teaspoon salt
- ⅛ teaspoon pepper
- 1 tablespoon bottled brown sauce
- 1 tablespoon water

Rinse fish well in cool water and pat dry; set aside. Place onion and butter in 1½-quart microproof bowl. Place in oven. Cook on HI, 2 minutes.

Stir in remaining ingredients except brown sauce and water. Spoon stuffing into cavity of bass. Place on oval microproof platter or in 11 × 7-inch microproof baking dish. Combine brown sauce and water; brush over fish.

Insert temperature probe into meatiest part of fish, parallel to spine. Place in oven. Cover dish lightly with plastic wrap, but wrap loosely around probe to vent. Plug in probe. Cook on HI, with probe set at 170°F.

Let stand 5 minutes before serving.

4 servings

Other whole fish can be substituted for bass, such as red snapper, lake trout, salmon, or whitefish. Whole stuffed fish can be cooked without the temperature probe; cook on HI, allowing 5 to 7 minutes per pound.

Shrimp Veracruz

Total Cooking Time: 16 minutes

- 1 large onion, cut into chunks
- 1 large green pepper, seeded and cut into chunks
- 2 cloves garlic, crushed
- 2 tablespoons vegetable oil
- 1 can (8 ounces) tomato sauce
- ¼ cup dry white wine
- ½ teaspoon oregano
- ½ teaspoon salt
- ¼ teaspoon cumin
  Dash hot pepper sauce
- 1 pound jumbo shrimp, shelled and deveined
- 2 tablespoons chopped parsley

Combine onion, green pepper, garlic, and oil in shallow oval microproof baking dish. Place in oven. Cook on HI, 3 minutes.

Stir through several times. Add tomato sauce, wine, oregano, salt, cumin, and hot pepper sauce. Cook on 80, 5 minutes.

Add shrimp. Spoon sauce mixture over shrimp. Cook on 70, 4 minutes.

Stir. Cook on 70, 4 minutes.

Garnish with parsley and serve over hot rice or noodles.

4 servings

Stuffed Mountain Trout →

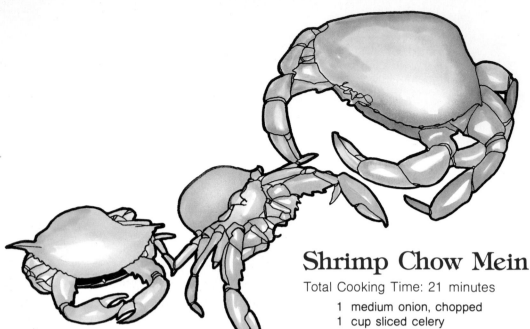

Shrimp Chow Mein

Total Cooking Time: 21 minutes

- 1 medium onion, chopped
- 1 cup sliced celery
- 1 green pepper, seeded and cut into thin strips
- 2 tablespoons butter or margarine
- 1 pound fresh bean sprouts, or 1 can (16 ounces) bean sprouts, drained
- 1 can (8 ounces) sliced water chestnuts, drained
- 8 to 10 ounces cooked deveined shelled shrimp
- ½ cup sliced mushrooms
- 2 tablespoons chopped pimiento
- 3 tablespoons cornstarch
- 3 tablespoons soy sauce
- 1 cup water
- 2 teaspoons chicken bouillon granules

Combine onion, celery, green pepper, and butter in 2-quart microproof casserole. Cover and place in oven. Cook on HI, 10 minutes.

Add bean sprouts, water chestnuts, shrimp, mushrooms, and pimiento; set aside. Dissolve cornstarch in soy sauce in 4-cup glass measure. Add water and bouillon and stir until bouillon is dissolved. Place mixture in oven. Cook on HI, 3 minutes.

Stir. Cook on HI, 3 minutes.

Stir sauce into shrimp mixture. Cover and place in oven. Cook on HI, 5 minutes.

Stir through several times. Serve over hot rice, topped with chow mein noodles, if desired.

5 to 6 servings

A7:0	&	A6	2

Crab Imperial

Preset Cooking Time: about 13 minutes

- ½ cup chopped onions
- 2 tablespoons butter or margarine
- 1½ cups half-and-half
- 1 cup sliced mushrooms
- 3 tablespoons all-purpose flour
- 3 tablespoons dry white wine
- ¼ teaspoon salt
- ⅛ teaspoon pepper
- 2 egg yolks, lightly beaten
- 1½ cups crab meat chunks

Place onions and butter in 2-quart glass measure. Place in oven. Touch A7. Touch START. (Oven cooks: HI, about 3 minutes.)

Add half-and-half, mushrooms, flour, wine, salt, and pepper; blend well. Touch A6. Touch 2. Touch START. (Oven cooks: 70, about 6 minutes.)

At Pause, stir and blend in egg yolks. Cover with waxed paper. Touch START. (Oven cooks: 70, about 2 minutes.)

At Pause, stir and add crab meat; blend well. Touch START. (Oven cooks: 70, about 2 minutes.)

Serve in au gratin dishes, individual custard cups, ramekins, or shells.

4 to 6 servings

A Visit to the Dairy Case

Eggs and cheese are great microwave partners, but they can stand by themselves, too. There's nothing quite like plain scrambled eggs or cheese fondue made in the microwave oven. From the most simple omelets to fancy quiches, the microwave oven can enliven an ordinary breakfast, Sunday brunch, or any meal. The recipes in this chapter are perfect for unexpected guests any time of day. Just remember to have on hand a carton of fresh eggs and some cheeses, like Cheddar or Swiss, that keep well. Then, a little onion and seasonings are all you need to make a

quick, easy, and delicious meal. As a special treat, we have included in this chapter a special recipe for Quiche Lorraine (page 138). One reminder: Do not hard-boil eggs in the microwave oven. Pressure builds up inside the shell, which causes the egg to burst. Eggs must be removed from their shells and egg yolks should always be carefully pierced before cooking to prevent them from popping. Keep in mind that eggs and cheese are delicate ingredients; handle them with care and you will have delectable results.

Omelet Classique (page 136) is cooked and served in the same dish (above left). Just a flip makes your Sunny-Side-Up Eggs (page 138) become "Over Easy" if that's your preference (above). Refrigerated cheese can be quickly brought to room temperature. Cook on 60, 1 minute (left).

Adapting Your Recipes

The best advice for adapting recipes that use eggs and cheese as primary ingredients is "better to undercook than overcook." Cheese and eggs cook so quickly that a few seconds can make the difference between airy excellence and a rubbery disaster. That's why we prefer to put you in charge of the timing instead of the sensors. Eggs and cheese are such delicate ingredients and must be handled with care for delectable results. That's not to make you shy away from developing your own recipes. You will be able to make countless variations on the recipes here, substituting vegetables and cooked meat, and adding your own spices and sauces. Conventional soufflé recipes do not adapt well to microwave cooking. Microwave soufflé recipes require a special form of stabilization because they cook so quickly; therefore, evaporated milk is used for the cream sauce base. The tips below will guide you to microwave success with all your egg and cheese recipes:

☐ Undercook eggs slightly and allow standing time to complete cooking. Eggs become tough when overcooked. Always check doneness to avoid overcooking.
☐ Cover poaching or baking eggs to trap steam and ensure even cooking.
☐ Eggs are usually cooked at 60 or 70.
☐ If you want a soft yolk, remove the egg from oven before whites are completely cooked. A brief standing time allows whites to set without overcooking yolks.
☐ Add 1/8 to 1/4 teaspoon vinegar to the water when poaching eggs to help the white coagulate.
☐ Cook bacon and egg combinations on HI, since most of the microwaves are attracted to the bacon because of its high fat content.
☐ Omelets and scrambled eggs should be stirred at least once during cooking. Fondues and sauces profit from occasional stirring during the cooking time.
☐ Cheese melts quickly and makes an attractive topping for casseroles and sandwiches.
☐ Cook cheese on 70 or a lower setting for short periods of time to avoid separation and toughening.

COOKING GUIDE — CONVENIENCE EGGS AND CHEESE

Food	Amount	Cook Control	Time (in minutes)	Special Notes
Omelet, frozen	10 oz.	80 (reheat)	4 - 5	Use microproof plate.
Egg substitute	8 oz.	50 (simmer)	4 - 4½	Turn carton over after 1 minute. Open carton after 1½ minutes. Stir every 30 seconds until smooth.
Soufflés: Corn, frozen	12 oz.	HI (max. power)	10 - 12	Use 1½-quart casserole, covered. Rotate casserole twice.
Cheese, frozen	12 oz.	HI (max. power)	11 - 13	Use 1½-quart casserole, covered. Rotate casserole twice.
Spinach, frozen	12 oz.	HI (max. power)	12 - 15	Use 1½-quart casserole, covered. Rotate casserole twice.
Welsh rabbit, frozen	10 oz.	70 (roast)	6 - 7	Use 1½-quart casserole, covered. Stir during cooking time.

COOKING GUIDE — SCRAMBLED EGGS
Cook on 60.

Number of Eggs	Liquid (Milk or Cream)	Butter	Minutes to Cook
1	1 tablespoon	1 teaspoon	1 to 1½
2	2 tablespoons	2 teaspoons	2 to 2½
4	3 tablespoons	3 teaspoons	4½ to 5½
6	4 tablespoons	4 teaspoons	7 to 8

- Break eggs into a microproof bowl or glass measure. Add milk or cream. Beat with a fork. Add butter. Cover with waxed paper. Stir at least once during cooking time from the outside to the center. Let stand 1 minute before serving.

COOKING GUIDE — POACHED EGGS
Cook on HI to boil water; on 60 after adding egg.

Number of Eggs	Water	Container	Minutes to Boil Water	Minutes to Cook
1	¼ cup	6-ounce microproof custard cup	1¾ to 2¾	1
2	¼ cup	6-ounce microproof custard cups	2¾	1½ to 2
3	¼ cup	6-ounce microproof custard cups	2¾ to 3¼	2 to 2¼
4	1 cup	1-quart microproof dish	2¼ to 4¼	2½ to 3

- Bring water to a boil with a pinch of salt and up to ¼ teaspoon vinegar. Break egg carefully into hot water. Pierce egg lightly with toothpick. Cover with waxed paper. Let stand, covered, 1 minute before serving.

Puffy Cheddar Omelet

Total Cooking Time: 7¾ minutes

- 4 large eggs, separated
- ⅓ cup mayonnaise
- 2 tablespoons water
- 1 tablespoon butter or margarine
- ½ cup (2 ounces) grated Cheddar cheese
- 1 tablespoon minced parsley

Beat egg whites with electric mixer until soft peaks form. Beat yolks, mayonnaise, and water. Gently fold whites into yolk mixture; set aside. Place butter in 9-inch microproof pie plate. Place in oven. Cook on HI, 45 seconds.

Tilt dish to coat evenly with butter. Pour in egg mixture. Cook on 60, 6 minutes. (If eggs begin to rise unevenly, open door and rotate dish one-quarter turn; touch START.)

Sprinkle mixture with cheese. Cook on 60, 1 minute.

Fold omelet in half, then cut in half. Slide onto serving plates. Sprinkle with parsley and serve.

2 servings

Eggs in Nests

Total Cooking Time: 5 minutes

- 2 very firm tomatoes (8 ounces each)
- 1 tablespoon parsley flakes
- 1 tablespoon onion flakes
- ⅛ teaspoon salt
  Dash pepper
- 2 large eggs

Slice tops off tomatoes. Carefully scoop out center pulp and seeds, leaving thick shells; discard seeds. Invert tomatoes onto paper towels to drain. Chop pulp. Transfer to bowl. Mix in parsley, onion, salt, and pepper. Fill shells half full with mixture. Place in shallow microproof dish. Break 1 egg into each tomato; carefully pierce yolks with toothpick. Place in oven. Cover with waxed paper. Cook on HI, 2 minutes.

Rotate dish one-half turn. Cook on 60, 3 minutes. Let stand 2 minutes before serving.

2 servings

Omelet Classique

Total Cooking Time: 5½ minutes

- 1 tablespoon butter or margarine
- 4 large eggs
- ¼ cup water
- ½ teaspoon salt
- ⅛ teaspoon pepper

Place butter in 9-inch microproof pie plate. Place in oven. Cook on HI, 30 seconds.

Beat remaining ingredients with fork. Pour over butter in pie plate. Cover with waxed paper. Cook on 60, 3 minutes.

Stir lightly; cover. Cook on 60, 2 minutes.

Let stand 2 minutes. Fold omelet in half, then cut in half. Slide onto serving plates and serve immediately.

2 servings

Before folding omelet, you can top with crumbled cooked bacon, grated cheese, chopped cooked ham, diced green chilies, or chopped tomato, if desired.

Shirred Eggs

Total Cooking Time: 2½ minutes

- 1 teaspoon butter or margarine
- 2 large eggs
- 1 tablespoon half-and-half
    Salt and pepper

Place butter in microproof ramekin or small bowl. Place in oven. Cook on 70, 30 seconds.

Carefully break eggs into ramekin. Gently pierce yolks in several places with toothpicks. Add half-and-half. Cover lightly with plastic wrap. Cook on 60, 2 minutes.

Let stand 1 minute. Season with salt and pepper before serving.

1 serving

Poached Egg

Total Cooking Time: 2½ minutes

- ¼ cup water
- ¼ teaspoon vinegar
    Pinch salt
- 1 large egg

Mix water, vinegar, and salt in 6-ounce microproof custard cup. Place in oven. Cook on HI, 1½ minutes.

Carefully break egg into hot liquid. Gently pierce yolk in several places with toothpick. Cover with waxed paper. Cook on 60, 1 minute. Let stand 1 minute before serving.

1 serving

Cheese Scramble

Total Cooking Time: 2½ minutes

- 1 large egg
- 2 tablespoons low-fat milk
- 6 tablespoons (1½ ounces) shredded Monterey Jack or Cheddar cheese
    Salt and pepper

Break egg into small microproof bowl. Add milk; mix well with fork. Mix in cheese, salt, and pepper. Place in oven. Cover with waxed paper. Cook on 60, 1 minute.

Stir. Cover. Cook on 60, 1½ minutes.

Stir before serving.

1 serving

Raisin Bran Muffins (page 73), Omelet Classique, Shirred Eggs →

Quiche Lorraine

Total Cooking Time: 24 minutes

- 6 slices bacon
- 3 green onions, thinly sliced
- 2 cups (8 ounces) shredded Swiss cheese
- 1 baked 9-inch Homemade Pie Shell (page 194)
- 1 can (13 ounces) evaporated milk, undiluted
- 4 large eggs, beaten
- 1 teaspoon prepared mustard
- ¼ teaspoon salt
- ¼ teaspoon nutmeg
  Dash cayenne

Arrange bacon on paper towel-lined microproof plate. Place in oven. Cover with another paper towel. Cook on HI, 7 minutes.

Crumble bacon. Reserve 1 tablespoon each bacon and green onion for topping. Sprinkle remaining bacon, green onions, and cheese in pie shell; set aside. Pour milk into 2-cup glass measure. Place in oven. Cook on HI, 3 minutes.

Combine eggs, mustard, salt, nutmeg, and cayenne. Gradually stir in milk. Pour into pie shell. Sprinkle with reserved bacon and green onion. Place in oven. Cook on 70, 14 minutes. Let stand 10 minutes before serving.

6 servings

If you are in a hurry and use a ready-made pie shell, be sure to place it in a microproof pie plate before filling.

Sunny-Side-Up Eggs

Total Cooking Time: 40 seconds

- 1 tablespoon butter or margarine
- 2 large eggs
  Salt and pepper

Preheat microwave browning dish according to manufacturer's directions. Add butter to dish and let stand until melted, then tilt dish carefully to coat evenly with butter. Carefully break eggs into dish. Gently pierce yolks in several places with toothpick. Season with salt and pepper. Cover. Place in oven. Cook on HI, 40 seconds.

Let stand 1 minute before serving.

1 to 2 servings

Cheddar and Onion Egg

Total Cooking Time: 2 minutes

- 1 teaspoon butter or margarine
- 1 green onion, thinly sliced
- 1 large egg
- 1 heaping tablespoon shredded Cheddar cheese

Combine butter and onion in microproof custard cup. Place in oven. Cook on HI, 1 minute.

Carefully break egg into same cup. Gently pierce yolk in several places with toothpick. Sprinkle with cheese. Cover with waxed paper. Place in oven. Cook on 60, 1 minute. Let stand 1 minute before serving.

1 serving

Quiche Lorraine →

Fiesta Scramble

Total Cooking Time: 10 minutes

  - 6 large eggs
  - 6 tablespoons milk
  - ¼ teaspoon salt
     Dash pepper
  - ⅛ teaspoon garlic powder
  - 2 small tomatoes, peeled and chopped
  - 1 can (4 ounces) diced green chilies, drained
  - 2 tablespoons butter or margarine, cut up
  - 1 tablespoon minced chives
  - 1 cup (4 ounces) grated sharp Cheddar cheese
  - 2 tablespoons minced parsley

Beat eggs, milk, salt, pepper, and garlic powder; set aside. Arrange tomatoes, chilies, butter, and chives evenly in bottom of 10-inch microproof pie plate. Place in oven. Cook on HI, 3 minutes.

Stir. Add egg mixture. Cook on 70, 3 minutes.

Stir outside of egg mixture toward center. Cook on 70, 3 minutes.

Stir outside of egg mixture toward center again. Sprinkle with cheese. Cook on HI, 1 minute.

Sprinkle with parsley before serving.

4 servings

Welsh Rabbit on Toast

Total Cooking Time: 12 minutes

  - 4 cups (1 pound) shredded sharp Cheddar cheese
  - 4 teaspoons butter or margarine
  - ¾ teaspoon Worcestershire sauce
  - ½ teaspoon paprika
  - ¼ teaspoon salt
  - ¼ teaspoon dry mustard
  - ¼ teaspoon cayenne
  - 2 large eggs, lightly beaten
  - 1 cup flat beer or ale, at room temperature
  - 4 to 6 slices French bread, toasted

Combine cheese, butter, Worcestershire, paprika, salt, mustard, and cayenne in 2-quart microproof casserole. Cover and place in oven. Cook on 50, 3 minutes.

Stir; cover. Cook on 50, 3 minutes.

Stir small amount cheese mixture into eggs, then stir eggs back into cheese mixture. Mix in beer. Cover and place in oven. Cook on 50, 3 minutes.

Stir through several times. Cook on 50, 3 minutes.

Stir thoroughly and briskly. Arrange toast in shallow bowls. Ladle cheese mixture over top and serve.

4 to 6 servings

Festival Eggs

Total Cooking Time: 6 minutes

  - 6 large eggs
  - ½ cup dairy sour cream
  - ¼ cup grated Parmesan cheese
  - 2 tablespoons chopped green pepper
  - 2 tablespoons chopped pimiento
  - 2 tablespoons butter or margarine
  - ½ teaspoon salt
  - ¼ teaspoon thyme
  - ¼ teaspoon dry mustard

Beat eggs in 2-quart microproof casserole until frothy. Carefully stir in remaining ingredients. Place in oven. Cover with waxed paper. Cook on HI, 2 minutes.

Stir. Cover. Cook on HI, 2 minutes, then on 10, 2 minutes.

4 servings

The microwave oven provides no significant saving of time when cooking pasta and rice. It takes just as long to rehydrate these products in the microwave oven as it does conventionally. While the oven can cook them separately, there is no advantage. Once the pasta is prepared and added to the rest of the ingredients according to the recipe, casseroles and similar dishes cook in speedy microwave time. And there are some wonderful recipes in this chapter that don't require advance preparation of the rice or pasta. Another great advantage the microwave oven offers is its ability to reheat pasta, rice, and cereal without adding water or having to stir. No worry about soggy noodles or starchy rice. And you'll find that pasta and rice taste as good reheated as when freshly cooked!

The microwave oven works wonders with pasta: simply top precooked rotini or macaroni with sauce, tomato slices, and cheese for a dandy lunch. Use surface-temperature sensor method, A1-5-HIGHER (top left). Cook frozen rice pouches on A3-2 (top right). One-Step Lasagna (page 146) is just one of several dishes that don't require precooked pasta. Double-wrapping with plastic wrap traps the moisture needed to reconstitute the pasta (above left). Hot cereal is now easy to prepare and serve in the same dish. Touch A2. Touch 2. Touch START. Stir at Pause. That's all there is to it! (above right).

Adapting Your Recipes

You will discover that your conventional rice or noodle-based casseroles can be easily adjusted to microwave cooking. When you find a similar recipe here, adapt your ingredients to the microwave method, but follow only about three-quarters of the recommended microwave cooking times in the similar recipe. Then check, and extend the cooking time at 1-minute intervals until done. Make a note of the final cooking time for a repeat of the dish. By "trial" and trying to avoid "error," you'll soon be able to add to our collection of pasta and rice dishes. Some tips:

☐ Casseroles may require occasional stirring to distribute heat.

☐ Cooked pasta or rice to be used in a casserole should be slightly firmer than if it is to be eaten at once. Simply cook a bit less.

☐ Quick-cooking rice may be substituted in converting from conventional recipes that call for uncooked rice, in order to make sure the rice will cook in the same short time as the rest of the ingredients. Otherwise, precook regular rice to a firm stage and add to the casserole.

☐ To reheat pasta, rice, and cereals in the microwave without drying them out, cover tightly with plastic wrap. Set at 80 for just a few minutes, depending upon amount.

☐ Pasta and rice are best when added to other ingredients, as in casseroles. However, the oven can cook them separately. Place spaghetti in 13×9-inch baking dish. Add 2½ cups hot water for 2 ounces of uncooked spaghetti; 4 cups for 4 ounces. Bring water to a boil on HI (6 minutes for 2 ounces; 10 minutes for 4 ounces of spaghetti). Then finish on 50 (6 minutes for 2 ounces; 8 minutes for 4 ounces).

☐ For rice, add 2 cups water to 1 cup of uncooked rice. Cook on HI, 4 to 5 minutes, or until water comes to a boil. Finish cooking on 50, 13 to 15 minutes. Allow 5 minutes standing time.

☐ Cook grits or other hot cereals on HI, 6 to 7 minutes for ⅓ cup grits (uncooked). Follow package directions for liquid. You can also use the surface-temperature sensor program A2-2 which has a built-in pause for stirring.

COOKING/DEFROSTING GUIDE — CONVENIENCE RICE AND PASTA
For Automatic Sensor Method see Page 29

Food	Amount	Cook Control Setting	Time (in minutes)	Special Notes
Rice, cooked refrigerated	1 cup	80 (reheat)	1½ - 2	Use covered bowl. Let stand 2 minutes, stir.
Cooked, frozen	1 cup 2 cups	80 (reheat) 80 (reheat)	2 - 3 3 - 4	
Pouch, frozen	11 oz.	80 (reheat)	6 - 7	Slit pouch.
Fried rice, frozen	10 oz.	HI (max. power)	5 - 6	Use covered casserole. Stir twice. Let stand 5 minutes.
Spanish rice, canned	12 oz.	HI (max. power)	4 - 5	Use covered casserole. Stir twice. Let stand 3 minutes.
Lasagna, frozen	21 oz.	70 (roast)	19 - 20	Use covered casserole. Let stand, covered, 5 minutes.
Macaroni and beef, frozen	11 oz.	HI (max. power)	7 - 9	Use covered casserole. Stir twice.
Macaroni and cheese, frozen	10 oz.	HI (max. power)	7 - 9	Use covered casserole. Stir twice.
Spaghetti and meatballs, frozen	14 oz.	HI (max. power)	8 - 10	Use covered casserole. Stir twice.

A1 2 & A1 6

Chinese Fried Rice

Preset Cooking Time: about 12 minutes

    2 tablespoons butter or margarine
    3 cups cooked rice
1½ tablespoons soy sauce
    3 large eggs
    1 tablespoon water
 ¼ teaspoon sugar
 ¼ cup thinly sliced green onions

Place butter in 3-quart microproof casserole. Place in oven. Touch A1. Touch 2. Touch START. *(Oven cooks: 80, about 1 minute.)*

Add rice and soy sauce; blend well. Beat eggs, water, and sugar until blended; pour over rice. Cover and place in oven. Touch A1. Touch 6. Touch START. *(Oven cooks: 80, about 8 minutes.)*

At Pause, stir in green onions. Cover. Touch START. *(Oven cooks: 80, about 3 minutes.)*

Stir before serving.

4 to 6 servings

A7:0

Rice Pilaf

Preset Cooking Time: about 14 minutes

    2 cups water
    1 cup long grain rice
 ¼ cup chopped green pepper
 ¼ cup chopped onion
 ¼ cup instant minced onion
    2 tablespoons butter or margarine
    2 teaspoons chicken bouillon
      granules

Combine all ingredients in 2-quart microproof casserole. Cover and place in oven. Touch A7. Touch START. *(Oven cooks: HI, about 14 minutes.)*

Stir through before serving.

4 servings

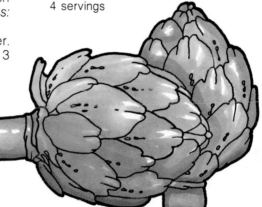

Artichoke Pilaf

Total Cooking Time: 7 minutes

    2 jars (6 ounces each) marinated
      artichoke hearts, drained,
      3 tablespoons liquid
      reserved
    1 cup chopped onions
 ½ cup thinly sliced celery
    1 clove garlic, minced
    1 cup chicken broth
    1 cup cooked rice
 ⅓ cup minced parsley
 ½ teaspoon salt
 ⅛ teaspoon pepper

Combine reserved artichoke liquid, onions, celery, and garlic in 2-quart microproof casserole. Place in oven. Cook on HI, 3 minutes.

Stir in remaining ingredients. Cover. Cook on HI, 2 minutes.

Stir; cover. Cook on HI, 2 minutes.

Remove cover. Let mixture stand 5 minutes before serving.

4 to 6 servings

Spanish Rice

Total Cooking Time: 35 minutes

1½ cups water
    1 can (16 ounces) whole tomatoes,
      drained and chopped
    1 can (6 ounces) tomato paste
 ¼ cup finely chopped onion
 ¼ cup chopped celery
    1 teaspoon sugar
    1 teaspoon salt
 ½ teaspoon oregano
    1 clove garlic, minced
 ⅔ cup long grain rice

Combine all ingredients except rice in 2-quart microproof casserole. Cover and place in oven. Cook on HI, 5 minutes.

Blend in rice. Cover. Cook on 50, 30 minutes. Let stand 5 minutes before serving.

6 to 8 servings

A8:0 HIGHER

Stroganoff Casserole

Preset Cooking Time: about 31 minutes

- 1 pound lean ground beef
- ¼ cup chopped onion
- 2 cloves garlic, minced
- 3 cups (4 ounces) uncooked medium-width egg noodles
- 1 cup sliced mushrooms
- 1 can (13¾ ounces) beef broth
- ⅛ teaspoon pepper
- 1 container (8 ounces) dairy sour cream
- 2 tablespoons chopped parsley

Combine beef, onion, and garlic in 2-quart microproof casserole. Place in oven. Touch A8. Touch HIGHER. Touch START. *(Oven cooks: HI, about 6 minutes.)*

At Pause, drain. Stir in noodles, mushrooms, broth, and pepper. Cover. Touch START. *(Oven cooks: 50, about 20 minutes; stands: 0, 5 minutes.)*

Blend in sour cream and sprinkle with parsley before serving.

6 servings

A7:0 & A8:0

San Francisco Dish

Preset Cooking Time: about 26 minutes

- 1 tablespoon beef bouillon granules
- 2½ cups hot water
- 1 medium onion, sliced
- 2 tablespoons butter or margarine
- 1 cup long grain rice
- ½ cup broken uncooked spaghetti (1-inch pieces)

Dissolve bouillon in hot water; set aside. Place onion and butter in 3-quart microproof casserole. Cover and place in oven. Touch A7. Touch START. *(Oven cooks: HI, about 2 minutes.)*

Stir in rice, spaghetti, and bouillon. Cover and place in oven. Touch A8. Touch START. *(Oven cooks: HI, about 4 minutes.)*

At Pause, stir through. Cover. Touch START. *(Oven cooks: 50, about 15 minutes; stands: 0, 5 minutes.)*

Fluff mixture with fork and serve.

5 servings

Noodles and Cheese

Total Cooking Time: 9 minutes

- ¼ cup butter or margarine
- ⅓ cup slivered almonds
- 2 cups (8 ounces) shredded Swiss cheese
- ½ cup milk
- 1 large egg, lightly beaten
- 1 teaspoon parsley flakes
- ¼ teaspoon pepper
- ¼ teaspoon nutmeg
- 3 cups cooked wide egg noodles

Place butter and almonds in 1½-quart microproof casserole. Place in oven. Cook on HI, 1 minute.

Stir in remaining ingredients except noodles. Add noodles and toss until separated and evenly coated. Cover. Cook on HI, 4 minutes.

Stir. Cover. Cook on HI, 4 minutes. Let stand 2 minutes before serving.

4 to 6 servings

A8:0 HIGHER

Mushroom-Pimiento Rice

Preset Cooking Time: about 31 minutes

- 12 mushrooms (about ½ pound)
- 6 shallots (about 12 ounces), minced
- 3 tablespoons butter or margarine
- 2½ cups chicken broth
- 1¼ cups long grain rice
- 1 jar (4 ounces) pimientos, drained and diced
-    Salt and pepper

Mince mushroom stems. Cut caps into ⅛-inch thick slices; set aside. Combine stems, shallots, and butter in 3-quart microproof casserole. Place in oven. Touch A8. Touch HIGHER. Touch START. *(Oven cooks: HI, about 6 minutes.)*

At Pause, stir in mushroom caps, broth, and rice. Cover. Touch START. *(Oven cooks: 50, about 20 minutes; stands: 0, 5 minutes.)*

Blend in pimientos. Cover and let stand until all liquid is absorbed. Season with salt and pepper before serving.

6 to 8 servings

All Seasons Rice (page 148), →
Stroganoff Casserole

```
A1   6   &   A8:0   HIGHER
```

One-Step Lasagna

Preset Cooking Time: about 42 minutes

- 1 pound lean ground beef
- 1 jar (15 ounces) spaghetti sauce
- 1 can (8 ounces) tomato sauce
- ½ cup water
- 1 teaspoon salt
- 1 package (8 ounces) lasagna noodles
- 2 cups ricotta cheese, drained
- 3 cups (12 ounces) shredded mozzarella cheese, divided
- ½ cup grated Parmesan cheese Chopped parsley

Crumble beef into 2-quart microproof casserole. Place in oven. Touch A1. Touch 6. Touch START. *(Oven cooks: 80, about 6 minutes.)*

At Pause, stir to break up beef. Touch START. *(Oven cooks: 80, about 3 minutes.)*

Remove from oven. Stir; drain. Add spaghetti sauce, tomato sauce, water, and salt. Blend well. Spread one-third of the beef mixture in 13 × 9-inch microproof baking dish. Arrange half of noodles over beef mixture. Spread with 1 cup ricotta cheese. Sprinkle with 1 cup mozzarella cheese. Repeat layers once. Top with remaining beef mixture, remaining mozzarella cheese, and Parmesan cheese. Double wrap with plastic wrap, and place in oven. Touch A8. Touch HIGHER. Touch START. *(Oven cooks: HI, about 8 minutes.)*

At Pause, rotate dish one-half turn. Touch START. *(Oven cooks: 50, about 20 minutes; stands: 0, 5 minutes.)*

Sprinkle with parsley, and serve with additional Parmesan cheese, if desired.

6 servings

This is one of several recipes that combine the benefits of two automatic cooking programs with one recipe. Simply follow the sequence given in the recipe for excellent results.

```
A8:0   &   A1   6
```

Macaroni and Cheese Vegetable Medley

Preset Cooking Time: about 38 minutes

- 1½ cups hot water
- 1 cup uncooked elbow macaroni
- 1 package (10 ounces) frozen chopped broccoli
- 1 package (10 ounces) frozen sliced carrots
- 4 tablespoons butter or margarine
- ½ cup milk
- 1 tablespoon cornstarch
- ½ teaspoon salt
- ¼ teaspoon pepper
- ¼ teaspoon garlic powder
- ¼ teaspoon dry mustard
- 2 cups (8 ounces) shredded Cheddar cheese

Combine hot water, macaroni, broccoli, and carrots in 2-quart microproof casserole. Dot with butter. Cover and place in oven. Touch A8. Touch START. *(Oven cooks: HI, about 8 minutes.)*

At Pause, stir. Cover. Touch START. *(Oven cooks: 50, about 15 minutes; stands: 0, 5 minutes.)*

Remove from oven and set aside. Combine milk, cornstarch, salt, pepper, garlic powder, and mustard; stir until cornstarch is dissolved. Blend into macaroni mixture. Cover and place in oven. Touch A1. Touch 6. Touch START. *(Oven cooks: 80, about 5 minutes.)*

At Pause, stir in cheese. Do not cover. Touch START. *(Oven cooks: 80, about 5 minutes.)*

Let stand, covered, until all liquid is absorbed. Serve hot.

6 to 8 servings

NOTE: Automatic cooking functions identified in charts and on oven control panel are representative. Some programs may be used to cook foods other than those listed. Follow recipe instructions.

One-Step Lasagna →

Casserole Italiano

Total Cooking Time: 25 minutes

- 1 pound lean ground beef
- 1½ cups spaghetti sauce
- 1½ cups water
- 1 can (16 ounces) green beans, drained
- 1 package (7 ounces) uncooked elbow macaroni
- 2 tablespoons onion flakes
- 1 tablespoon sugar
- 1 teaspoon Italian seasoning
- ½ teaspoon salt
- ⅛ teaspoon pepper
- 1 clove garlic, minced
- 1 cup (4 ounces) shredded mozzarella cheese

Crumble beef into 3-quart microproof casserole. Place in oven. Cook on HI, 3 minutes.

Stir to break up beef; drain. Add remaining ingredients except cheese and blend well. Cover and place in oven. Cook on HI, 12 minutes.

Stir. Cover. Cook on 60, 10 minutes.

Sprinkle with cheese. Cover and let stand 10 minutes before serving.

6 to 8 servings

Chicken Noodle au Gratin

Total Cooking Time: 15 minutes

- 1½ cups broken uncooked thin egg noodles
- 1 cup chicken broth
- ½ cup milk
- ½ teaspoon salt
- ⅛ teaspoon pepper
- 2 to 3 cups coarsely chopped cooked chicken or turkey
- 1 cup (4 ounces) shredded Cheddar cheese
- ¼ cup sliced stuffed green olives

Combine noodles, broth, milk, salt, and pepper in 2-quart microproof casserole; stir lightly. Cover and place in oven. Cook on 70, 5 minutes.

Stir in chicken, cheese, and olives. Cover. Cook on 70, 5 minutes.

Stir. Cover. Cook on 20, 5 minutes.

4 to 6 servings

Mexican Macaroni

Total Cooking Time: 51 to 55 minutes

- 3 tablespoons olive oil
- 1 large onion, sliced
- 2 cups sliced carrots
- 1 cup chopped celery
- 1 clove garlic, crushed
- 2 cups cubed peeled tomatoes
- ½ teaspoon cumin
- ½ teaspoon chili powder
- ¼ teaspoon cayenne
- ¼ teaspoon basil
- ⅛ teaspoon thyme
- ⅛ teaspoon rosemary
- 1 package (7 ounces) shell macaroni, cooked
- 2 cans (16 ounces each) pinto beans, drained
- Salt and pepper
- Grated Parmesan Cheese

Pour oil into 4-quart microproof casserole. Place in oven. Cook on HI, 2 minutes.

Stir in onion, carrots, celery, and garlic. Cook on HI, 10 to 12 minutes, or until vegetables are tender.

Stir in tomatoes and seasonings. Cover and cook on 70, 7 minutes.

Blend in macaroni and beans. Cover and cook on HI, 14 minutes.

Stir. Cook on 70, 18 to 20 minutes, or until heated through, stirring occasionally.

Season with salt and pepper, and sprinkle with Parmesan cheese.

8 servings

A7:0

All Seasons Rice

Preset Cooking Time: about 14 minutes

- 2 cups chicken or beef broth
- 1 cup long grain rice
- ¼ cup minced onion
- 2 tablespoons minced parsley

Combine all ingredients in 3-quart microproof casserole. Cover and place in oven. Touch A7. Touch START. *(Oven cooks: HI, about 14 minutes.)*

Let stand 5 minutes before serving.

4 servings

Complements for Your Meal

Your microwave oven enables you to enter one of the most exciting areas of the culinary arts: The world of succulent crisp-cooked vegetables. Because very little water is used, sometimes none at all, vegetables emerge from the microwave oven with bright, fresh color, full of flavor, tender and nutritious. Even reheated, fresh vegetables retain their original flavor and color. They do not dry out, because the steam that heats them is primarily generated within the vegetables themselves. Canned vegetables heat well too, because they can be drained before cooking so that they retain their full fresh taste after cooking.

You'll truly be amazed at how easy it is to cook whole vegetables, like acorn squash or cauliflower. Try Savory Cauliflower (page 159) for an exciting introduction to microwave vegetable cookery. Like most of our vegetable recipes, it uses the surface-temperature sensor method.

Arrange asparagus with the tender tips overlapped in the center of the dish. Carrots cook a bit more quickly and are more interesting when cut diagonally (above). A nice variation for Corn-on-the-Cob (page 166) calls for cooking without the aid of the sensors. If you like to prepare your corn in the husks, it's the choice for you (above right). For best results, cut vegetables in equal-size pieces (right).

Adapting Your Recipes

Vegetables are best when eaten at the crisp stage — tender, yet resilient to the bite. If you prefer a softer texture, simply cook a bit longer (use the HIGHER option with automatic surface-temperature sensor method). Because of the importance of vegetable cookery and the personal preferences involved, we have provided you with complete timing information plus instructions for automatic cooking with the surface-temperature sensor. You can experiment with your favorite vegetables and decide which method you prefer to use. To adapt a conventional recipe, find a similar recipe in this chapter and also check the cooking *Guides*. The following tips offer additional thoughts for you:

☐ Celery, onions, green peppers, and carrots are usually precooked before being added to other vegetable casserole ingredients. The surface-temperature sensor program A7-0 is excellent for such precooking functions.

☐ The temperature probe can also be used for cooking vegetables. Insert probe in center of dish with temperature set at 150°F.

☐ Check doneness after the shortest recommended cooking times. Add more cooking time to suit individual preferences.

☐ If necessary, frozen vegetables may be used in recipes calling for fresh vegetables. It is not necessary to thaw frozen vegetables before cooking.

☐ Freeze small portions of your favorite vegetable dishes in boilable plastic pouches. If you use metal twist ties, be sure to replace with string or rubber band before cooking.

☐ To prevent boiling over when preparing vegetable dishes with cream sauces, use a baking dish large enough to allow for bubbling. Use a lower power level such as 60 or 70.

☐ To cook mashed potatoes, cube potatoes. Add a small amount of water. Cook, tightly covered, until soft. Season and mash.

☐ To reheat mashed potatoes, set at 80, stirring once during cooking time.

Using the Cooking Guide

1. All fresh or frozen vegetables are cooked and reheated on HI.

2. Choose a dish that keeps vegetables together for best results.

3. Add ¼ cup water for each 1 pound fresh vegetables. Do not add water for spinach, corn-on-the-cob, whole potatoes, or eggplant.

4. Cover all vegetables tightly.

5. Some vegetables should be stirred or rearranged during cooking. Sensor programs A7-3 and A7-4 include automatic pauses.

6. A3-1 offers an automatic method for vegetables in boilable pouches. At Pause, shake down ingredients and cut off one top corner. Place bag on plate, upright. Touch START.

7. Frozen vegetables in foil-wrapped or lined cartons must be removed from their original packaging. Cook others in their original packages. Exception: vegetables in sauce. Remove from carton; place in microproof dish.

8. Additional frozen vegetable information is provided in chapter 18.

9. All vegetables profit from standing time of 2 to 3 minutes before serving.

COOKING GUIDE — VEGETABLES
USES HI THROUGHOUT

Food	Amount	Fresh Vegetable Preparation	Time (in minutes)	Water	Automatic Sensor Method	Special Notes
Artichokes 3½" in diameter	Fresh: 1 2 4 Frozen: 10 oz.	Wash thoroughly. Cut tops off each leaf. Slit pouch	7 - 8 11 - 12 5 - 6	¼ cup ½ cup	A7-0 A7-0 A7-4	When done, a leaf peeled from whole comes off easily.
Asparagus: spears and cut pieces	Fresh: 1 lb. Frozen: 10 oz.	Wash thoroughly. Snap off tough base and discard.	2 - 3 7 - 8	¼ cup None	A7-1 A7-4	
Beans: green, wax, French-cut	Fresh: 1 lb. Frozen: 6 oz.	Remove ends. Wash well. Leave whole or break in pieces.	12 - 14 7 - 8	¼ cup None	A7-0 Lower A7-4	Stir once if necessary.
Beets	4 medium	Scrub beets. Leave 1" of top on beet.	16 - 18	¼ cup	A7-3	After cooking, peel. Cut or leave whole.
Broccoli	Fresh, whole 1 - 2½ lbs. Frozen, whole Fresh, chopped, 1 - 1½ lbs. Frozen, chopped 10 oz.	Remove outer leaves. Slit stalks.	9 - 10 8 - 10 12 - 14 8 - 9	¼ cup ¼ cup ¼ cup None	A7-0 A7-4 A7-0 Lower A7-4	
Brussels sprouts	Fresh: 1 lb. Frozen: 10 oz.	Remove outside leaves if wilted. Cut off stems. Wash	8 - 9 6 - 7	¼ cup None	A7-0 A7-4	
Cabbage	½ medium head, shredded 1 medium head, wedges	Remove outside wilted leaves.	5 - 6 13 - 15	¼ cup ¼ cup	A7-0 Lower A7-0	
Carrots	4: sliced or diced 6: sliced or diced 8: tiny, whole Frozen: 10 oz.	Peel and cut off tops. Fresh young carrots cook best.	7 - 9 9 - 10 8 - 10 8 - 9	1 Tb. 2 Tbs. 2 Tbs. None	A7-0 A7-0 A7-0 A7-4	
Cauliflower	1 medium, in flowerets 1 medium, whole Frozen: 10 oz.	Cut tough stem. Wash, remove outside leaves. Remove core.	7 - 8 8 - 9 8 - 9	¼ cup ½ cup ¼ cup	A7-0 A7-0 Higher A7-4	
Celery	2½ cups, 1" slices	Clean stalks thoroughly.	8 - 9	¼ cup	A7-0	
Corn: kernel	Frozen: 10 oz.		5 - 6	¼ cup	A7-4	
On the cob	1 ear 2 ears 3 ears 5 ears Frozen, 2 ears 4 ears	Husk, wrap each in waxed paper. Place on glass tray in oven. Flat dish, covered.	3 - 4 6 - 7 9 - 10 11 - 12 5½ - 6 10 - 11	None None None None None None	A7-2 A7-2 A7-2 A7-2 A7-0 A7-0	Rearrange halfway through cooking time unless cooked on microwave rack. Rearrange halfway through cooking time.
Eggplant	1 medium, sliced 1 medium, whole	Wash and peel. Cut into slices or cubes. Pierce skin.	5 - 6 6 - 7	2 Tb.	Not applicable Not applicable	Place on microwave rack.
Greens: collard, kale, etc.	Fresh: 1 lb. Frozen: 10 oz.	Wash. Remove wilted leaves or tough stem.	6 - 7 7 - 8	None None	A7-1 Lower A7-4	

COOKING GUIDE — VEGETABLES
USES HI THROUGHOUT

Food	Amount	Fresh Vegetable Preparation	Time (in minutes)	Water	Automatic Sensor Method	Special Notes
Mushrooms	Fresh: ½ lb., sliced	Add butter or water.	2 - 4	2 Tbs.	A7-1 Lower	Stir halfway through cooking time, if desired.
Okra	Fresh: ½ lb.	Wash thoroughly. Leave whole or cut	3 - 5	¼ cup	A7-0	
	Frozen: 10 oz.	in thick slices.	7 - 8	None	A7-4	
Onions	1 lb., tiny whole	Peel. Add 1 Tb. butter.	6 - 7		A7-0 Lower	Stir once during cooking time, if
	1 lb., medium to large	Peel and quarter. Add 1 Tb. butter.	7 - 9	¼ cup	A7-0	desired.
Parsnips	4 medium, quartered	Peel and cut.	8 - 9	¼ cup	A7-0	Stir once during cooking time, if desired.
Peas: green	Fresh: 1 lb.	Shell peas. Rinse well.	7 - 8	¼ cup	A7-1	Stir once during cooking time if,
	Fresh: 2 lbs.		8 - 9	½ cup	A7-1	desired.
	Frozen: 6 oz.		5 - 6	None	A7-4	
Peas and onions	Frozen: 10 oz.		6 - 8	2 Tbs.	A7-4	
Pea pods	Frozen: 6 oz.		3 - 4	2 Tbs.	A7-4	
Potatoes, sweet 5 - 6 oz. ea.	1	Scrub well. Pierce with fork. Place on rack or paper towel in circle, 1" apart.	4 - 4½	None	A7-3 all quantities	Rearrange halfway through cooking time.
	2		6 - 7	None		
	4		8 - 10	None		
	6		10 - 11	None		
Potatoes, white baking 6 - 8 oz. ea.	1	Wash and scrub well. Pierce with fork. Place on rack or paper towel in circle, 1" apart.	4 - 6	None	A7-3 all quantities	Rearrange halfway through cooking time.
	2		6 - 8	None		
	3		8 - 12	None		
	4		12 - 16	None		
	5		16 - 20	None		
russet, boiling	3	Peel potatoes, cut in quarters.	12 - 16	½ cup	A7-3 Higher	
Rutabaga	Fresh: 1 lb.	Wash well. Remove tough stems or any	6 - 7	None	A7-0	
	Frozen: 10 oz.	wilted leaves.	7 - 8	None	A7-4	
Spinach	Fresh: 1 lb.	Wash well. Remove touch stems.	6 - 7	None	A7-1 Lower	
	Frozen: 10 oz.		7 - 8	None	A7-4	
Squash, acorn or butternut	1 - 1½ lbs. whole	Scrub. Pierce with fork.	10 - 12	None	A7-3 Higher	Cut and remove seeds to serve.
Spaghetti squash	2 - 3 lbs.	Scrub, pierce. Place on rack.	6 per lb.	None	A7-3 Higher	Serve with butter, Parmesan cheese, or spaghetti sauce.
Turnips	4 cups cubed	Peel, wash.	9 - 11	¼ cup	A7-0	Stir, if desired.
Zucchini	3 cups sliced	Wash; do not peel.	7 - 8	¼ cup	A7-1	Stir, if desired.

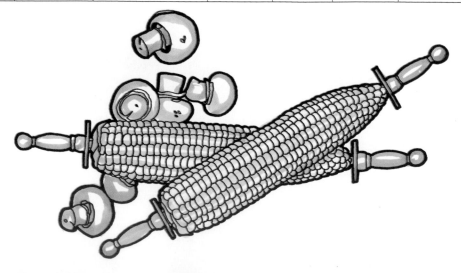

COOKING GUIDE — CONVENIENCE VEGETABLES

Food	Amount	Cook Control Setting	Time (in minutes)	or	Automatic Sensor Method	Special Notes
Au gratin vegetables, frozen	11½ oz.	70 (roast)	10 - 12	or	A7-4	Use glass loaf dish, covered. Stir once.
Baked beans, frozen	6 oz.	70 (roast)	8 - 10	or	A3-2	Use 1½-quart casserole, covered. Stir once.
Corn, scalloped frozen	12 oz.	70 (roast)	7 - 8	or	A3-0	Use 1-quart casserole, covered. Stir once.
Potatoes stuffed, frozen	2	70 (roast)	10 - 12	or	A3-2	Use shallow dish. Cover with waxed paper. Rotate dish once.
Tots, frozen	16 oz. 32 oz.	80 (reheat) 80 (reheat)	9 - 10 12 - 14	or	A7-4	Use 2-quart round or oval baking dish.
Creamed potato mix	4 - 5 oz.	70 (roast)	20 - 24	or	A8-0	Stir once.
Au gratin, frozen	11½ oz.	70 (roast)	12	or	A7-4	Use 1½-quart casserole, covered with waxed paper.
Instant mashed	3½ oz. packet	HI (max. power)	5 - 6	or	not applicable	Use covered casserole. Follow package directions. Reduce liquid by 1 tablespoon.
Peas, pea pods, chestnuts, frozen	10 oz.	HI (max. power)	6 - 7	or	A7-4	Place pouch on plate. Slit pouch.
Stuffing mix	6 oz.	HI (max. power)	8	or	not applicable	Use 1½-quart casserole, covered. Follow package directions.

Using the Blanching Guide

The microwave oven can be a valuable and appreciated aid in preparing fresh vegetables for the freezer. (The oven is *not* recommended for canning.) Some vegetables don't require any water at all and, of course, the less water used the better. You'll have that "fresh picked" color and flavor for your produce. Here are some tips in preparing vegetables for blanching:

☐ Choose young, tender vegetables.
☐ Clean and prepare for cooking according to cooking *Guide.*
☐ Measure amounts to be blanched; place by batches, in microproof casserole.
☐ Add water according to chart.
☐ Cover and cook on HI for time indicated on chart.
☐ Stir vegetables halfway through cooking.
☐ Let vegetables stand, covered, 1 minute after cooking.
☐ Place vegetables in ice water at once to stop cooking. When vegetables feel cool, spread on towel to absorb excess moisture.
☐ Package in freezer containers or pouches. Seal, label, date, and freeze quickly.

BLANCHING GUIDE — VEGETABLES
USES HI THROUGHOUT

Food	Amount	Water	Approximate Time (in minutes)	Casserole Size
Asparagus (cut in 1-inch pieces)	4 cups	¼ cup	4½	1½ quart
Beans, green or wax (cut in 1-inch pieces)	1 pound	½ cup	5	1½ quart
Broccoli (cut in 1-inch pieces)	1 pound	⅓ cup	6	1½ quart
Carrots (sliced)	1 pound	⅓ cup	6	1½ quart
Cauliflower (cut in florets)	1 head	⅓ cup	6	2 quart
Corn (cut from cob)	4 cups	none	4	1½ quart
Corn-on-the-cob (husked)	6 ears	none	5½	1½ quart
Onion (quartered)	4 medium	½ cup	3 - 4½	1 quart
Parsnips (cubed)	1 pound	¼ cup	2½ - 4	1½ quart
Peas (shelled)	4 cups	¼ cup	4½	1½ quart
Snow peas	4 cups	¼ cup	3½	1½ quart
Spinach (washed)	1 pound	none	4	2 quart
Turnips (cubed)	1 pound	¼ cup	3 - 4½	1½ quart
Zucchini (sliced or cubed)	1 pound	¼ cup	4	1½ quart

A7:0   LOWER

Cabbage

Preset Cooking Time: about 6 minutes

   ½ medium head cabbage, shredded
   ¼ cup water

Place cabbage and water in 1-quart microproof casserole. Cover and place in oven. Touch A7. Touch LOWER. Touch START. *(Oven cooks: HI, about 6 minutes.)*

Stir through several times. Drain before serving.

4 servings

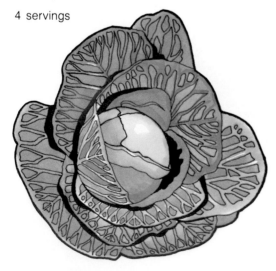

Carrot-Brocccoli Casserole

Total Cooking Time: 15¾ minutes

   1 package (10 ounces) frozen
        broccoli spears
   1 can (10¾ ounces) cream of
        chicken soup, undiluted
   1 cup finely shredded carrots
   ½ cup dairy sour cream
   1 tablespoon all-purpose flour
   1 tablespoon minced onion
   ¼ teaspoon salt
   ⅛ teaspoon pepper
   2 tablespoons butter or margarine
   ¾ cup herb-seasoned stuffing cubes

Place broccoli in package on microproof plate. Place in oven. Cook on HI, 3 minutes.

Combine soup, carrots, sour cream, flour, onion, salt, and pepper in 1½-quart microproof casserole. Cut broccoli into 1-inch pieces. Stir into soup mixture. Cover and place in oven. Cook on HI, 6 minutes.

Stir through soup and set aside. Place butter in 2-cup glass measure. Place in oven. Cook on HI, 45 seconds.

Mix stuffing into butter. Spoon over broccoli mixture. Place in oven. Cook on HI, 6 minutes. Serve immediately.

5 to 6 servings

```
A7:0
```

Cauliflower

Preset Cooking Time: about 8 minutes

>   1 head cauliflower (1⅓ pounds)
>   ¼ cup water

Remove stem and outer leaves from cauliflower; discard. Rinse cauliflower well. Break into florets. Place in 1½- to 2-quart microproof casserole. Add water. Cover and place in oven. Touch A7. Touch START. *(Oven cooks: HI, about 8 minutes.)*

Drain before serving.

5 to 6 servings

If you prefer a firmer texture, touch LOWER just before START.

```
A7:0    HIGHER
```

Carrots

Preset Cooking Time: about 9 minutes

>   1 pound carrots, peeled and
>   thinly sliced
>   2 tablespoons water

Place carrots in 1-quart microproof casserole. Add water. Cover and place in oven. Touch A7. Touch HIGHER. Touch START. *(Oven cooks: HI, about 9 minutes.)*

Let stand 2 to 3 minutes. Drain before serving.

4 servings

Eggplant

Total Cooking Time: 7 minutes

>   1 eggplant (1 pound)

Wash eggplant and pierce skin in several places. Place on microwave roasting rack. Place in oven. Cook on HI, 7 minutes.

Let stand 3 minutes before slicing.

4 to 6 servings

```
A7   3   &   A1   6   HIGHER
```

Candied Sweet Potatoes

Preset Cooking Time: about 17 minutes

>   5 sweet potatoes (5 to 6 ounces
>   each)
>   1 cup firmly packed brown sugar
>   ⅓ cup water
>   2 tablespoons butter or margarine
>   ½ teaspoon salt

Scrub potatoes and pierce at intervals with fork. Place 1 potato on microwave roasting rack and arrange remaining 4 potatoes in ring around center potato. Place in oven, with center potato over circle on glass tray. Touch A7. Touch 3. Touch START. *(Oven cooks: HI, about 3 minutes.)*

At Pause, turn potatoes over and rearrange. Touch START. *(Oven cooks: HI, about 7 minutes.)*

Let potatoes stand 3 minutes before peeling and slicing. Arrange slices in 2-quart microproof casserole; set aside. Combine brown sugar, water, butter, and salt in 2-cup glass measure. Place in oven over circle on glass tray. Touch A1. Touch 6. Touch HIGHER. Touch START. *(Oven cooks: 80, about 3 minutes.)*

At Pause, pour sauce over potatoes. Cover and place in oven. Touch START. *(Oven cooks: 80, about 4 minutes.)*

Spoon sauce over potatoes before serving.

6 servings

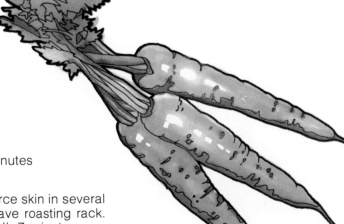

```
A7   3   &   A1   4   HIGHER
```

Twice-Baked Potatoes

Preset Cooking Time: about 25 minutes

> 4 potatoes (6 ounces each)
> ½ cup butter or margarine, cut up
> ½ cup dairy sour cream
> ½ teaspoon salt
> Dash pepper
> Paprika

Scrub potatoes and rinse well. Pierce at intervals with fork. Place 1 potato on microwave roasting rack and arrange remaining 3 potatoes in ring around center potato. Place in oven, with center potato over circle on glass tray. Touch A7. Touch 3. Touch START. *(Oven cooks: HI, about 10 minutes.)*

At Pause, turn potatoes over and rearrange. Touch START. *(Oven cooks: HI, about 12 minutes.)*

Remove ¼-inch horizontal slice from top of each potato. Carefully remove pulp with teaspoon; place pulp in mixing bowl. Set shells aside. Add butter, sour cream, salt, and pepper to pulp; beat with electric mixer until smooth. Divide mixture evenly and spoon back into shells. Arrange potatoes as above on microwave roasting rack in oven. Touch A1. Touch 4. Touch HIGHER. Touch START. *(Oven cooks: 80, about 3 minutes.)*

Sprinkle with paprika before serving.

4 servings

```
A1   1
```

Baby Food

Preset Cooking Time: about 2 minutes

> 1 jar (4 to 6 ounces) baby
>   food (vegetable, meat,
>   or fruit)

Place baby food in microwave mug or custard cup. Place in oven over circle on glass tray. Touch A1. Touch 1. Touch START. *(Oven cooks: 80, about 2 minutes.)*

```
A2   4   &   A7   4   HIGHER
```

Green Beans Italiano

Preset Cooking Time: about 12 minutes

> 3 slices bacon, chopped
> 1 small onion, chopped
> 2 packages (10 ounces each) frozen
>   cut green beans
> ⅓ cup Italian dressing

Place bacon and onion in 2-quart microproof casserole. Place in oven. Cover with paper towel. Touch A2. Touch 4. Touch START. *(Oven cooks: HI, about 3 minutes.)*

Add beans and cover with casserole lid. Touch A7. Touch 4. Touch HIGHER. Touch START. *(Oven cooks: HI, about 5 minutes.)*

At Pause, add dressing. Stir through. Touch START. *(Oven cooks: HI, about 4 minutes.)*

Let stand 3 minutes. Stir before serving.

6 servings

```
A7:0   HIGHER   &   A1   6   LOWER
```

Cranberry Carrots

Preset Cooking Time: about 12 minutes

> 1 pound carrots, thinly sliced
> 2 tablespoons water
> ¼ cup butter or margarine
> ¼ cup jellied cranberry sauce
>   Salt

Place carrots and water in 1½- to 2-quart microproof casserole. Cover and place in oven. Touch A7. Touch HIGHER. Touch START. *(Oven cooks: HI, about 9 minutes.)*

At Pause, drain. Stir in butter and cranberry sauce. Season with salt. Cover and place in oven. Touch A1. Touch 6. Touch LOWER. Touch START. *(Oven cooks: 80, about 2 minutes.)*

At Pause, stir. Cover. Touch START. *(Oven cooks: 80, about 1 minute.)*

4 servings

This is one of several recipes that combine the benefits of two automatic cooking programs with one recipe. Simply follow the sequence given in the recipe for excellent results.

← *Twice-Baked Potatoes, Green Beans Italiano, Cranberry Carrots*

A7 1 LOWER

Corn-Mushroom Scallop

Preset Cooking Time: about 10 minutes

- 1 can (17 ounces) cream-style corn
- ¼ pound mushrooms, sliced
- 1 large egg, lightly beaten
- ¾ cup soda-cracker crumbs, divided
- 1 tablespoon chopped chives
- ¼ teaspoon white pepper
- 2 tablespoons butter or margarine

Combine corn, mushrooms, and egg in 1-quart microproof casserole; blend well. Combine ½ cup cracker crumbs, chives, and pepper. Spread evenly in casserole over corn mixture. Sprinkle with remaining ¼ cup cracker crumbs. Dot with butter. Place in oven. Touch A7. Touch 1. Touch LOWER. Touch START. *(Oven cooks: HI, about 10 minutes.)*

Let stand 5 minutes before serving.

4 servings

A7 4 HIGHER

Green Beans Amandine

Preset Cooking Time: about 9 minutes

- ½ cup sliced almonds
- 2 tablespoons butter or margarine
- 1 package (10 ounces) frozen French cut green beans
  Salt and pepper

Combine all ingredients in 2-quart microproof casserole. Cover and place in oven. Touch A7. Touch 4. Touch HIGHER. Touch START. *(Oven cooks: HI, about 6 minutes.)*

At Pause, stir. Cover. Touch START. *(Oven cooks: HI, about 3 minutes.)*

3 to 4 servings

Any recipe that uses either the surface-temperature sensor or internal-temperature sensor can be increased or decreased in quantity to suit your needs. The oven will automatically determine the correct cooking time. The settings you enter are not changed from those provided with the recipe.

A7 4 HIGHER

Creamy Cabbage

Preset Cooking Time: about 8 minutes

- 1 medium head cabbage, shredded
- ¼ cup water
- 1 package (3 ounces) cream cheese, cut into cubes
- 2 tablespoons milk
- ½ teaspoon salt
- ½ teaspoon celery seed
  Dash pepper
  Chopped parsley

Place cabbage and water in 3-quart microproof casserole. Cover and place in oven. Touch A7. Touch 4. Touch HIGHER. Touch START. *(Oven cooks: HI, about 5 minutes.)*

At Pause, add remaining ingredients except parsley. Stir. Cover. Touch START. *(Oven cooks: HI, about 3 minutes.)* Let stand 2 minutes. Stir and sprinkle with parsley before serving.

5 to 6 servings

If you prefer your vegetables a bit softer, continue to cook on HI, 2 to 3 minutes, or until cabbage is done the way you like it.

Corn and Pepper Pudding

Total Cooking Time: 19 minutes

- 2 tablespoons butter or margarine
- 2 tablespoons chopped green pepper
- 2 tablespoons chopped pimiento
- 2 cans (17 ounces each) cream-style corn
- 2 large eggs, lightly beaten
- 3 tablespoons all-purpose flour
- 1 tablespoon instant minced onion
- ¼ teaspoon salt
- ¼ teaspoon pepper

Combine butter, green pepper, and pimiento in shallow 1½-quart round or oval microproof baking dish. Place in oven. Cook on 90, 2 minutes.

Stir in remaining ingredients. Cover. Cook on 70, 9 minutes.

Stir through several times. Cook on 70, 8 minutes.

Let stand 5 minutes before serving.

6 servings

Crumb Topped Tomatoes

Total Cooking Time: 4½ minutes

>   4 medium tomatoes
> 1½ tablespoons butter or margarine,
>   melted
> 1½ tablespoons dry bread crumbs
>   1 tablespoon onion soup mix
>   1 tablespoon chopped parsley
>   1 tablespoon chopped fresh basil,
>   or 1 teaspoon dried basil

Cut slice from top of each tomato; discard. Arrange tomatoes, cut-sides up, in circle on microproof plate. Combine remaining ingredients. Divide among tomatoes, spreading onto cut surfaces. Place in oven. Cook on HI, 4½ minutes.

4 servings

A7   1

Spinach

Preset Cooking Time: about 6 minutes

>   1 pound spinach, tough stems
>   removed
>   Salt and pepper

Rinse spinach and drain well. Place in wide shallow microproof baking dish. Cover and place in oven. Touch A7. Touch 1. Touch START. *(Oven cooks: HI, about 6 minutes.)*
Let stand 2 minutes before draining. Season with salt and pepper before serving.

2 servings

A7:0   HIGHER   &   A1   4

Savory Cauliflower

Preset Cooking Time: about 7 minutes

>   1 head cauliflower (1⅓ pounds)
>   ¼ cup water
>   ½ cup mayonnaise
>   1 tablespoon instant minced onion
>   ½ teaspoon dry mustard
>   ¼ teaspoon salt
>   4 slices Cheddar cheese
>   Paprika

Cut cone-shaped wedge from cauliflower core. Place cauliflower in 1½-quart microproof casserole. Add water. Cover and place in oven. Touch A7. Touch HIGHER. Touch START. *(Oven cooks: HI, about 6 minutes.)*
At Pause, drain cauliflower. Combine mayonnaise, onion, mustard, and salt; spoon over cauliflower. Lay cheese slices on top. Place in oven. Do not cover. Touch A1. Touch 4. Touch START. *(Oven cooks: 80, about 1 minute.)*
Sprinkle with paprika. Let stand 2 minutes before serving.

6 servings

It really doesn't matter what size cauliflower you use. The oven will automatically adjust the cooking time.

A7:0   HIGHER

Onions

Preset Cooking Time: about 14 minutes

>   1 pound onions, peeled and cut
>   into quarters
>   ¼ cup water

Place onions and water in wide shallow microproof baking dish. Cover and place in oven. Touch A7. Touch HIGHER. Touch START. *(Oven cooks: HI, about 14 minutes.)*
Stir; cover. Let stand 5 minutes before serving.

3 to 4 servings

For onions with a firmer texture, use the LOWER touch pad instead of HIGHER.

Harvard Beets

Total Cooking Time: 8 minutes

- 1 can (16 ounces) diced or sliced beets
- ¼ cup sugar
- ¼ cup wine vinegar
- 1 tablespoon cornstarch
- ½ teaspoon salt
- ⅛ teaspoon pepper

Drain beet liquid into 1-cup glass measure. Add water to equal 1 cup liquid; set aside. Combine sugar, vinegar, cornstarch, salt, and pepper in 1-quart micro-proof casserole; stir until cornstarch is dissolved. Stir in beet-water mixture. Place in oven. Cook on HI, 1½ minutes.

Stir through several times. Cook on HI, 1½ minutes.

Add beets and stir to coat. Cover. Cook on HI, 5 minutes.

4 servings

A7 3

Pan Baked Potato Halves

Preset Cooking Time: about 12 minutes

- ¼ cup grated Parmesan cheese
- ½ teaspoon salt
- ¼ teaspoon white pepper
- 4 medium baking potatoes (4 to 5 ounces each), cut in half lengthwise
- 2 tablespoons butter or margarine, melted
  Paprika

Combine cheese, salt, and pepper. Dip cut sides of potatoes in butter, then in cheese mixture. Arrange potatoes, cut-sides up, in circle in large shallow micro-proof baking dish. Place in oven, with 1 potato over circle on glass tray. Touch A7. Touch 3. Touch START. *(Oven cooks: HI, about 4 minutes.)*

At Pause, rotate dish one-half turn. Touch START. *(Oven cooks: HI, about 8 minutes.)*

Let stand 5 minutes. Sprinkle with paprika and serve.

8 servings

A7 3

Parsley New Potatoes

Preset Cooking Time: about 10 minutes

- 12 new potatoes (1 pound)
- ¼ cup water
- 2 tablespoons butter
- 1 tablespoon minced parsley
  Dash salt and pepper

Peel a ½-inch strip around middle of each potato. Place potatoes in 2-quart micro-proof casserole. Add water. Cover and place in oven. Touch A7. Touch 3. Touch START. *(Oven cooks: HI, about 5 minutes.)*

At Pause, stir carefully. Touch START. *(Oven cooks: HI, about 5 minutes.)*

Drain potatoes. Add butter, parsley, salt and pepper. Cover and let stand 3 minutes. Stir through once and serve.

4 servings

You can reduce or increase quantities with any vegetable recipe which uses the surface-temperature sensor method. The oven automatically determines the correct cooking time required for perfect doneness. For variety, substitute dillweed, celery seed, or tarragon for the parsley in this recipe.

Harvard Beets →

Sweet-Sour Red Cabbage

Total Cooking Time: 23 minutes

- 1 head red cabbage (1½ pounds), shredded
- 1 tart apple, peeled, cored, and diced
- 5 tablespoons wine vinegar
- 1 tablespoon butter or margarine
- 3 tablespoons sugar
- 1 teaspoon salt

Combine cabbage, apple, vinegar, and butter in 3-quart microproof casserole. Cover and place in oven. Cook on HI, 6 minutes.

Stir through several times. Cover. Cook on HI, 6 minutes.

Stir; cover. Cook on HI, 6 minutes.

Stir in sugar and salt. Cover. Cook on HI, 5 minutes.

6 servings

Green Peas

Total Cooking Time: 8 minutes

- 1 pound peas in shells
- ¼ cup water

Shell peas; rinse and drain. Place peas and water in wide shallow microproof baking dish. Cover and place in oven. Cook on HI, 4 minutes.

Stir through several times. Cover. Cook on HI, 4 minutes.

Let peas stand 2 minutes before draining. Serve seasoned with butter and salt, if desired.

2 servings

Peas Francine

Total Cooking Time: 10 minutes

- 2 cups shelled green peas
- ¼ cup water
- 1 teaspoon sugar
- 3 or 4 large lettuce leaves
  Dash salt and pepper

Combine peas, water, and sugar in 1½-quart microproof casserole. Cover and place in oven. Cook on HI, 4 minutes.

Stir; cover with lettuce, overlapping leaves as necessary. Cover. Cook on HI, 6 minutes.

Discard lettuce. Drain peas; stir in salt and pepper. Cover and let stand 2 to 3 minutes before serving.

4 servings

A7	3

Potato Salad

Preset Cooking Time: about 12 minutes

- 2 pounds potatoes, peeled and cut into 1-inch cubes
- ½ cup water
- ¼ teaspoon salt
- ¼ cup Italian dressing
- 6 large hard-cooked eggs, chopped, divided
- ½ cup chopped pimiento, divided
- 1 cup mayonnaise
- 1 cup chopped celery
- ½ cup chopped onions
  Salt and pepper
  Minced parsley

Place potatoes, water, and salt in 4-quart microproof casserole. Cover and place in oven. Touch A7. Touch 3. Touch START. (Oven cooks: HI, about 4 minutes.)

At Pause, stir. Cover. Touch START. (Oven cooks: HI, about 8 minutes.)

Drain potatoes. Pour dressing over potatoes and toss lightly. Set aside ¼ cup egg for garnish; add remaining eggs to potatoes; toss lightly. Set aside 1 tablespoon pimiento; add remaining pimiento to potato mixture. Blend in mayonnaise, celery, and onions. Season with salt and pepper. Spoon into serving bowl. Garnish with reserved egg, pimiento, and parsley.

6 servings

`A7  3`

Baked Potatoes

Preset Cooking Time: about 9 minutes

2 potatoes (6 ounces each)

Scrub potatoes and rinse well. Pierce at intervals with fork. Place potatoes about 1 inch apart on microwave roasting rack. Place in oven, with 1 potato over circle on glass tray. Touch A7. Touch 3. Touch START. *(Oven cooks: HI, about 3 minutes.)*

At Pause, turn potatoes over. Touch START. *(Oven cooks: HI, about 6 minutes.)*

Let stand 3 minutes before serving.

2 servings

You can cook as many as 5 potatoes using the A7-3 setting. Be sure to arrange potatoes in a circle with 1 potato in the center, and position the center potato in the oven over the circle on the glass tray. The oven will automatically adjust the cooking time to accommodate the increased number of potatoes.

If you do not have a microwave roasting rack, you can place the potatoes directly on the glass tray. We recommend the rack because it does not permit the underside of the potato to become moist from steam that develops.

`A4  4`

Creamed Potato Mix

Preset Cooking Time: about 20 minutes

1 package (5 ounces) creamed potato mix

Prepare potato mix as directed on package in 3-quart microproof casserole. Insert temperature probe. Cover lightly with plastic wrap. (The plastic wrap should be placed so that it will help keep the probe in position.) Place in oven. Plug in probe. Touch A4. Touch 4. Touch START. *(Oven cooks: 70, to 90°F.)*

At Pause, stir. Cover. Touch START. *(Oven cooks: 70, to 145°F; stands: 0, 5 minutes.)*

4 servings

`A7  3  HIGHER`

Country Style Potatoes

Preset Cooking Time: about 17 minutes

5 medium potatoes, peeled and shredded (about 6 cups)
¼ cup water
1½ cups milk
¼ cup chopped chives
¼ cup butter or margarine, cut up
1 teaspoon salt
¼ cup grated Parmesan cheese
   Paprika

Place potatoes and water in 2-quart microproof casserole. Cover and place in oven. Touch A7. Touch 3. Touch HIGHER. Touch START. *(Oven cooks: HI, about 6 minutes.)*

At Pause, add milk, chives, butter, and salt; stir carefully. Stir in cheese. Sprinkle with paprika. Do not cover. Touch START. *(Oven cooks: HI, about 11 minutes.)*

6 servings

Scalloped Potato Mix

Total Cooking Time: 14 minutes

1 package (7 ounces) scalloped potato mix

Prepare potatoes as directed on package in 3-quart microproof casserole. Cover and place in oven. Cook on HI, 4 minutes, then on 50, 10 minutes. Let stand 5 minutes. Stir through several times before serving.

6 servings

Ratatouille

Total Cooking Time: 21 minutes

- 1 eggplant (1 pound)
- ¼ cup olive oil
- 1 medium onion, sliced
- 2 cloves garlic, minced
- 3 medium zucchini, sliced (about 3 cups)
- 1 green pepper, seeded and cut into strips
- 4 medium-size firm tomatoes, cut into quarters
- 1 teaspoon basil
- ½ teaspoon salt
- ¼ teaspoon pepper
  Pinch thyme
- ¼ cup minced parsley
- 2 tablespoons grated Parmesan cheese

Wash eggplant and pierce skin in several places. Place on microwave roasting rack. Place in oven. Cook on HI, 6 minutes.

Remove from oven; set aside. Combine oil, onion, and garlic in 2½-quart microproof casserole. Cover and place in oven. Cook on HI, 4 minutes.

Peel eggplant, if desired, and cut into 1½-inch cubes. Add to onion mixture. Add remaining ingredients except parsley and cheese; blend well. Cover and place in oven. Cook on HI, 5 minutes.

Stir. Do not cover. Cook on HI, 6 minutes.

Stir in parsley and sprinkle with cheese before serving.

6 to 8 servings

Parmesan Potatoes

Total Cooking Time: 9 minutes

- 8 buttery crackers
- ¼ cup grated Parmesan cheese
- 1 teaspoon garlic powder
- ½ teaspoon paprika
- ½ teaspoon salt
- ⅛ teaspoon pepper
- ¼ cup butter or margarine
- 1 pound potatoes, peeled and cut into 1-inch cubes
- 1 tablespoon grated Parmesan cheese
- 3 tablespoons minced parsley

Combine crackers, cheese, garlic powder, paprika, salt, and pepper in blender or food processor to make fine crumbs. Transfer mixture to plastic bag; set aside. Place butter in 8-inch round microproof baking dish. Place in oven. Cook on HI, 1 minute. Add potatoes and stir to coat. Drain any remaining butter and reserve.

Add potatoes to crumb mixture in batches and shake to coat evenly. Arrange potatoes in single layer in shallow microproof baking dish or pie plate just large enough to accommodate. Cover with plastic wrap. Place in oven. Cook on HI, 5 minutes.

Stir in reserved butter. Cook on HI, 3 minutes.

Sprinkle with 1 tablespoon cheese. Garnish with parsley before serving.

4 servings

← Ratatouille, Veal Cutlets (Guide, page 82)

A7	2	HIGHER

Corn-on-the-Cob

Preset Cooking Time: about 6 minutes

  2 ears of corn (about 14 ounces
        each), husked and rinsed
     Butter or margarine
     Salt

Wrap each ear of corn in waxed paper. Place on microwave roasting rack. Place in oven, with portions of each ear over circle on glass tray. Touch A7. Touch 2. Touch HIGHER. Touch START. *(Oven cooks: HI, about 6 minutes.)*

Serve with butter and salt.

2 servings

If you are cooking more than 2 ears of corn, place 1 ear in center of roasting rack and arrange others in circle around center ear of corn. Place in oven with center ear of corn over circle on glass tray.

Do you like to prepare your corn in-the-husk? You can, but the surface-temperature sensor method cannot be used. To cook corn in-the-husk, soak corn in cold water for 5 to 10 minutes after discarding any soiled outer leaves. Drain. Place on microwave roasting rack in oven. Cook on HI, 7 minutes for 2 ears; 9 minutes for 3 ears; or, 11 minutes for 4 ears. Let stand, in husks, 3 to 5 minutes before serving.

A7	3

Sweet Potatoes

Preset Cooking Time: about 4 minutes

  1 sweet potato (about 5 ounces)

Scrub potato and rinse well. Pierce at intervals with fork. Place on microwave roasting rack. Place in oven, with potato over circle on glass tray. Touch A7. Touch 3. Touch START. *(Oven cooks: HI, about 2 minutes.)*

At Pause, turn potato over. Touch START. *(Oven cooks: HI, about 2 minutes.)*

Let stand 3 minutes before serving.

1 serving

You can cook as many as 5 sweet potatoes at a time using the A7-3 setting. Be sure to arrange potatoes in a circle with 1 potato in the center, and position the center potato in the oven over the circle on the glass tray. The oven will automatically adjust the cooking time to accommodate the increased number of potatoes.

A7	5

Canned Vegetables

Preset Cooking Time: about 2 minutes

  1 can (8 ounces) canned vegetables,
        drained

Pour vegetables into 1-quart microproof casserole. Cover and place in oven. Touch A7. Touch 5. Touch START. *(Oven cooks: HI, about 2 minutes.)*

Let stand 2 to 3 minutes before serving.

2 servings

Mushroom-Pimiento Rice (page 144), Corn-on-the-Cob →

A7	1

Spinach Oriental

Preset Cooking Time: about 5 minutes

- 10 ounces spinach, tough stems removed
- 1 can (8 ounces) sliced water chestnuts, drained
- 4 green onions, sliced
- 2 tablespoons vegetable oil
- 2 tablespoons wine vinegar
- 2 tablespoons soy sauce
- 1 teaspoon sugar

Rinse spinach and drain; tear into bite-size pieces. Combine spinach and remaining ingredients in 2-quart microproof casserole. Cover and place in oven. Touch A7. Touch 1. Touch START. *(Oven cooks: HI, about 5 minutes.)*

Stir through and serve.

4 servings

A7	1	LOWER

Sautéed Mushrooms

Preset Cooking Time: about 3 minutes

- ½ pound mushrooms, cleaned and sliced
- ¼ cup butter or margarine
- 1 clove garlic, minced

Combine all ingredients in 8-inch microproof baking dish. Place in oven. Touch A7. Touch 1. Touch LOWER. Touch START. *(Oven cooks: HI, about 3 minutes.)*

Stir through several times before serving.

2 to 4 servings

Serve with roast beef or steak, or as a "surprise" side dish with any meal. Sautéed Mushrooms are also a delicious main dish when served on toast and sprinkled with Parmesan cheese.

Sauces are a cinch in your Sanyo Automatic Cuisine-Master microwave oven. They are definitely a microwave success story. For those of us who have slaved over a hot stove with whisk in hand and double boiler at full speed, those days are gone forever. Sauces simply do not stick or scorch as they do when prepared on the stove top. They heat evenly and require less time and attention. You don't have to stir constantly and can simply retire that double boiler. Usual- ly, just an occasional stirring is all that is required to prevent lumping. Sometimes, a quick beating after cooking can be added to make a sauce velvety-smooth. You can measure, mix, and cook all in the same cup, or in the serving pitcher itself! Choose Tarragon Sauce (page 175) or Béarnaise Sauce (page 170) to perk up meat or vegetables, others for desserts. Just try making a sauce the microwave way and you'll turn an ordinary food into an elegant treat.

Basic White Sauce (page 171) is typical of the preparation ease the microwave method provides. The simple steps are illustrated (right and above right). The addition of herbs or spices turns Basic White Sauce into something new each time you use it (above).

Adapting Your Recipes

All those sauces generally considered too difficult for the average cook are easy in the microwave oven. When looking for a sauce recipe similar to the conventional one you want to convert, find a recipe with a similar quantity of liquid and similar main thickening ingredient such as cornstarch, flour, egg, cheese, or jelly. Read the directions carefully to determine procedure, timing, and cook control setting. Then, when you stir, notice the progress of the sauce, and remove when the right consistency or doneness is reached. Keep notes to help you the next time. The following tips will help:

☐ Use a microproof container about twice the volume of ingredients to safeguard against the sauce boiling over — so easy with milk- and cream-based sauces.

☐ Sauces and salad dressings with ingredients not sensitive to high heat should be cooked on HI. Basic White Sauce is an example.

☐ Bring cornstarch-thickened mixtures to a boil and remove as soon as thickened. Remember, overcooking will destroy the thickening agent.

☐ You will notice that more flour or cornstarch is required in microwave cooking than in conventional cooking to thicken sauces and gravies, since they will not be reduced by evaporation.

☐ Stirring quickly two or three times during cooking is sufficient to assure even cooking. Too many stirrings may slow cooking.

☐ To reheat sauces: Dessert sauces to 125°F with temperature probe. Main dish sauces, such as gravy or canned spaghetti sauce, to 150°F.

☐ When sauces require time to develop flavor or if they contain eggs, which might curdle, they should be cooked slowly, on 50 or even 30. Don't allow delicate egg yolk sauces to boil.

A2:0

Béarnaise Sauce
Preset Cooking Time: about 2 minutes

- 4 egg yolks
- 2 teaspoons tarragon vinegar
- 1 teaspoon instant minced onion
- ½ teaspoon chervil
  Dash white pepper
- ½ cup butter or margarine
- 1 teaspoon minced parsley

Combine egg yolks, vinegar, onion, chervil, and pepper in blender or food processor container; set aside. Place butter in 1-cup glass measure. Place in oven over circle on glass tray. Touch A2. Touch START. *(Oven cooks: HI, about 2 minutes.)*

With blender at high speed, gradually add melted butter to yolk mixture through cover opening; process until thick and creamy. Stir in parsley. Serve warm over broiled steak, green vegetables, poached eggs, or fish.

½ cup

A2	2	HIGHER

Easy Gravy
Preset Cooking Time: about 6 minutes

- ¼ cup fat-free meat or poultry drippings
- ¼ cup all-purpose flour
- 2 cups warm broth, water, or pan drippings
  Salt and pepper

Pour drippings into 2-quart glass measure. Add flour; stir until smooth. Pour in broth; stir briskly with wire whisk until blended. Place in oven. Touch A2. Touch 2. Touch HIGHER. Touch START. *(Oven cooks: HI, about 3 minutes.)*

At Pause, stir. Touch START. *(Oven cooks: HI, about 3 minutes.)*

Season with salt and pepper; blend until smooth. Serve hot with meat, poultry, potatoes, or dressing.

2½ cups

A2	2	&	A2	2	HIGHER

Basic White Sauce

Preset Cooking Time: about 8 minutes

    1 cup milk
    2 tablespoons butter
    2 tablespoons all-purpose flour
       Dash white pepper
       Dash nutmeg

Pour milk into 4-cup glass measure. Place in oven over circle on glass tray. Touch A2. Touch 2. Touch START. *(Oven cooks: HI, about 2 minutes.)*

At Pause, remove from oven. Place butter in 2-cup glass measure. Place in oven over circle on glass tray. Touch START. *(Oven cooks: HI, about 1½ minutes.)*

Stir flour into butter until smooth. Touch A2. Touch 2. Touch HIGHER. Touch START. *(Oven cooks: HI, about 2 minutes.)*

At Pause, whisk in warm milk, pepper, and nutmeg, blending well. Touch START. *(Oven cooks: HI, about 2½ minutes.)* If sauce isn't quite thick enough, cook on HI an additional 30 seconds.

Serve over cooked broccoli or cauliflower, or use as base for other sauces.

1 cup

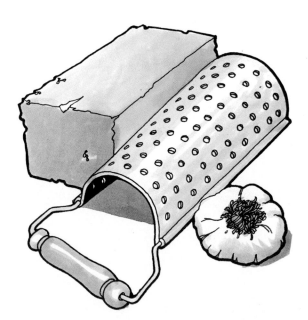

A9	6

Cranberry Sauce

Preset Cooking Time: about 7 minutes

    3 cups (1 pound) cranberries
    ½ cup sugar
    ⅓ cup water

Combine all ingredients in 2-quart micro-proof casserole. Place in oven. Touch A9. Touch 6. Touch START. *(Oven cooks: HI, about 4 minutes.)*

At Pause, stir. Touch START. *(Oven cooks: HI, about 3 minutes.)*

Remove from oven. Stir through several times. Let stand until cool. Chill before serving.

2 cups

For a festive touch, cut 4 oranges in half, scoop out orange segments and cut shells in a zig-zag pattern. Fill with Cranberry Sauce. Sprinkle with chopped pecans or walnuts. Place on platter with your favorite poultry.

A9	6	LOWER

Spicy Barbecue Sauce

Preset Cooking Time: about 6 minutes

    1 can (8 ounces) tomato sauce
    ¼ cup wine vinegar
    2 tablespoons brown sugar
    2 tablespoons prepared mustard
    1 tablespoon instant minced onion
    1 tablespoon Worcestershire sauce
    1 teaspoon celery seed
    ¼ teaspoon salt
    1 clove garlic, minced (optional)
       Dash hot pepper sauce

Combine all ingredients in 4-cup glass measure. Cover with plastic wrap. Place in oven. Touch A9. Touch 6. Touch LOWER. Touch START. *(Oven cooks: HI, about 4 minutes.)*

At Pause, stir through several times. Cover. Touch START. *(Oven cooks: HI, about 2 minutes.)*

Stir through before serving.

1⅓ cups

Hollandaise Sauce

Total Cooking Time: 2 minutes

- ¼ cup butter
- ¼ cup half-and-half
- 2 egg yolks, well beaten
- 1 tablespoon lemon juice
- ½ teaspoon dry mustard
- ¼ teaspoon salt

Place butter in 4-cup glass measure. Place in oven. Cook on HI, 1 minute.

Add remaining ingredients and beat with electric mixer or wire whisk until smooth. Cook on 70, 30 seconds.

Beat until blended. Cook on 70, 15 seconds.

Stir. Cook on 70, 15 seconds.

Beat until smooth. Serve immediately over cooked asparagus or broccoli.

¾ cup

If sauce curdles, beat in 1 teaspoon hot water, and continue beating until smooth.

To reheat Hollandaise Sauce, cook on 20 for 15 to 30 seconds. Stir; let stand 1 minute. Repeat until hot.

A2	2

Raisin Brandy Sauce

Preset Cooking Time: about 5 minutes

- ½ cup raisins
- ¼ cup apple brandy
- 3 tablespoons brown sugar
- 1 tablespoon cornstarch
- 1 cup apple juice
- 2 tablespoons lemon juice
- ⅛ teaspoon ground cloves
- ⅛ teaspoon nutmeg

Combine raisins and brandy in small bowl; set aside.

Combine brown sugar and cornstarch in 4-cup glass measure. Add apple and lemon juices and stir until cornstarch is dissolved. Place in oven. Touch A2. Touch 2. Touch START. *(Oven cooks: HI, about 3 minutes.)*

At Pause, stir in cloves, nutmeg, and undrained raisins. Touch START. *(Oven cooks: HI, about 2 minutes.)*

Serve warm with ham, beef tongue, baked squash, gingerbread, or Baked Apples (page 184).

1½ cups

← *Hollandaise Sauce on Asparagus (Guide, page 151), Raisin Brandy Sauce on Center Cut Ham Slice (Guide, page 82)*

Orange Sauce

Total Cooking Time: 3 minutes

- ⅔ cup orange juice
- 3 tablespoons fat-free duckling drippings
- 2 tablespoons brown sugar
- 1 tablespoon cornstarch
- 2 teaspoons grated orange peel
- 2 tablespoons orange-flavored liqueur

Combine all ingredients except liqueur in 2-cup glass measure, stirring until brown sugar and cornstarch are dissolved. Place in oven. Cook on HI, 1½ minutes.

Stir through several times. Cook on HI, 1½ minutes.

Stir in liqueur. Serve hot with Roast Orange Duckling (page 118).

1¼ cups

Not having duckling? Any poultry drippings will do. Or, simply increase orange juice by 3 tablespoons, and use as a dessert sauce.

A2	LOWER

Best Ever French Dressing

Preset Cooking Time: about 9 minutes

- ½ cup lemon juice
- ¼ cup wine vinegar
- 1 small onion, sliced
- 1 clove garlic, cut in half
- ¾ cup sugar
- ½ cup water
- 2 tablespoons corn syrup
- 1 cup vegetable oil
- ½ cup catsup
- 1 teaspoon salt
- 1 teaspoon paprika
- 1 teaspoon celery salt
- 1 teaspoon dry mustard

Combine lemon juice, vinegar, onion, and garlic; set aside. Combine sugar, water, and corn syrup in 4-cup glass measure. Place in oven. Touch A2. Touch LOWER. Touch START. *(Oven cooks: HI, about 9 minutes.)*

Remove from oven; let stand until cool. Strain lemon-vinegar mixture, discarding onion and garlic. Add to cooled syrup along with remaining ingredients. Beat with electric mixer until thick.

Serve chilled over salad or your favorite combination of raw or blanched vegetables.

2½ cups

A2	2	LOWER

Lemon Butter Sauce

Preset Cooking Time: about 3 minutes

- ½ cup butter
- 2 tablespoons lemon juice
- ⅛ teaspoon salt
- ⅛ teaspoon white pepper

Combine all ingredients in 2-cup glass measure. Place in oven over circle on glass tray. Touch A2. Touch 2. Touch LOWER. Touch START. *(Oven cooks: HI, about 2 minutes.)*

At Pause, stir. Touch START. *(Oven cooks: HI, about 1 minute.)*

Stir sauce and serve immediately with seafood, hot green vegetables, or Simple Salmon Ring (page 127).

⅔ cup

Tarragon Sauce

Total Cooking Time: 4 minutes

- ½ cup unsalted butter
- ⅓ cup dry white wine
- 2 tablespoons minced fresh tarragon or 2 teaspoons dried tarragon
- 1 tablespoon chopped chives
- 1 tablespoon tarragon vinegar
- ½ teaspoon salt
- ¼ teaspoon pepper
- 3 egg yolks, beaten

Combine all ingredients except egg yolks in 4-cup glass measure. Place in oven. Cook on HI, 2 minutes.

Stir small amount of mixture into yolks. Gradually stir yolks back into remaining mixture. Cook on 50, 1 minute.

Stir through several times. Cook on 50, 1 minute.

Beat with wire whisk until smooth. Serve immediately with poached eggs, broiled meat, cooked cauliflower or carrots.

1½ cups

Hot Lemony Dill Sauce

Total Cooking Time: 5 minutes

- ½ cup butter or margarine
- 2 tablespoons all-purpose flour
- 1 teaspoon chicken bouillon granules
- ½ teaspoon dillweed
- ½ teaspoon salt
- 1 cup chicken broth
- 2 tablespoons lemon juice

Place butter in 2-cup glass measure. Place in oven. Cook on HI, 1½ minutes.

Stir in flour, bouillon, dillweed, and salt. Whisk in broth. Cook on HI, 1½ minutes.

Stir through several times. Cook on HI, 1 minute.

Stir. Cook on HI, 1 minute.

Blend in lemon juice. Serve with broiled or Poached Salmon (page 125), or Simple Salmon Ring (page 127).

1½ cups

Clarified Butter

Total Cooking Time: 2½ minutes

- 1 cup butter

Place butter in 2-cup glass measure. Place in oven. Cook on 20, 2½ minutes.

Let stand 3 to 4 minutes. Skim foam from top. Slowly pour off yellow oil (this is the clarified butter). Discard any remaining impurities. Serve as a dipping sauce for steamed clams, crab legs, or shrimp.

⅓ cup

```
A9   6
```

Apricot Dessert Sauce

Preset Cooking Time: about 7 minutes

> 1 cup apricot nectar
> ¼ cup sugar
> 1 tablespoon cornstarch
> 1 teaspoon grated lemon peel
> 3 tablespoons apricot-flavored brandy

Combine apricot nectar, sugar, cornstarch, and lemon peel in 2-cup glass measure. Stir until sugar and cornstarch are dissolved. Place in oven over circle on glass tray. Touch A9. Touch 6. Touch START. *(Oven cooks: HI, about 4 minutes.)*

At Pause, add brandy; stir. Touch START. *(Oven cooks: HI, about 3 minutes.)*

Stir through several times. Serve warm or chilled over ice cream, rice pudding, Fluffy Tapioca (page 190), or pound cake.

1⅓ cups

To make a Lemon Dessert Sauce, substitute ½ cup water for the 1 cup apricot nectar, lemon juice for the brandy, and add 1 egg yolk and 1 tablespoon butter.

```
A2   2   HIGHER
```

Butterscotch Sauce

Preset Cooking Time: about 5 minutes

> 1¼ cups firmly packed brown sugar
> 1½ tablespoons cornstarch
> ½ cup half-and-half
> ¼ cup butter
> 2 tablespoons corn syrup
> ⅛ teaspoon salt
> 1 teaspoon vanilla

Combine brown sugar and cornstarch in 1½-quart microproof casserole. Add half-and-half, butter, corn syrup, and salt; stir until cornstarch and brown sugar are dissolved. Place in oven. Touch A2. Touch 2. Touch HIGHER. Touch START. *(Oven cooks: HI, about 2 minutes.)*

At Pause, stir until butter is melted. Touch START. *(Oven cooks: HI, about 3 minutes.)*

Stir through. Stir in vanilla. Serve hot or chilled over ice cream or cake.

1½ cups

Rum Custard Sauce

Total Cooking Time: 11 minutes

> 1½ cups milk
> ½ cup half-and-half
> ⅓ cup sugar
> ⅛ teaspoon salt
> 3 large eggs, lightly beaten
> 3 tablespoons dark rum

Combine milk, half-and-half, sugar, and salt in 2-quart glass measure. Place in oven. Cook on 70, 4 minutes.

Stir ½ cup milk mixture into eggs. Gradually stir eggs back into milk mixture. Cook on 50, 2 minutes.

Stir through several times. Cook on 30, 2½ minutes.

Stir. Cook on 30, 2½ minutes.

Let sauce stand until cooled to room temperature. Sitr in rum. Serve over bread pudding, banana pudding, or poached peaches.

2½ cups

← *Apricot Dessert Sauce with Fluffy Tapioca (page 190), Lemon Dessert Sauce variation on pound cake*

A9	6

Raspberry Sauce

Preset Cooking Time: about 7 minutes

- 1 package (12 ounces) frozen raspberries
- 1 teaspoon cornstarch
- 1 tablespoon water

Place raspberries in 1½-quart microproof bowl. Place in oven. Touch A9. Touch 6. Touch START. *(Oven cooks: HI, about 4 minutes.)*

At Pause, remove from oven. Break up berries with wooden spoon. Strain, if desired. Return to bowl. Dissolve cornstarch in water. Stir into berries. Place in oven. Touch START. *(Oven cooks: HI, about 3 minutes.)*

Stir through several times. Serve over angel food cake, poached pears, or ice cream.

1½ cups

Remember that you can increase the quantity of the recipe to suit your own family's needs — the surface-temperature sensor will automatically do the work.

A2	2	HIGHER

Hot Fudge Sauce

Preset Cooking Time: about 4 minutes

- 1 cup sugar
- 2 squares (1 ounce each) unsweetened chocolate
- ⅓ cup milk
- 3 tablespoons light corn syrup
- 1 large egg, well beaten
- 1 teaspoon vanilla

Combine all ingredients except vanilla in 4-cup glass measure; blend well. Place in oven. Touch A2. Touch 2. Touch HIGHER. Touch START. *(Oven cooks: HI, about 2 minutes.)*

At Pause, stir until chocolate is melted. Touch START. *(Oven cooks: HI, about 2 minutes.)*

Blend in vanilla. Briskly stir with wire whisk until clear and shiny. Refrigerate until cool; sauce will thicken as it stands. Serve over ice cream, chocolate cake, fresh fruit, or as a fondue for dipping pound cake or fresh berries.

1 cup

Hot Fudge Sauce on banana splits, Raspberry Sauce on poached pears →

Fresh Strawberry Sauce

Total Cooking Time: 4 minutes

- 1 pint strawberries, hulled
- 1 cup water
- ½ cup sugar
- 2 tablespoons cornstarch
- 2 tablespoons butter
- ½ cup lemon juice

Set aside several whole berries for garnish. Press remaining berries through food mill or purée in blender or food processor. Strain purée and set aside. Combine water, sugar, and cornstarch in 4-cup glass measure until sugar and cornstarch are dissolved. Place in oven. Cook on HI, 2 minutes.

Stir through several times. Cover. Cook on HI, 1 minute.

Stir. Cover. Cook on HI, 1 minute.

Add butter and stir until melted. Blend in lemon juice and strawberry purée. Fold in whole berries. Refrigerate. Serve over pound cake, vanilla pudding, custard, or as a parfait sauce.

2½ cups

A2	2	HIGHER

Choco-Peanut Butter Sauce

Preset Cooking Time: about 3 minutes

- 1 cup sugar
- ⅓ cup peanut butter
- ¼ cup milk
- 1 square (1 ounce) unsweetened chocolate
- 1 tablespoon light corn syrup
- ¼ teaspoon vanilla

Place all ingredients except vanilla in 4-cup glass measure. Place in oven. Touch A2. Touch 2. Touch HIGHER. Touch START. *(Oven cooks: HI, about 1½ minutes.)*

At Pause, stir until chocolate is melted. Touch START. *(Oven cooks: HI, about 1½ minutes.)*

Add vanilla; blend well. Serve hot or chilled over ice cream, cake, or sliced bananas.

1 cup

How Sweet It Is!

Desserts can transform a simple meal into a delectable feast. From baked fresh fruit to fudgy chocolate cake, they make the perfect ending to any meal. Here are some traditional family favorites, glamorous party desserts, and spur-of-the-moment treats. All are quick and easy with your microwave oven. In no time at all, cakes will rise before your eyes, custards will become thick and creamy, and pie fillings will bubble and thicken. Brownies and bar cookies are delicious, fast and fun to make, and if you've never tried home-made candies, now is the time! It's impossible to fail when you make candy the microwave way.

An egg wash brushed on Homemade Pie Shell (page 194) will enhance the appearance. Chocolate wafer or graham cracker Crumb Crust (page 194) is a quick dessert when filled with pudding (top left). Rich Chocolate Fudge (page 196) is easy. A candy thermometer can be used to check the soft ball stage (234°F on the thermometer) when making candy (top right). Other ingredients are added after cooking (above left). Microwave cakes rise higher than conventional cakes. Fill cake pans only half-full (above right).

Adapting Your Recipes

How easy it is! Puddings and custards can be baked without the usual water bath, and they need only occasional stirring. Fruits retain their bright color and fresh-picked flavor. Cakes cook so quickly; yet they are superior in texture, taste, and height. When you discover how effortless it is to make candy, you'll be trying all those recipes you've been longing to do. Because cakes and pie crusts cook so fast, they do not brown. If you like a browned surface, there are many ways to give desserts a browned look. So try adapting your dessert recipes following the guidance of a similar recipe in this chapter and these tips:

AUTOMATIC COOKING GUIDE — DESSERTS

No.	Food	Cover	Special Notes
A9-0	Cakes, Thin Batter	NO	Place batter portion over circle on glass tray. Rotate if rising unevenly. See pages 71, 73, 74, 76, 190, 191.
A9-1	Cakes, Heavy Batter	NO	
A9-2	Muffins, Cupcakes	NO	Place muffin ring with 1 muffin over circle on glass tray. See pages 27, 76.
A9-3	Bars, Brownies	NO	At Pause, rotate pan one-quarter turn. See pages 188, 190.
A9-4	Firm Fruit	NO	See pages 184, 186. If a cover is specified in a recipe, cover must be used.
A9-5	Delicate Fruit	NO	
A9-6	Pudding	NO	At Pause, stir. See page 191.

☐ You can enhance your light-colored cookies and cakes with cinnamon, nutmeg, brown sugar, coffee, nuts, toppings, frostings, glazes, food coloring, etc.

☐ Small drop cookies and slice 'n bake cookies don't do as well as the larger bar cookies. Drop cookies must be cooked in small batches; they tend to cook unevenly, and need to be removed individually from the oven when finished.

☐ A serviceable cookie sheet can be made by covering cardboard with waxed paper.

☐ Layer cakes are generally baked one layer at a time. Baking is usually begun on 50 or 60 for the first 7 minutes, then finished on HI. If cake appears to be rising unevenly, rotate the dish one-quarter turn as necessary. Denser batters, such as fruit cakes, require slower, gentler cooking. Set at 30 for good results.

☐ A pie shell is cooked when surface appears opaque and dry.

☐ For even cooking, select fruit of uniform size to be cooked whole, as in baked apples, or cut uniformly to be cooked in pieces, as in apple pie.

☐ Remove baked custards from oven when centers are nearly firm. They will continue to cook and set after removal.

☐ To avoid lumping, puddings should be stirred once or twice during the second half of cooking.

☐ To use the surface-temperature sensor, follow the guidelines in the recipes here. Placement of the dish is important: batter must be over the circle on the glass tray.

☐ For best results, choose a recipe from this collection that is quite like yours. Should the dessert be underdone, use HIGHER option next time; if overdone, use LOWER option.

☐ Cook egg custards on 70. Prepared from a 3-ounce package, custard requires 8 to 10 minutes. Use 4-cup glass measure and stir 3 times.

☐ Tapioca cooks on HI. Prepared from a 3¼-ounce package, tapioca requires 6 to 7 minutes. Use 4-cup glass measure and stir twice.

COOKING/DEFROSTING GUIDE — CONVENIENCE DESSERTS

Food	Amount	Cook Control Setting	Time	Special Notes
Brownies, other bars, frozen	12 - 13 oz.	30 (defrost)	2 - 3 minutes	In original ¾" foil tray, lid removed. Let stand 5 minutes.
Cookies, frozen	6	30 (defrost)	50 - 60 seconds	Place on paper plate or towels.
Pineapple upside-down cake mix	21½ oz.	50 (simmer) HI (max. power)	3 minutes 4 minutes	Use 9" round glass dish. Remove enough batter for 2 cupcakes, bake separately. Rotate if rising unevenly.
Cupcakes or crumb cakes, frozen	1 or 2	30 (defrost)	½ - 1 minute	Place on shallow plate.
Cheesecake, frozen	17 - 19 oz.	30 (defrost)	4 - 5 minutes	Remove from foil pan to plate. Let stand 1 minute.
Pound cake, frozen	10¾ oz.	30 (defrost)	2 minutes	Remove from foil pan to plate. Rotate once. Let stand 5 minutes.
Cake, frozen 2- or 3-layer	17 oz.	30 (defrost)	2½ - 3 minutes	Remove from foil pan to plate. Watch carefully, frosting melts fast. Let stand 5 minutes.
Custard pie, frozen	9" pie	70 (roast)	4 - 5½ minutes	Remove from foil pan to plate. Center should be nearly set.
Fruit pie, frozen, unbaked, 2 crusts	9" pie	HI (max. power)	13 - 15 minutes	On glass pie plate. Brown, if desired, in preheated 425° conventional oven 8 - 10 minutes.
Frozen fruit	10 oz.	HI (max. power)	5 - 5½ minutes	On microproof plate. Slit pouch. Flex halfway through cooking time to mix.
	16 oz.	HI (max. power)	7 - 9 minutes	Remove from bag. Place in glass casserole, cover. Stir halfway through cooking time.

A9:0   LOWER

Cake Mix

Preset Cooking Time: about 7 minutes

> 1 package (9 ounces) single-layer
> cake mix

Line bottom of 9-inch round microproof baking dish with waxed paper. Prepare cake batter as directed on package. Pour into prepared baking dish. Place in oven. Touch A9. Touch LOWER. Touch START. *(Oven cooks: 50, about 5 minutes; HI, about 2 minutes.)* If cake begins to rise unevenly, open door and rotate pan one-quarter turn; touch START.

Let cool in pan 3 to 5 minutes before inverting cake onto serving plate. Carefully peel off waxed paper.

1 layer

A9   3   LOWER

Brownie Mix

Preset Cooking Time: about 6 minutes

> 1 package (16 ounces) brownie mix
> 1 tablespoon confectioners sugar

Butter 8-inch round microproof pie plate. Prepare brownie batter as directed on package. Pour into prepared pie plate. Place in oven. Touch A9. Touch 3. Touch LOWER. Touch START. *(Oven cooks: HI, about 3 minutes.)*

At Pause, rotate pie plate one-quarter turn. Touch START. *(Oven cooks: HI, about 3 minutes.)*

Let stand in pie plate until cool. Sprinkle with confectioners sugar and cut into wedges or squares.

16 brownies

A9	4	LOWER

Baked Apples

Preset Cooking Time: about 5 minutes

  2 baking apples (1 pound)
    Lemon juice
  2 teaspoons slivered almonds
  2 teaspoons raisins
  2 teaspoons brown sugar
  1/4 teaspoon cinnamon
  2 tablespoons water
  2 teaspoons butter or margarine

Core apples, starting from tops, without cutting all the way through. Remove a thin circle of peel around tops. Sprinkle with lemon juice. Combine almonds, raisins, brown sugar, and cinnamon; mix lightly. Fill apples with mixture. Place each apple in microproof custard cup. Add 1 tablespoon water to each cup. Dot each apple with 1 teaspoon butter. Place in oven with portions of each apple over circle on glass tray. Cover with waxed paper. Touch A9. Touch 4. Touch LOWER. Touch START. *(Oven cooks: HI, about 5 minutes.)*

2 servings

A9	5

Fresh Peaches in Raspberry Liqueur

Preset Cooking Time: about 5 minutes

  2 large peaches, cut in half
    and pitted
  3 tablespoons raspberry liqueur

Place peaches and liqueur in small glass microproof bowl. Place in oven over circle on glass tray. Touch A9. Touch 5. Touch START. *(Oven cooks: HI, about 5 minutes.)*

Gently stir peaches to coat with liqueur. Serve hot over ice cream, or, for a special occasion, divide mixture between 2 wine glasses and fill glasses with Champagne.

2 servings

A9	5	LOWER

Baked Maple Bananas

Preset Cooking Time: about 3 minutes

  3 tablespoons maple syrup
  2 tablespoons butter or margarine,
    melted
  4 bananas, cut in half lengthwise
  2 tablespoons chopped walnuts
  1 tablespoon lemon juice
  1/4 teaspoon cinnamon

Combine maple syrup and butter; blend well. Pour into shallow microproof baking dish just large enough to accommodate bananas. Add bananas. Spoon some of the maple syrup mixture over bananas. Touch A9. Touch 5. Touch LOWER. Touch START. *(Oven cooks: HI, about 3 minutes.)*

Sprinkle with walnuts, lemon juice and cinnamon. Serve warm.

4 servings

Don't tell anyone this dessert took only 3 minutes! For an elegant variation, pour 3 tablespoons warm rum over bananas at the table and ignite. Bananas Flambé! The butter can be melted in the microwave as a preparation step. Use a 1-cup glass measure. Touch A1. Touch 1. Touch START. (Oven cooks: 80, about 30 seconds.)

A9   3

Fresh Strawberry Jam

Preset Cooking Time: about 36 minutes

- 5 cups crushed hulled strawberries
- 2 teaspoons lemon juice
- 1 package (1¾ ounces) powdered fruit pectin
- 7 cups sugar

Combine strawberries, lemon juice, and pectin in 6-quart microproof casserole. Place in oven. Touch A9. Touch 3. Touch START. *(Oven cooks: HI, about 15 minutes.)*

At Pause, add sugar; blend well. Touch START. *(Oven cooks: HI, about 21 minutes.)*

Skim foam with metal spoon. Pour into hot sterilized jars and seal.

2 quarts

A9   3

Cranapple Jelly

Preset Cooking Time: about 32 minutes

- 4 cups cranapple juice
- 1 package (1¾ ounces) powdered fruit pectin
- 4 cups sugar

Combine juice and pectin in 4-quart microproof casserole. Cover and place in oven. Touch A9. Touch 3. Touch START. *(Oven cooks: HI, about 13 minutes.)*

At Pause, add sugar; blend well. Do not cover. Touch START. *(Oven cooks: HI, about 19 minutes.)*

Skim foam with metal spoon. Pour into hot sterilized jars and seal.

6 cups

A9   4   HIGHER

Applesauce

Preset Cooking Time: about 9 minutes

- 6 cups sliced peeled cooking apples
- ½ cup water
- 1 tablespoon lemon juice
- ¼ cup sugar
- ½ teaspoon cinnamon or nutmeg

Place apples, water, and lemon juice in 2-quart microproof casserole. Cover and place in oven. Touch A9. Touch 4. Touch HIGHER. Touch START. *(Oven cooks: HI, about 9 minutes.)*

Stir in sugar and cinnamon. Serve warm or chilled with pork or as a light dessert.

4 to 6 servings

A9   4   HIGHER

Golden Apple Chunks

Preset Cooking Time: about 7 minutes

- 4 medium-size tart cooking apples, peeled, cored, and cut into quarters
- ¼ cup firmly packed brown sugar
- 1 teaspoon cinnamon
- 2 tablespoons butter or margarine

Place apples in 1-quart microproof casserole. Combine brown sugar and cinnamon and sprinkle over apples. Dot with butter. Cover and place in oven. Touch A9. Touch 4. Touch HIGHER. Touch START. *(Oven cooks: HI, about 7 minutes.)*

4 servings

`| A2 | 1 | HIGHER |`

Chocolate Fudge Frosting

Preset Cooking Time: about 2 minutes

- 1 square (1 ounce) unsweetened chocolate
- 1 cup sugar
- ⅓ cup milk
- ¼ cup butter or margarine
- ⅛ teaspoon salt
- 1 teaspoon vanilla
- ¼ cup chopped walnuts or pecans

Combine chocolate, sugar, milk, butter, and salt in 4-cup glass measure. Place in oven. Touch A2. Touch 1. Touch HIGHER. Touch START. (Oven cooks: 70, about 2 minutes.)

Add vanilla and beat with electric mixer until almost cool. Add nuts and beat until mixture is spreading consistency.

1 cup

Peanut Crispy Bars

Total Cooking Time: 3½ minutes

- ¼ cup butter or margarine
- 5 cups miniature or 40 regular marshmallows
- ⅓ cup peanut butter
- 5 cups crispy rice cereal
- 1 cup unsalted dry-roasted peanuts, chopped

Lightly grease 11×7-inch baking dish. Place butter in 3-quart microproof bowl. Place in oven. Cook on HI, 1 minute.

Stir in marshmallows. Cover. Cook on HI, 2½ minutes.

Stir in peanut butter until smooth. Stir in cereal and peanuts. Press warm mixture into prepared baking dish. Let cool before cutting into bars.

36 bars

Cherry Crunch

Total Cooking Time: 15 minutes

- 1 package (9 ounces) single-layer white or yellow cake mix
- ¼ cup chopped nuts
- 2 tablespoons brown sugar
- 2 teaspoons cinnamon
- 1 can (21 ounces) cherry pie filling
- ½ cup butter or margarine
  Whipped cream or vanilla ice cream

Combine cake mix, nuts, brown sugar, and cinnamon. Spoon pie filling evenly into 8-inch round microproof baking dish. Sprinkle evenly with cake mix mixture; set aside. Place butter in 1-cup glass measure. Place in oven. Cook on HI, 1 minute.

Drizzle butter over cake mix mixture. Place in oven. Cook on HI, 7 minutes.

Rotate dish one-quarter turn. Cook on HI, 7 minutes.

Let stand 5 minutes. Serve warm, topped with whipped cream.

6 to 8 servings

Coconut Squares

Total Cooking Time: 8 minutes

- ¼ cup butter or margarine
- 1 cup graham-cracker crumbs
- 1 teaspoon sugar
- 1 cup flaked coconut
- ⅔ cup sweetened condensed milk
- ½ cup chopped walnuts or pecans
- 1 cup semisweet chocolate pieces

Place butter in 9-inch round microproof baking dish. Place in oven. Cook on HI, 1 minute.

Stir in cracker crumbs and sugar. Pat mixture firmly into bottom of dish. Cook on HI, 2 minutes.

Let cool slightly. Combine coconut, milk, and nuts. Carefully spoon into crust. Place in oven. Cook on HI, 4 minutes.

Sprinkle with chocolate. Cook on HI, 1 minute.

Spread melted chocolate evenly over top. Cool before cutting into squares or wedges.

16 to 20 squares

| A1 | 1 | & | A9 | 3 |

Chocolate Chip Bars

Preset Cooking Time: about 8 minutes

- ½ cup butter or margarine
- ¾ cup firmly packed brown sugar
- 2 large eggs, lightly beaten
- 1 teaspoon vanilla
- 1 cup chopped nuts
- 1 cup semisweet chocolate pieces
- ½ cup all-purpose flour
- 1 teaspoon baking powder
  Confectioners sugar or instant cocoa drink mix

Place butter in 2-quart glass measure. Place in oven. Touch A1. Touch 1. Touch START. *(Oven cooks: 80, about 1 minute.)*

Add brown sugar, eggs, and vanilla; blend well. Stir in nuts, chocolate, flour, and baking powder. Spread in 9-inch round microproof baking dish. Place in oven. Touch A9. Touch 3. Touch START. *(Oven cooks: HI, about 3 minutes.)*

At Pause, rotate dish one-quarter turn. Touch START. *(Oven cooks: HI, about 4 minutes.)*

Let stand in pan until cool. Sprinkle with confectioners sugar, and cut into bars or wedges.

24 bars

| A1 | 1 | HIGHER | & | A9 | 3 |

Chocolate Nut Brownies

Preset Cooking Time: about 11 minutes

- 2 squares (1 ounce each) unsweetened chocolate
- ½ cup unsalted butter
- 2 large eggs
- ¾ cup sugar
- ½ cup all-purpose flour
- 1 tablespoon vanilla
- 1 teaspoon baking powder
- ¼ teaspoon salt
- 1 cup coarsely chopped walnuts
- 1 cup semisweet chocolate pieces
  Confectioners sugar

Place chocolate squares and butter in 4-cup glass measure. Place in oven. Touch A1. Touch 1. Touch HIGHER. Touch START. *(Oven cooks: 80, about 2 minutes.)*

Remove from oven. Stir until chocolate is melted; set aside. Break eggs into large bowl; beat with fork until blended. Add chocolate mixture, sugar, flour, vanilla, baking powder, and salt; blend well. Stir in walnuts and chocolate pieces. Pour into 9-inch microproof deep-dish pie plate or quiche dish. Place in oven. Touch A9. Touch 3. Touch START. *(Oven cooks: HI, about 4 minutes.)*

At Pause, rotate dish one-quarter turn. Touch START. *(Oven cooks: HI, about 5 minutes.)*

Let cool completely before sprinkling with confectioners sugar. Cut into wedges.

10 brownies

| A9 | 3 | HIGHER |

Chewy Coconut Bars

Preset Cooking Time: about 7 minutes

- 2 large eggs
- ½ cup butter or margarine, melted
- ¾ cup firmly packed brown sugar
- ½ cup all-purpose flour
- 1 teaspoon baking powder
- 1 teaspoon vanilla
- 1 cup chopped nuts
- 1 cup flaked coconut
  Confectioners sugar

Break eggs into mixing bowl. Beat with electric mixer until lemon-colored. Add butter, brown sugar, flour, baking powder, and vanilla; blend well. Stir in nuts and coconut. Pour into 8-inch round microproof baking dish. Place in oven. Touch A9. Touch 3. Touch HIGHER. Touch START. *(Oven cooks: HI, about 3 minutes.)*

At Pause, rotate dish one-quarter turn. Touch START. *(Oven cooks: HI, about 4 minutes.)*

Sprinkle with confectioners sugar. Let cool completely before cutting into bars or wedges.

18 to 20 bars

*Chocolate Nut Brownies, Chewy Coconut →
Bars, Chocolate Chip Bars, Date Oatmeal
Bars (page 190)*

A1	5	&	A9	3	HIGHER

Date Oatmeal Bars

Preset Cooking Time: about 11 minutes

- 1 cup chopped dates
- ½ cup raisins
- ½ cup water
- 2 tablespoons sugar
- 1 tablespoon all-purpose flour
- ½ cup chopped walnuts or pecans
- ¼ teaspoon baking soda
- 1 tablespoon water
- 1 cup firmly packed brown sugar
- 1 cup all-purpose flour
- 1 cup rolled oats
- ½ cup butter or margarine, melted
- ¼ teaspoon salt
- 1 teaspoon cinnamon

Grease 9-inch round microproof baking dish. Combine dates, raisins, ½ cup water, sugar, and 1 tablespoon flour in microproof bowl. Place in oven. Touch A1. Touch 5. Touch START. *(Oven cooks: 80, about 3 minutes.)*

Stir nuts into mixture and set aside. Dissolve baking soda in 1 tablespoon water in large bowl. Add brown sugar, 1 cup flour, oats, butter, and salt. Firmly pat two-thirds of oat mixture into prepared baking dish. Spread with date mixture. Stir cinnamon into remaining oat mixture; crumble over date mixture. Place in oven. Touch A9. Touch 3. Touch HIGHER. Touch START. *(Oven cooks: HI, about 3 minutes.)*

At Pause, rotate dish one-half turn. Touch START. *(Oven cooks: HI, about 5 minutes.)*

Cover with aluminum foil, and let stand until cool. Cut into bars or wedges.

24 bars

Fluffy Tapioca

Total Cooking Time: 11 minutes

- 2 cups milk
- 3 tablespoons quick-cooking tapioca
- 5 tablespoons sugar, divided
- 1 large egg, separated
- ⅛ teaspoon salt
- 1 teaspoon vanilla

Combine milk, tapioca, 3 tablespoons sugar, egg yolk, and salt in 2-quart microproof casserole; blend well. Place in oven. Cook on HI, 6 minutes.

Beat with wire whisk until well blended. Cook on 70, 5 minutes.

Beat egg white in small mixing bowl with electric mixer until foamy. Gradually beat in remaining 2 tablespoons sugar until soft peaks form. Stir vanilla into tapioca. Fold egg whites into tapioca a little at a time until just blended. Serve topped with Apricot Dessert Sauce (page 177).

5 servings

A9	1

Carrot Cake

Preset Cooking Time: about 16 minutes

- 1½ cups all-purpose flour
- 2 teaspoons cinnamon
- 1½ teaspoons baking soda
- 1 teaspoon nutmeg
- ½ teaspoon salt
- 3 cups grated carrots
- 1½ cups sugar
- 1 cup vegetable oil
- 1 cup chopped walnuts
- 3 eggs, beaten

Frosting:

- 1 package (8 ounces) cream cheese, softened
- ½ cup butter or margarine, softened
- ¼ cup chopped walnuts
- 2 teaspoons vanilla
- 3 cups confectioners sugar, sifted

Lightly grease 6-cup microproof bundt pan; set aside. Sift together flour, cinnamon, baking soda, nutmeg, and salt. Combine carrots, sugar, oil, nuts, and eggs in large bowl. Add dry ingredients and mix thoroughly. Pour into prepared pan. Place in oven with batter positioned over circle on glass tray. Touch A9. Touch 1. Touch START. *(Oven cooks: 70, about 16 minutes.)* If cake begins to rise unevenly, open door and rotate pan one-quarter turn; touch START. Let cool in pan in oven or on flat surface.

Beat cream cheese and butter in large bowl. Add nuts and vanilla, and blend well. Gradually beat in sugar. Invert cake onto serving platter. Frost cake. Sprinkle with additional chopped walnuts, if desired.

8 to 10 servings

Pumpkin Cupcakes

Total Cooking Time: 12 minutes

- ½ cup firmly packed brown sugar
- ¼ cup sugar
- 1 large egg
- 6 tablespoons vegetable oil
- ½ cup canned or mashed cooked pumpkin
- ½ teaspoon vanilla
- 1 cup all-purpose flour
- 2 tablespoons milk
- ½ teaspoon cinnamon
- ½ teaspoon salt
- ¼ teaspoon baking powder
- ¼ teaspoon baking soda
- ⅛ teaspoon ginger

Beat sugars, egg, and oil until smooth. Stir in pumpkin and vanilla. Add remaining ingredients and beat until smooth. Spoon batter into 6 paper-lined microproof muffin cups, filling cups half full. Place in oven. Cook on 30, 6 minutes. If cupcakes begin to rise unevenly, open door and rotate cups one-quarter turn; touch START.

Remove cupcakes from oven. Spoon remaining batter into muffin cups as above. Place in oven. Cook on 30, 6 minutes. If cupcakes begin to rise unevenly, rotate cups as above.

Let cool completely before serving.

12 cupcakes

Top with your favorite cream cheese frosting for a delectable treat.

```
A9    6    HIGHER
```

Pudding Mix

Preset Cooking Time: about 7 minutes

- 1 package (3¼ ounces) pudding and pie filling mix
- 2 cups milk

Place pudding mix in 2-quart microproof bowl. Stir in milk. Place in oven. Touch A9. Touch 6. Touch HIGHER. Touch START. *(Oven cooks: HI, about 3 minutes.)*

At Pause, stir through several times. Touch START. *(Oven cooks: HI, 4 minutes.)*

Pour pudding into individual dessert dishes. Chill before serving.

4 servings

```
A9:0    HIGHER
```

Scotch Nut Oatmeal Cake

Preset Cooking Time: about 8 minutes

- 2 tablespoons butter or margarine
- ¾ cup firmly packed brown sugar, divided
- ¼ cup butterscotch pieces
- ¼ cup chopped walnuts
- ¾ cup hot water
- ½ cup rolled oats
- ¼ cup butter or margarine
- ½ cup sugar
- 1 large egg
- ¾ cup all-purpose flour
- ½ teaspoon baking soda
- ½ teaspoon salt
- ½ teaspoon cinnamon
- ½ teaspoon nutmeg

Spread 2 tablespoons butter over bottom of 6-cup shallow microproof ring mold. Combine ¼ cup brown sugar, butterscotch, and walnuts; spread evenly over butter in ring mold. Set aside. Combine hot water, oats, and butter; stir. Add sugar, remaining ½ cup brown sugar, and egg; blend well. Add remaining ingredients; stir just until blended. Pour over nut mixture in ring mold. Place in oven, with batter positioned over circle on glass tray. Touch A9. Touch HIGHER. Touch START. *(Oven cooks: 50, about 4 minutes; HI, about 4 minutes.)* If cake begins to rise unevenly, open door and rotate mold one-half turn; touch START.

Let stand 5 minutes before inverting cake onto serving plate. Serve warm or chilled, topped with whipped cream, if desired.

8 servings

A9	1	HIGHER

Chocolate Cherry Bundt Cake

Preset Cooking Time: about 21 minutes

> 1 package (18½ ounces) chocolate cake mix with pudding
> 1 cup cherry pie filling
> 3 large eggs
> ¾ cup water
> ¼ cup vegetable oil
> 1 teaspoon almond extract

Combine all ingredients according to directions on cake package. Carefully pour batter into 12-cup microproof bundt pan. Place in oven with batter positioned over circle on glass tray. Touch A9. Touch 1. Touch HIGHER. Touch START. *(Oven cooks: 70, about 21 minutes.)* If cake begins to rise unevenly, open door and rotate pan one-quarter turn; touch START. Let stand 10 minutes before inverting onto serving plate to cool.

9 servings

For an extra festive treat, top cooled cake with ring of additional cherries from remaining pie filling, and drizzle some of the cherry juice over top and sides.

Snow White Frosting

Total Cooking Time: about 5 minutes

> 1 cup sugar
> ½ cup water
> ¼ teaspoon cream of tartar
> Dash salt
> 2 egg whites
> 1 teaspoon vanilla

Combine sugar, water, cream of tartar, and salt in 2-cup glass measure. Place in oven. Insert temperature probe. Plug in probe. Cook on 70, with probe set at 200°F.

Beat egg whites with electric mixer until soft peaks form. Gradually beat hot syrup into egg whites. Add vanilla and continue beating 5 minutes, or until thick and fluffy.

1½ to 2 cups

A9:0	&	A9:0

Devil's Food Cake

Preset Cooking Time: about 20 minutes

> 2 cups sifted all-purpose flour
> 1¼ teaspoons baking soda
> ¼ teaspoon salt
> 2 cups sugar
> ½ cup shortening
> ½ cup unsweetened cocoa powder
> 1 teaspoon vanilla
> 1 cup boiling water
> ½ cup buttermilk
> 2 large eggs, beaten

Grease bottoms of two 8½- or 9-inch round microproof baking dishes. Line bottoms with waxed paper. Sift together flour, baking soda, and salt; set aside. Cream sugar, shortening, cocoa, and vanilla in large mixing bowl with electric mixer. Stir in boiling water, buttermilk, and eggs; blend well. Gradually beat in flour mixture until smooth. Divide mixture between prepared baking pans. Place 1 dish in oven. Touch A9. Touch START. *(Oven cooks: 50, about 8 minutes; HI, about 2 minutes.)* If cake begins to rise unevenly, open door and rotate dish one-quarter turn; touch START.

Remove from oven. Place second layer in oven. Touch A9. Touch START. *(Oven cooks: 50, about 8 minutes; HI, about 2 minutes.)* If cake begins to rise unevenly, rotate dish as above.

After removing from oven, let each layer stand 5 minutes before inverting onto wire rack. Remove waxed paper and let cool completely before frosting.

8 to 10 servings

To frost and fill, try Chocolate Fudge Frosting (page 187) or Snow White Frosting (page 192).

Lemon Pineapple Crème

Total Cooking Time: 6 minutes

- 1 can (8 ounces) crushed pineapple
- ¾ cup sugar, divided
- ⅔ cup water
- 3 tablespoons cornstarch
- 2 large eggs, separated
- 1 package (3 ounces) cream cheese, cut into cubes
- 2 tablespoons lemon juice
- 1 teaspoon grated lemon peel

Combine pineapple, ½ cup sugar, water, and cornstarch in 4-cup glass measure; stir until cornstarch is dissolved. Place in oven. Cook on HI, 2½ minutes.

Stir through several times. Cook on HI, 2½ minutes.

Beat egg yolks with electric mixer until lemon-colored. Stir into pineapple mixture. Blend in cream cheese, lemon juice, and lemon peel. Cook on 80, 1 minute.

Beat pineapple mixture with electric mixer until blended. Let stand until cool. Beat egg whites until foamy. Gradually beat in remaining ¼ cup sugar until soft peaks form. Fold into pineapple mixture. Spoon into individual dessert dishes. Chill before serving.

5 to 6 servings

Crumb Crust

Total Cooking Time: 3 minutes

- 5 tablespoons butter or margarine
- 1¼ cups fine graham-cracker crumbs
- 1 tablespoon sugar

Place butter in 9-inch microproof pie plate. Place in oven. Cook on HI, 1½ minutes.

Blend in cracker crumbs and sugar. Set aside 2 tablespoons crumb mixture to sprinkle over top of pie, if desired. Press remaining crumb mixture firmly into bottom and sides of plate. Cook on HI, 1½ minutes.

Let cool completely before filling.

One 9-inch pie shell

Vanilla wafers, gingersnaps, or chocolate wafers also make delicious crumb crusts.

Homemade Pie Shell

Total Cooking Time: 6 minutes

- 1 cup all-purpose flour
- 1 teaspoon salt
- 6 tablespoons shortening
- 2 tablespoons ice water
- 1 large egg, lightly beaten

Combine flour and salt. Cut in shortening with pastry blender or 2 knives until mixture is consistency of small peas. Sprinkle with ice water. Mix with fork until dough holds together. Gather into ball. Roll out on lightly floured surface to 12-inch circle. Fit into 9-inch microproof pie plate. Trim and flute edge. Prick at intervals with fork. Brush with egg. Place in oven. Cook on HI, 6 minutes. Cool completely before filling.

One 9-inch pie shell

If you want to save time by using a ready-made pie shell, be sure to place it in a microproof pie plate before filling.

Raisin Bread Pudding

Total Cooking Time: 18½ minutes

- 4 slices raisin bread, cut into cubes (about 4 cups)
- ¼ cup raisins
- 3 large eggs
- ½ cup firmly packed brown sugar
- 1 teaspoon vanilla
  Dash salt
- 2 cups milk
- 2 tablespoons butter or margarine
  Cinnamon or nutmeg

Toss bread and raisins in 2-quart round microproof baking dish; set aside. Beat eggs, brown sugar, vanilla, and salt until well blended; set aside. Combine milk and butter in 2-quart glass measure. Place in oven. Cook on HI, 4½ minutes.

Gradually whisk egg mixture into milk mixture. Pour over bread mixture. Sprinkle with cinnamon. Place in oven. Cover with waxed paper. Cook on 50, 14 minutes. (Center may be slightly soft but will set as pudding cools.) Serve warm or chilled.

6 servings

Yogurt Pumpkin Pie

Total Cooking Time: 3 minutes

  1 cup canned or cooked mashed
      pumpkin
 ¼ cup firmly packed brown sugar
  1 teaspoon cinnamon
 ½ teaspoon nutmeg
 ¼ teaspoon ginger
 ¼ teaspoon salt
  1 container (9 ounces) frozen
      whipped topping
  1 container (8 ounces) vanilla
      yogurt
  1 9-inch Crumb Crust Pie Shell
      (page 194)

Combine pumpkin, brown sugar, cinnamon, nutmeg, ginger, and salt in 3-quart microproof bowl. Place in oven. Cook on HI, 2 minutes. Remove from oven and let stand 10 minutes.

Remove cover from whipped topping. Place in oven. Defrost on 30, 1 minute.

Carefully stir topping. Fold topping and yogurt into cooled pumpkin mixture. Spoon into pie shell. Refrigerate about 4 hours, or until set.

6 servings

A9   4   HIGHER

Danish Apple Pie

Preset Cooking Time: about 12 minutes

  7 tart cooking apples, peeled,
      cored, and sliced (about
      6 cups)
 ¾ cup sugar
  2 tablespoons all-purpose flour
  1 teaspoon cinnamon
 ⅛ teaspoon salt
  1 baked 9-inch Homemade Pie Shell
      (page 194)
 ¼ cup all-purpose flour
 ¼ cup firmly packed brown sugar
  2 tablespoons butter or margarine

Place apples in large bowl. Combine sugar, 2 tablespoons flour, cinnamon, and salt. Sprinkle over apples and toss lightly to coat. Arrange apples evenly in pie shell; set aside. Combine ¼ cup flour and brown sugar. Cut in butter with pastry blender or 2 knives. Sprinkle evenly over apples. Place in oven. Touch A9. Touch 4. Touch HIGHER. Touch START. *(Oven cooks: HI, about 12 minutes.)* If pie begins to cook unevenly, open door and rotate plate one-quarter turn; touch START.

Let cool before serving.

6 to 8 servings

Pecan Pie

Total Cooking Time: 13 minutes

 ¼ cup butter or margarine
1¼ cups pecan halves
  1 cup sugar
 ½ cup dark corn syrup
  3 large eggs, lightly beaten
  1 teaspoon vanilla
 ⅛ teaspoon salt
  1 baked 9-inch Homemade Pie Shell
      (page 194)

Place butter in microproof bowl. Place in oven. Cook on HI, 1 minute.

Stir in remaining ingredients except pie shell and blend thoroughly. Pour into pie shell. Place in oven. Cook on 70, 12 minutes. If pie begins to cook unevenly, open door and rotate plate one-quarter turn; touch START.

Let cool to room temperature or chill before serving.

8 servings

Rocky Road Candy

Total Cooking Time: 5 minutes

    1 package (12 ounces) semisweet
          chocolate pieces
    1 package (12 ounces) butterscotch
          pieces
    ½ cup butter
    1 package (10½ ounces) miniature
          marshmallows
    1 cup chopped walnuts or pecans

Butter 13×9-inch baking dish. Combine chocolate, butterscotch, and butter in 4-quart microproof bowl. Place in oven. Cook on 70, 5 minutes.

Stir until blended. Beat in marshmallows and nuts. Pour into prepared baking dish and spread evenly. Refrigerate 2 hours, or until set. Cut into squares to serve.

45 squares

Try these variations: Substitute ½ cup chopped nuts plus ½ cup chopped dried fruit, or 1 cup chopped dried fruit for the cup chopped nuts. Dried apricots, pitted prunes, or candied fruit would be delicious.

Rich Chocolate Fudge

Total Cooking Time: 20 minutes

    4 cups sugar
    1 can (13 ounces) evaporated milk,
          undiluted
    1 cup butter or margarine
    1 package (12 ounces) semisweet
          chocolate pieces
    1 jar (7 ounces) marshmallow
          creme
    1 cup chopped walnuts or pecans
    1 teaspoon vanilla

Butter 9-inch square or 11×7-inch baking dish. Combine sugar, milk, and butter in 4-quart microproof bowl. Place in oven. Cook on HI, 10 minutes.

Stir through several times. Cook on HI, 10 minutes.

Stir in chocolate and marshmallow creme. Stir in nuts and vanilla. Pour into prepared baking dish. Let cool before cutting into squares.

48 squares

Deluxe Mints

Total Cooking Time: 6 minutes

    2 cups sugar
    ¼ cup light corn syrup
    ¼ cup milk
    ¼ teaspoon cream of tartar
    8 to 10 drops peppermint extract,
          or to taste
       Red or green food coloring

Combine sugar, corn syrup, milk, and cream of tartar in 2-quart glass measure. Place in oven. Cook on HI, 6 minutes.

Let stand 3 minutes, or until slightly cooled. Beat with electric mixer until creamy, flavoring with peppermint extract and tinting with food coloring. Drop by teaspoonfuls onto sheets of aluminum foil. Let stand until cool and firm. Store in airtight container.

36 mints

Almond Bark

Total Cooking Time: 7½ minutes

    1 cup whole blanched almonds
    1 teaspoon butter or margarine
    1 pound white chocolate

Line large baking sheet with waxed paper; set aside. Place almonds and butter in 9-inch microproof pie plate. Place in oven. Cook on HI, 2½ minutes.

Stir through several times. Cook on HI, 2 minutes.

Remove from oven. Place chocolate in large microproof bowl. Place in oven. Cook on HI, 3 minutes.

Stir almonds into chocolate. Pour onto prepared sheet. Spread to desired thickness. Refrigerate until set. Break into pieces. Store in airtight container.

1½ pounds

Rocky Road Candy, Almond Bark, →
Deluxe Mints

Chocolate-Raisin Nut Clusters

Total Cooking Time: 2½ minutes

>   1 pound semisweet chocolate
>   1 cup cashews
>   ½ cup plump raisins

Place chocolate in 2-quart glass measure. Place in oven. Cook on HI, 2½ minutes.

Add cashews and raisins; stir until blended. Drop mixture by teaspoonfuls onto waxed paper. Let stand until firm. (If mixture in bowl becomes too firm, cook on 30, 1 to 2 minutes.)

1½ pounds

Peanut Brittle

Total Cooking Time: 10 minutes

>   1 cup sugar
>   ½ cup corn syrup
>   1¾ to 2 cups unsalted dry-roasted peanuts
>   1 teaspoon butter or margarine
>   1 teaspoon vanilla
>   1 teaspoon baking soda

Generously grease large baking sheet. Combine sugar and corn syrup in 2-quart glass measure. Place in oven. Cook on HI, 4 minutes.

Stir in peanuts with wooden spoon. Cook on HI, 4 minutes.

Stir in butter and vanilla. Cook on HI, 2 minutes.

Add baking soda and stir until light and foamy. Pour onto prepared baking sheet, spreading quickly to edges using back of wooden spoon. As candy cools, stretch into thin sheet using palms of hands. Cool completely before breaking into pieces. Store in airtight container in cool place.

1 pound

Caramel Nut Candy

Total Cooking Time: 3 minutes

>   1 pound light caramels
>   2 tablespoons water
>   2 cups (12 ounces) mixed nuts

Lightly butter 8-inch square baking pan. Place caramels and water in 2-quart glass measure. Place in oven. Cook on HI, 3 minutes.

Stir with wooden spoon until caramels are completely melted. Blend in nuts. Pour into prepared baking pan and refrigerate until firm. Cut into 1-inch squares. Wrap each piece in plastic wrap before storing.

64 pieces

From Freezer to Table — Fast!

One of the most important functions designed into this microwave oven is its superior ability to defrost food. It uses all the latest technology to speed and simplify one of our most-frequent and aggravating kitchen chores. Detailed defrosting *Guides* are provided throughout the book to aid in your preparation of the food discussed in the recipe chapters. Here, as a special convenience, many common and frequently used items have been presented in detail — all using the surface-temperature sensor. You'll also want to spend more time reviewing the defrosting instructions in your Use and Care Manual. Many of the same principles and techniques that apply to micro-wave cooking also apply to micro-wave defrosting and heating. Micro-waves are attracted to water or moisture molecules. As soon as microwaves have thawed a portion of the item, they are more attracted to the thawed portion. The frozen por-tion continues to thaw, but this is due to the warmth produced in the thawed portion. Special techniques, such as shielding and rotating, are helpful to

Defrosting is one of the major benefits of the surface-temperature sensor. If you prefer, poultry and meat can begin defrosting in their original wrappers but remove packaging as soon as possible. Fruit and vegetables can be thawed in their packages (above left). Thawed portions of ground beef are removed from the oven so cooking does not start (above). Most food is turned over during defrosting to assist even thawing (left).

be sure the thawed portion does not cook before the rest defrosts. It is often necessary to turn, stir, and separate to assist the defrosting process. Defrosting requires standing time to complete. Because food differs in size, weight, and density, recommended defrosting times can only be approximate. Additional standing time may be necessary to defrost completely. Read the defrosting *Guides* throughout the book for times, temperature, and special instructions about defrosting specific foods. Here are some tips to aid you toward fast and easy defrosting:

```
AUTOMATIC DEFROSTING GUIDE
A0-0   Ground Meat
A0-1   Roasts
A0-2   Stew Meat, Steaks
A0-3   Chops, Bacon
A0-4   Chicken, Duck, Turkey Parts
A0-5   Whole Turkey, Whole Ham
A0-6   Whole Fish, Fish Steaks
A0-7   Fish Fillets, Shrimp
```

☐ Plastic-wrapped packages from the supermarket meat department may not be wrapped with a plastic wrap recommended for microwave use. If in doubt, unwrap package and place food on a microwave plate.

☐ Poultry, seafood, fish, and meat will defrost more evenly if removed from their original package. However, if you wish, you may begin defrosting in the original package, then finish defrosting by removing packaging and placing food on a plate. Metal clips in poultry may be left in until it becomes possible to remove them. They should always be removed before cooking. Metal twists on bags should be replaced with rubber bands.

☐ Vegetables are usually packaged to go right into the microwave for defrosting and heating to serving temperature. It is not necessary to use a defrost setting for frozen vegetables; they may be defrosted on HI.

☐ Poultry wings, legs, and the small or bony ends of meat or fish may need to be covered with pieces of aluminum foil for part of the thawing time to prevent cooking while the remainder thaws.

☐ Large items should be turned and rotated halfway through defrosting time to provide more even thawing.

☐ Food textures influence thawing time. Because of air space, porous foods like cake and bread defrost more quickly than a solid mass, such as a sauce, or roast.

☐ Do not thaw food wrapped in aluminum or in foil dishes except as approved, page 19.

☐ The edges will begin cooking if meat, fish, and seafood are completely thawed in the microwave oven. Therefore, food should still be icy in the center when removed from oven. It will finish thawing while standing.

☐ Remove portions of ground meat as soon as thawed, returning frozen portions to the oven.

☐ To thaw half of a frozen vegetable package, wrap half the package with aluminum foil. When unwrapped side is thawed, separate and return balance to freezer.

☐ Thin or sliced items, such as fish fillets, meat patties, etc., should be separated as soon as possible. Remove thawed pieces and allow others to continue thawing.

☐ Casseroles, saucy foods, vegetables, and soups should be stirred once or twice during defrosting to redistribute heat.

☐ Frozen fried foods may be defrosted but will not be crisp when heated in the microwave oven.

☐ Freezing tips: It is helpful to freeze in small quantities rather than in one large piece. When freezing casseroles, it's a good idea to insert an empty paper cup in the center so no food is present there. This speeds thawing. Depressing the center of ground meat when freezing also hastens thawing later.

A0:0

Ground Beef

Preset Defrost Time: about 11 minutes

1 pound frozen lean ground
beef

Remove beef from package and place in microproof baking dish. Place in oven, with beef over circle on glass tray. Touch A0. Touch 0. Touch START. *(Oven defrosts: 30, about 3 minutes.)*

At Pause, turn beef over. Remove thawed portions from oven. Touch START. *(Oven defrosts: 30, about 3 minutes; stands: 0, 5 minutes.)*

A0   2   HIGHER

Stew Beef

Preset Defrost Time: about 20 minutes

2 pounds frozen beef for stew

Remove beef from package and place in shallow microproof baking dish. Place in oven. Touch A0. Touch 2. Touch HIGHER. Touch START. *(Oven defrosts: 30, about 10 minutes; stands: 0, 10 minutes.)*

Separate beef into pieces. Let stand 30 minutes before cooking.

You can also use the A0-2-HIGHER setting for defrosting beef steaks. Two pounds of steak will take about the same length of time to defrost as 2 pounds of stew beef.

A0   2

Steak

Preset Defrost Time: about 30 minutes

1 frozen steak (2 pounds)

Remove steak from package and place in microproof baking dish. Place in oven. Touch A0. Touch 2. Touch START. *(Oven defrosts: 30, about 20 minutes; stands: 0, 10 minutes.)*

A0   1   LOWER

Rolled Rib Roast

Preset Defrost Time: about 1 hour
5 minutes

1 frozen rolled rib roast
(3 pounds)

Remove all wrapping and place roast in microproof baking dish. Place in oven. Touch A0. Touch 1. Touch LOWER. Touch START. *(Oven defrosts: 30, about 10 minutes.)*

At Pause, turn roast over. Cover any warm areas with aluminum foil, keeping foil at least 1 inch away from oven wall. Touch START. *(Oven defrosts: 30, about 5 minutes; stands: 0, 50 minutes.)*

The oven has been programmed to let the roast stand for the additional 50 minutes needed to complete defrosting. If you want to use your oven during that time, simply touch STOP and then CLEAR, and remove the roast to the countertop for the balance of standing time.

A3:0

Frozen Dinner

Preset Defrost/Cooking Time:
about 9 minutes

1 chicken, beef, or pasta frozen
dinner (8½ ounces)

Remove foil or other cover from dinner and discard. If dinner container is not microproof, pop frozen contents out of container and place on microproof plate. Cover with waxed paper. Place in oven. Touch A3. Touch START. *(Oven defrosts: 80, about 6 minutes.)*

At Pause, stir contents, if necessary. Touch START. *(Oven cooks: 80, about 3 minutes.)*

Here's a nifty idea: save frozen dinner containers approved for microwave use. Refill with your own leftovers and freeze. A good way to stretch your food dollar while keeping the convenience of packaged foods. Reheat as directed above.

```
AO    3
```

Pork Chops

Preset Defrost Time: about 10 minutes

> 2 pounds frozen pork chops,
> ½ inch thick

Remove chops from package and place in microproof baking dish. Place in oven. Touch A0. Touch 3. Touch START. *(Oven defrosts: 30, about 2 minutes.)*

At Pause, turn chops over and separate. Touch START. *(Oven defrosts: 30, about 3 minutes; stands: 0, 5 minutes.)*

You can use the A0-3 setting to defrost bacon, too. The oven will adjust defrosting time, depending on the weight and thickness of the slices.

```
AO    4
```

Cut Up Chicken

Preset Defrost Time: about 11 minutes

> 2 pounds frozen chicken parts

Remove chicken from package and place in microproof baking dish. Place in oven. Touch A0. Touch 4. Touch START. *(Oven defrosts: 30, about 4 minutes.)*

At Pause, turn parts over and separate. Cover any warm areas with small strips of aluminum foil, keeping foil at least 1 inch away from oven wall. Touch START. *(Oven defrosts: 30, about 2 minutes; stands: 0, 5 minutes.)*

Immediately rinse parts in cold water.

```
AO    4    HIGHER
```

Whole Chicken

Preset Defrost Time: about 25 minutes

> 1 frozen broiler-fryer
> chicken (3 pounds)

Remove chicken from package. Place chicken in microproof baking dish. Place in oven. Touch A0. Touch 4. Touch HIGHER. Touch START. *(Oven defrosts: 30, about 10 minutes.)*

At Pause, turn chicken over. Touch START. *(Oven defrosts: 30, about 15 minutes.)*

Let stand 25 minutes.

```
AO    6    LOWER
```

Whole Fish

Preset Defrost Time: about 8 minutes

> 1 frozen fish (10 ounces)

Remove fish from package. Place fish in shallow microproof baking dish. Place in oven, with fish over circle on glass tray. Cover head with aluminum foil, keeping foil at least 1 inch away from oven wall. Touch A0. Touch 6. Touch LOWER. Touch START. *(Oven defrosts: 30, about 3 minutes; stands: 0, 5 minutes.)*

You can also use the A0-6 setting — without the LOWER touch pad — to defrost frozen fish steaks. The oven will automatically adjust defrosting time according to the size of the fish.

---

*Frozen foods come in an increasingly wide variety of microproof packages that make defrosting in →
the microwave more simple and convenient than ever. Other frozen foods can be placed in a
microproof container for thawing.*

A7	4

Vegetables in Sauce

Preset Defrost/Cooking Time:
about 5 minutes

1 package (10 ounces) frozen vegetables in sauce

Place pouch on microproof plate. Place in oven, with pouch over circle on glass tray. Touch A7. Touch 4. Touch START. *(Oven defrosts: HI, about 3 minutes.)*

At Pause, shake pouch to settle ingredients on bottom. Snip off 1 top corner. Place pouch upright on plate. Touch START. *(Oven cooks: HI, about 2 minutes.)* Pour into serving bowl and stir once before serving.

This cooking technique is quick and convenient. If you wish, you can set the pouch right in your microproof serving dish. Be sure the contents are moved to one end of the pouch before the cooking stage. Otherwise, the pouch won't stand upright.

A3	1

Frozen Entree

Preset Defrost/Cooking Time:
about 6 minutes

1 package (12 ounces) beef,
chicken, or seafood with
sauce or gravy

Place pouch on microproof plate. Place in the oven with pouch over circle on glass tray. Touch A3. Touch 1. Touch START. *(Oven defrosts: 80, about 4 minutes.)*

At Pause, shake pouch to settle ingredients on bottom. Snip off 1 top corner. Place pouch upright on plate. Touch START. *(Oven cooks: 80, about 2 minutes.)* Stir once before serving.

A0	7

Fish Fillets

Preset Defrost Time: about 7 minutes

1 pound frozen fish fillets

Remove fillets from package and place in shallow microproof baking dish. Place in oven, with fillets over circle on glass tray. Touch A0. Touch 7. Touch START. *(Oven defrosts: 30, about 2 minutes; stands: 0, 5 minutes.)*

Separate fillets and rinse in cold water.

A7	4

Broccoli, Carrots, Cauliflower

Preset Defrost/Cooking Time:
about 4 minutes

1 package (10 ounces) frozen broccoli, carrots, or cauliflower

Place vegetables in package on microproof plate. Place in oven, with package over circle on glass tray. Touch A7. Touch 4. Touch START. *(Oven defrosts/cooks: HI, about 3 minutes.)*

At Pause, turn package over. Touch START. *(Oven cooks: HI, about 1 minute.)* Let stand 5 minutes before serving.

A7	4

Green Peas

Preset Defrost/Cooking Time:
about 4 minutes

1 package (10 ounces) frozen green peas

Place peas in package on microproof plate. Place in oven, with package over circle on glass tray. Touch A7. Touch 4. Touch START. *(Oven defrosts/cooks: HI, about 3 minutes.)*

At Pause, turn package over. Touch START. *(Oven cooks: HI, about 1 minute.)* Let stand 5 minutes before serving.

A7	4	HIGHER

Spinach

Preset Defrost/Cooking Time:
about 5 minutes

1 package (10 ounces) frozen chopped or leaf spinach

Place spinach in package on microproof plate. Place in oven, with package over circle on glass tray. Touch A7. Touch 4. Touch HIGHER. Touch START. *(Oven defrosts/cooks: HI, about 3 minutes.)*

At Pause, turn package over. Touch START. *(Oven cooks: HI, about 2 minutes.)* Let stand 5 minutes before serving.

AO 7

Crab Meat

Preset Defrost Time: about 7 minutes

1 package (6 ounces) frozen
crab meat

Remove crab meat from package and place in microproof baking dish. Place in oven. Touch A0. Touch 7. Touch START. *(Oven defrosts: 30, about 2 minutes; stands: 0, 5 minutes.)*

AO 6

Brownies and other frozen bar cookies

Preset Defrost Time: about 2 minutes

1 package (12 ounces) frozen brownies
or other bar cookies

Remove lid from tray and place in oven. Touch A0. Touch 6. Touch START. *(Oven defrosts: 30, about 2 minutes.)*
Let stand 5 minutes before serving.

AO 7

Shrimp

Preset Defrost Time: about 7 minutes

1 package (1 pound) frozen
shrimp

Remove shrimp from package and arrange in round shallow microproof baking dish with tails toward center. Place in oven with shrimp over circle on glass tray. Touch A0. Touch 7. Touch START. *(Oven defrosts: 30, about 2 minutes; stands: 0, 5 minutes.)*

AO 7

Bread, Rolls

Preset Defrost Time: about 7 minutes

1 loaf (1 pound) frozen bread,
or 1 pound frozen rolls

Remove bread from package and place on microproof plate. Place in oven. Touch A0. Touch 7. Touch START. *(Oven defrosts: 30, about 2 minutes; stands: 0, 5 minutes.)*

REMINDER

Additional defrosting information is provided in the Use & Care Manual and in the following Guides:

☐ Convenience Breads	Page 70
☐ Defrosting Guide - Meat	Pages 79-80
☐ Cooking/Defrosting Guide - Convenience Meat	Page 84
☐ Defrosting Guide - Poultry	Page 107
☐ Defrosting Guide - Seafood	Page 123
☐ Cooking/Defrosting Guide - Convenience Seafood	Page 123
☐ Cooking/Defrosting Guide - Convenience Rice and Pasta	Page 142
☐ Cooking/Defrosting Guide - Convenience Desserts	Page 183

Dinner's in the Oven

Dinner's in the oven! Who doesn't look forward to hearing this familiar saying as mealtime approaches? You'll find that just as in conventional cooking, you can prepare a whole two- or three-dish meal at the same time in your microwave oven. For the most successful whole meal, it is important to consider the placement of dishes in the oven, the size and shape of the microproof containers, the kinds of food you select, the timing, and the sequence of cooking. This chapter provides you with all the necessary information and step-by-step instructions for organizing your own whole meals as well as seven different whole meals that have been presented with complete instructions and diagrams. Start by reading the following basic tips on how to approach whole meal planning:

☐ Since microwaves enter from the top of the oven, they are primarily attracted to food placed on the middle metal rack; a smaller amount reaches the bottom tray. It is logical then to place delicate, quick-cooking food on the bottom glass tray and longer-cooking food on the middle metal rack.

☐ Whenever the metal middle rack is not being used, remove it from oven.

☐ When using a browning dish, place it on the bottom glass tray. Do not cook other foods on the bottom glass tray at the same time.

☐ An ideal procedure for whole-meal cooking is to place two foods with similar cooking times on the middle metal rack and one shorter-cooking food on the bottom tray.

☐ If all foods require the same cooking time, reverse the location of dishes in the oven halfway through cooking time.

☐ While the middle rack can be used in two positions, the upper position is generally best. Use the lower position whenever greater capacity on the top is needed. This does limit the usable space below.

☐ Check your cooking dishes to be sure they will fit on the same shelf before filling with food.

☐ Often covers with knobs are too high to fit easily when the middle metal rack is used. Use plastic wrap instead of casserole lids when necessary.

☐ All whole-meal cooking is done on HI. The automatic sensors are not used.

IMPORTANT GUIDELINES FOR TIMING AND PLANNING

☐ If all foods take no more than 15 minutes individually, add cooking times together and cook the menu for the total time.

☐ If all foods take 15 to 35 minutes individually, add cooking times together and subtract about 5 minutes.

☐ If any one food takes over 35 minutes, all the food can be cooked in the time suggested for food taking the longest time.

← *Seasoned Pork Chops, Parsley Potatoes, and Mixed Vegetables can all be cooked at the same time in the microwave (page 215).*

In order to make the timing and planning easier, we have divided the menus into two types: one-stage and two-stage. For one-stage menus, all the dishes are cooked for the same length of time. The two-stage menus require partial cooking of one main dish and then the addition of other dishes to the oven.

Tips to remember in planning a one- or two-stage menu:

1. Choose a menu from the chart.
2. Review the individual recipe. Occasionally you will find that an ingredient should be prepared ahead; for example, the green pepper and pimiento need to be sautéed before adding the remaining ingredients to Corn and Pepper Pudding (page 158).
3. Check microproof dishes to be sure they fit in the oven together. Change dish sizes, if needed.
4. Place dishes in oven with food from column "A" on the middle metal rack; "B" and "C" are placed on the bottom glass tray.
5. Apply the rules in *Important Guidelines for Timing and Planning*. Cooking time for each recipe follows the recipe title in the menu charts. Standing time is not included.
6. Most recipes in whole-meal cooking benefit from stirring, rearranging, or turning over about halfway through cooking time.

ONE-STAGE MENUS

Pick one dish from each column in any combination.

A	B	C
All-American Meatballs (15) (page 95)	Corn-Mushroom Scallop (10) (page 158)	Crumb Topped Tomatoes (4½) (page 159)
Favorite Meatloaf (17) (page 89)	Parsley New Potatoes (10) (page 160)	Frozen Fruit 10 oz. (5) (page 183)
Simple Salmon Ring (35) (page 127)	Broccoli Spears 10 oz. Frozen (8) (page 151)	Lemon Butter Sauce (3) (page 174)
Pot Roast in Sherry (65) (page 85)	Corn and Pepper Pudding (19) (page 158)	Cherry Crunch (15) (page 187)
Orange Ginger Pork Chops (16) (page 99)	Pan Baked Potato Halves (12) (page 160)	Carrots 10 oz. Frozen (8) (page 151)
Barbecued Chicken (25) (page 114)	Stuffing Mix 6 oz. pkg. (8) (page 153)	Broccoli 10 oz. Frozen (8) (page 151)

To demonstrate one-stage menu planning we have chosen:

(A) All-American Meatballs
    page 95 . . . . 15 min.
(B) Corn-Mushroom Scallop
    page 158 . . . . 10 min.
(C) Crumb Topped Tomatoes
    page 159 . . . . 4½ min.

Note that each individual cooking time takes no more than 15 minutes. Using the *Guidelines* (page 207), this one-stage meal will cook in 29½ minutes.

Let's take it step by step:

1. Prepare the All-American Meatballs according to the recipe, omitting the cornstarch and water at this time. Cover with plastic wrap; set aside.
2. Prepare Corn-Mushroom Scallop in 8×4-inch loaf pan. Omit topping of ¼ cup of crumbs and butter at this time. Cover with plastic wrap; set aside.
3. Prepare Crumb Topped Tomatoes on 9-inch pie plate.

4. Place middle metal rack in oven. Place meatballs on rack. Place corn dish and tomato dish on bottom glass tray. Cook on HI, 10 minutes.

5. Stir cornstarch and water into meatballs and cover. Stir scalloped corn and cover. Cook on HI, 19½ minutes.

6. Remove from oven and top corn with ¼ cup of crumbs dotted with butter. Let all dishes stand,

covered, on heat-resistant surface for 5 minutes before serving.

TWO-STAGE MENUS

Pick one dish from each column in any combination.

A	B	C
Tomato Swiss Steak (70) (page 89)	Parsley New Potatoes (10) (page 160)	Honey Corn Bread Ring (13) (page 74)
Lamb Ragout (40) (page 97)	Pineapple-Zucchini Bread (16) (page 74)	Frozen Fruit 10 oz. (5) (page 183)
Baked Ham with Pineapple (27) (page 104)	Acorn Squash (11) (page 152)	Golden Apple Chunks (7) (page 186)
Chicken and Vegetables (20) (page 116)	Baked Apple (5) (page 184)	Hard Roll, heat - last 3 min.

Standing time is especially important in whole meal cooking. The Swiss Steak whole meal (above) finishes cooking during standing time (left).

The two-stage procedure is designed to give one recipe a longer time to cook. To demonstrate this we have chosen:

(A) Tomato Swiss Steak
    page 89 .... 1 hour 10 min.
(B) Parsley New Potatoes
    page 160 .... 10 min.
(C) Honey Corn Bread Ring
    page 74 .... 13 min.

Using the *Guidelines* (page 207), all foods will be cooked in the time it takes Tomato Swiss Steak, 1 hour 10 minutes.

Let's take it step by step:

1. Prepare Tomato Swiss Steak. Place on bottom glass tray and cook, covered, on HI, 10 minutes.
2. Meanwhile, prepare Parsley New Potatoes. Place in 8 × 4-inch loaf pan, covered with plastic wrap, and set aside.
3. Prepare Honey Corn Bread Ring.
4. Place middle metal rack in oven. Place steak on middle rack, potatoes and cake on bottom glass tray.
5. Cook on HI, 35 minutes. Re-arrange steak, cover. Stir potatoes, cover. If cake is rising unevenly, rotate dish.
6. Cook on HI, 25 minutes, or until steak is cooked. Remove from oven. Drain potatoes, stir in butter, parsley, salt, and pepper. Let all dishes stand 5 minutes before serving.

TEMPERATURE PROBE MENUS

Pick one dish from each column in any combination.

A	B	C
Pork Loin, boneless (165°) 3 to 4 lb. (page 82)	Pan-Baked Potato Halves (page 160)	Applesauce (page 186)
Beef Rib-eye Roast (130°) 2½ to 3 lbs. (page 81)	Twice-Baked Potatoes 2 to 2½ lbs. (page 157)	Peas Francine (page 162)
Turkey Roast - thawed (170°) 2 to 3 lbs. (page 108)	Candied Sweet Potatoes (pre-bake potato) (page 155)	Stuffing Mix 6 oz. pkg. (page 153)
Whole Chicken (180°) 3 lbs. (page 108)	Creamed Potato Mix 5 - oz. pkg. (page 163)	Green Beans Italiano (page 157)

Another whole meal method is the use of the temperature probe. All the food will be finished when the meat is ready. HI power is used, even though the individual recipes may call for lower power settings. The temperature setting to use follows the meat recipe title.

Protect top of meat with a narrow strip of foil, and place on middle metal rack. Arrange accompanying dishes on bottom glass tray. Turn meat over halfway through cooking time, being careful not to remove probe. Stir or rearrange vegetables or other dishes at the same time. Cover as required by the individual recipe.

Special Menu

With practice and imagination you will enjoy trying different combinations. For example, here is a special menu method that puts the meat on the bottom glass tray for the second stage to give it a simmer effect, while the microwave energy is concentrated on the vegetables.

Country Style Ribs
     page 99 .... 1 hour 10 min.
4 Corn-on-the-Cob
     page 151 .... 12 min.
4 Baked Potatoes (6 oz. each)
     page 152 .... 14 min.

Let's take it step by step:

1. Prepare Country Style Ribs. Cook on 50, 40 minutes; drain.
2. Meanwhile, remove husks and silk from each ear of corn. Wrap each ear individually in waxed paper.

3. Wash and remove any blemishes from potatoes; pierce. Brush both sides of ribs with sauce; cover with plastic wrap.

4. Place middle metal rack in oven. Place ribs on bottom glass tray. Place corn, spoke fashion, on middle metal rack; place one potato between each ear of corn. Cook on HI, 30 minutes, or until cooked. Turn vegetables over after 15 minutes.
5. Let stand, covered, 5 minutes before serving.

Now you know the basics for preparing your own whole meals. The following pages give you seven additional wonderful whole meals to enhance your enjoyment of your Sanyo Automatic Cuisine-Master microwave oven. Be sure to observe the recommended dish placements.

Scrambled Eggs, Bacon, and Sweet Rolls

Total Cooking Time: 10 minutes

- 6 large eggs
- 1/3 cup milk
- 2 tablespoons butter, melted
- 6 slices bacon
- 6 sweet rolls

Position metal rack in oven. Combine eggs, milk, and butter in 1-quart microproof casserole; beat with fork until blended. Cover and set aside. Arrange bacon on paper towel-lined microproof plate. Cover with another paper towel; set aside. Arrange rolls in circle on microproof plate; set aside. Arrange egg mixture and bacon in oven as shown in "A." Cook on HI, 8 minutes.

Stir eggs; cover. Place rolls in oven as shown in "B." Cook on HI, 2 minutes.

Let stand 3 minutes before stirring eggs and serving.

4 to 6 servings

Beef Stew, Garlic Bread, and Pudding

Total Cooking Time: 13 minutes

- 1 can (24 ounces) beef stew
- 1/4 cup butter, melted
- 1/2 teaspoon garlic powder
- 1/2 pound French bread, cut into 1-inch thick slices
- 1 package (3 1/4 ounces) pudding mix
- 2 cups milk

Position metal rack in oven. Pour stew into 1-quart microproof casserole. Cover and set aside. Combine butter and garlic powder. Brush both sides of bread slices with garlic butter mixture. Reshape into loaf and wrap in paper towels. Place on microproof plate and set aside. Place pudding mix in 1-quart microproof casserole. Stir in milk; set aside. Arrange stew and pudding mixture in oven as shown in "A." Cook on HI, 5 minutes.

Stir stew and pudding. Cover stew. Cook on HI, 3 1/2 minutes.

Stir pudding. Place bread in oven as shown in "B." Cook on HI, 4 1/2 minutes.

3 servings

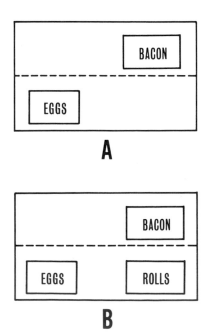

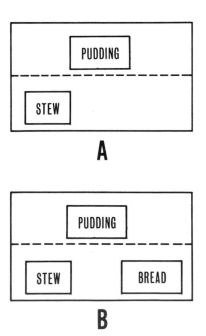

Chili, Corn Muffins, and Apple Crisp

Total Cooking Time: 13 minutes

    1 can (24 ounces) chili
    3 corn muffins
    1 recipe Apple Crisp (below)

Position metal rack in oven. Pour chili into 1½-quart microproof casserole. Cover and set aside. Wrap corn muffins in paper towels; set aside. Prepare Apple Crisp batter as directed below. Cover with waxed paper. Arrange chili and Apple Crisp in oven as shown in "A." Cook on HI, 5 minutes.

Stir chili; cover. Rotate dishes as shown in "B." Cook on HI, 3½ minutes.

Stir chili again; cover. Place muffins in oven as shown in "C." Cook on HI, 4½ minutes.

Let Apple Crisp stand 3 minutes before serving.

3 servings

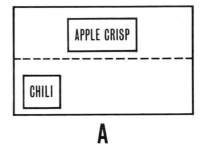

A

Apple Crisp

    4 cups sliced tart apples
    ½ cup rolled oats
    ¼ cup butter or margarine
    ¼ cup all-purpose flour
    ¼ cup firmly packed brown sugar
    1 teaspoon lemon juice
    ½ teaspoon cinnamon
    ⅛ teaspoon nutmeg

Arrange apple slices in 8-inch square microproof baking dish. Combine remaining ingredients; blend well. Crumble over apples.

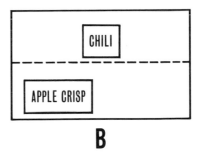

B

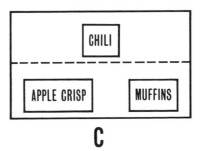

C

Baked Chicken, Rice, and Asparagus

Total Cooking Time: 26 minutes

- ¾ cup cornflake crumbs
- ⅓ cup grated Parmesan cheese
- 1 broiler-fryer chicken (2½ to 3 pounds), quartered
- ¼ cup butter or margarine, melted
- 1 package (11 ounces) frozen rice in pouch
- 2 cans (14½ ounces each) asparagus spears, drained

Position metal rack in oven. Combine cornflake crumbs and cheese. Brush chicken lightly with butter; coat with crumb mixture. Arrange chicken in large micro-proof baking dish, skin-side up, with thickest parts toward outside of dish. Cover with waxed paper and set aside. Place rice in pouch on small microproof plate; slit pouch; set aside. Place asparagus in 8 × 4-inch microproof loaf pan. Cover lightly with plastic wrap. Arrange all 3 dishes in oven as shown in "A." Cook on HI, 20 minutes.

Rotate rice one-quarter turn. Cook on HI, 4 minutes.

Remove chicken and asparagus from oven. Rotate rice as shown in "B." Cook on HI, 2 minutes.

3 to 4 servings

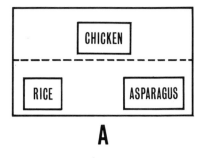

A

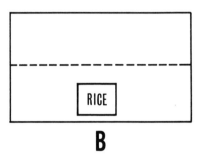

B

Seasoned Pork Chops, Parsley Potatoes, and Mixed Vegetables

Total Cooking Time: 26 minutes

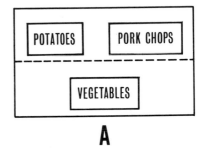

A

- 1 envelope (2¼ ounces) seasoned coating mix for pork
- 4 pork chops (1¼ pounds)
- 3 potatoes (5 ounces each), peeled and cut into ¾-inch cubes
- ¼ cup water
- 1 can (16 ounces) mixed vegetables, drained
  Butter or margarine
- 1 tablespoon chopped parsley

Position metal rack in oven. Empty coating mix into plastic bag. Shake pork chops, 1 at a time, in coating mix. Place chops in 12 × 7-inch microproof baking dish. Cover with waxed paper and set aside. Place potatoes and water in 8 × 4-inch microproof loaf pan. Cover with plastic wrap and set aside. Place mixed vegetables in 1-quart microproof casserole. Arrange all 3 dishes in oven as shown in "A." Cook on HI, 20 minutes.

Stir potatoes; cover. Cook on HI, 4 minutes.

Check pork chops and remove from oven if done. Cook on HI, 2 minutes.

Remove all dishes from oven. Stir vegetables. Dot potatoes with butter, and sprinkle with parsley before serving.

3 to 4 servings

Beef & Spaghetti Casserole, Green Peas, and Baked Apple Chunks

Total Cooking Time: 25 minutes

    1 package (7½ ounces) spaghetti
        meat-noodle main dish mix
    1 pound lean ground beef
    4 cups hot water
    1 package (10 ounces) frozen
        green peas
    1 recipe Baked Apple Chunks (below)

Position metal rack in oven. Prepare meat-noodle mix, adding beef and hot water as directed on package. Place in 2-quart microproof casserole. Cover and set aside. Place peas in 1-quart microproof casserole. Cover and set aside. Prepare Baked Apple Chunks as directed below. Cover with plastic wrap. Arrange beef mixture, peas, and Baked Apple Chunks in oven as shown in "A." Cook on HI, 20 minutes.

Stir beef mixture and Baked Apple Chunks. Cover both dishes. Cook on HI, 5 minutes. Let stand 5 minutes before serving.

4 servings

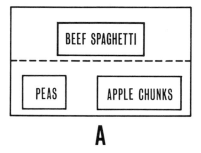

A

Baked Apple Chunks

    4 medium-size tart apples,
        peeled, cored, and cut into
        quarters
    ¼ cup firmly packed brown sugar
    1 teaspoon cinnamon
    2 tablespoons butter or margarine

Place apples in 8 × 4-inch microproof loaf pan. Combine brown sugar and cinnamon; blend well. Crumble over apples. Dot with butter.

Meatloaf, Yellow Squash, and Chocolate Fudge Layer Cake

Total Cooking Time: 23 minutes

    1 recipe Meatloaf (below)
    1 recipe Chocolate Fudge Layer
       Cake (below)
    1 medium yellow squash, peeled and
       thinly sliced
    1 tablespoon butter
    ¼ teaspoon salt
       Whipped cream

A

Position metal rack in oven. Prepare Meatloaf and Chocolate Fudge Layer Cake as directed below; set aside. Place squash in 8 × 4-inch microproof loaf pan. Cover with plastic wrap. Arrange all 3 dishes in oven as shown in "A." Cook on HI, 15 minutes.

Rotate meatloaf and cake dishes one-half turn. Stir squash; cover. Cook on HI, 7 minutes.

Insert toothpick into cake. If toothpick comes out clean, remove cake from oven. Cook remaining dishes on HI, 1 minute.

Stir butter and salt into squash. Let cake stand 3 to 5 minutes before inverting onto serving plate. Slice and serve topped with whipped cream.

6 servings

Chocolate Fudge Layer Cake

    1 package (15 ounces) snacking
       chocolate fudge cake mix

Prepare cake batter as directed on package. Pour into 6-cup microproof ring mold.

Meatloaf

    1½ pounds lean ground beef
     2 cups soft bread crumbs
     1 can (8 ounces) tomato sauce, divided
     ½ cup finely chopped onions
     ¼ cup finely chopped green pepper
     1 large egg
    1½ teaspoons salt

Combine beef, bread crumbs, ½ cup tomato sauce, onions, green pepper, egg, and salt; blend well. Pack into 6-cup microproof ring mold. Pour remaining sauce over beef mixture.

Index

A

All-American Meatballs, 95
All Seasons Rice, 148
Almond Bark, 196
Altitudes, Adjusting For, 26
Appetizers, 11, 39-47
  Convenience Cooking Guide, 40
Apple(s)
  Baked, 184
  Baked Apple Chunks, in whole
    meal, 216
  Cranapple Jelly, 186
  Crisp, in whole meal, 213
  Danish Apple Pie, 195
  Golden Apple Chunks, 186
  Spicy Apple Drink, 60
Applesauce, 186
Apricot Dessert Sauce, 177
Arrangement of Food, 15, 22
Artichoke(s), 151
  Pilaf, 143
  Shrimp and, 44
Asparagus, 149, 151, 154, 172
  in whole meal, 214
Automatic Cooking, 6-8, 14-15, 27,
  28-31
  Internal Temperature Sensor, 7,
    8, 30-31, 33, 49
  Positioning of Food, 8, 14, 15,
    22, 23, 28, 29, 49, 105, 121
  Surface Temperature Sensor, 7,
    8, 28-29, 32-34
  Timing, 14-15
Automatic Cooking Guides
  Convenience Foods, 28
  Desserts, 182
  Instant Foods, 28
  Meat, 31
  Poultry, 31
  Reheat, 28
  Seafood, 29, 124
  Slow-Cook, 29
  Vegetables, 29, 151-52
Automatic Cooking/Defrosting
  Guide
  Convenience Rice and Pasta, 142
Automatic Defrosting Guides, 28
  Defrost, 200
  Meat, 79-80
  Poultry, 107
  Seafood, 123

B

Baby Food, 28, 157
Bacon, 10, 11, 31, 79, 83, 98
  Cheesewiches, 62
  in whole meal, 212

Baked Apple Chunks, in whole
  meal, 216
Baked Apples, 184
Baked Chicken, in whole meal, 214
Baked Ham with Pineapple, 104
Baked Maple Bananas, 184
Baked Potatoes, 152, 163
  Twice-Baked Potatoes, 157
Bananas, Baked Maple, 184
Barbecue Sauce, Spicy, 171
Barbecued Beef, Chili, Stew, Hash
  Meatballs, 84
Barbecued Beef-on-a-Bun, 65
Barbecued Chicken, 114
Barbecued Spareribs, 100
Bar Cookies, 182, 183
  Chewy Coconut, 188
  Chocolate Chip, 188
  Date Oatmeal, 190
  Peanut Crispy, 187
Basic White Sauce, 169, 171
Beans, 151, 153, 154, see also
  Green Beans, dried, 50
Béarnaise Sauce, 170
Beef; 77-81, 84-95; see also Ham-
  burger(s), Meatball(s), Meatloaf,
  Roast(s), Steak(s)
  Barbecued, 84
  Barbecued Beef-on-a-Bun, 65
  Boiled Beef Carbonnade, 85
  Chili con Carne, 93
  Cooking Guide, 80-81
  Cooking/Defrosting Guide
    Convenience Beef, 84
  Defrosting Guide, 79
  Ground, defrosting, 79, 200-201
  Horseradish-Onion Beef Roast, 84
  Hungarian Goulash, 92
  Oriental, 88
  Pot Roast in Sherry, 77, 85
  Roast Beef 'n Swiss Rolls, 63
  Roulade, 88
  Shanghai, 90
  Shish Kabobs, 96
  Short Ribs of, 90
  & Spaghetti Casserole, in whole
    meal, 216
  Stew, 93
  Stew Beef, defrosting, 201
  Stew, in whole meal, 212
  Stuffed Cabbage, 93
  Tacos, 62
  Tenderloin of Beef Supreme, 85
Beets, 151
  Harvard, 160
Best Ever French Dressing, 174
Beverage(s), 49-50, 57-60
Blanching Vegetables, 153-54

Blueberry Muffins, 76
Boiled Beef Carbonnade, 85
Bratwurst, Precooked, 63, 83
Breads, Rolls, & Muffins, 69-76
  Convenience Guide, 70
  defrosting, 205
  English Muffin, 74
  Garlic, in whole meal, 212
  Garlic Parmesan, 71
  heating and reheating, 10, 28,
    63, 69
  Honey Corn Bread Ring, 74
  Molasses Buttermilk Bread, 71
  Pineapple Zucchini, 74
  raising of dough, 69, 70
  Zucchini-Nut, 69, 73
Breast of Turkey Jardiniere, 120
Broccoli, 22, 151, 154
  Carrot-Broccoli Casserole, 154
  cooking frozen, 204
Brownie(s)
  and other bar cookies, 29
    defrosting, 183, 205
  Chocolate Nut, 188
  Mix, 183
Browning, 26
  of Meat, 78
Browning Dish, 19-21
  61, 122, 207
Brussels sprouts, 151
Burgers; see Hamburger(s)
Butterscotch Sauce, 177
Butter
  Clarified, 175
  Lemon Butter Sauce, 174
  Melting, 184

C

Cabbage, 151, 154
  Creamy, 158
  Stuffed, 93
  Sweet-Sour Red, 162
Cake(s), 29, 181-83
  Carrot, 190
  Chocolate Cherry Bundt, 192
  Chocolate Fudge Layer, in
    whole meal, 217
  Devil's Food, 192
  Mix, 183
  Scotch Nut Oatmeal, 191
Calories; see Low or Reduced
  Calories
Canadian Green Pea Soup, 52
Candied Sweet Potatoes, 155
Candy, 181-82; see also Fudge
  Almond Bark, 11, 196

Caramel Nut, 198
Chocolate-Raisin Nut
   Clusters, 198
Deluxe Mints, 196
Peanut Brittle, 198
Rocky Road, 196
Canned Foods, 28
Ham, 82
Soup, 55
Vegetables, 166
Capon, 107
Cappuccino, 58
Caramel
Nut Candy, 198
Nut Sticky Buns, 71
Carrots, 149, 151, 154, 155
-Broccoli Casserole, 154
Cranberry, 157
cooking frozen, 204
Casserole(s), 37
Beef & Spaghetti, in whole
   meal, 216
Carrot-Broccoli, 154
Enchilada, 89
Italiano, 148
Macaroni and Cheese Vegetable
   Medley, 146
Stroganoff, 144
Cauliflower, 22, 151, 154, 155
cooking frozen, 204
Japanese Cauliflower Soup, 56
Savory, 149, 159
Center Cut Ham Slice, 82
Cereals, hot, 28, 141, 142
Cheddar (Cheese)
and Onion Egg, 138
Canapés, 41
Puffy Cheddar Omelet, 135
Cheese, 133-36, 138-40; see also
   Swiss, Cheddar, Parmesan
Bacon Cheesewiches, 62
Cooking Guide, 134
Hearty Cheese and Frank Soup, 55
Macaroni and Cheese Vegetable
   Medley, 146
Noodles and, 144
Scramble, 135
Warming, 133
Cheeseburgers, 63
Cheesecake, frozen, 183
Cherry
Chocolate Cherry Bundt Cake, 192
Crunch, 187
-Glazed Ham Slice, 104
Chewy Coconut Bars, 188
Chicken, 105-117
Arrangement of, 15, 22, 23, 105
Automatic Cooking Guide, 31
Baked, in whole meal, 214
Barbecued, 114
Cacciatore, 114

Cooking Guide, 108
with Cornbread Stuffing, 111
Croissant, 66
Cut Up, 108
Cut Up, defrosting, 202
Defrosting Guide, 107
Garlic Chicken Italiano, 112
Honey-Glazed, 113
Liver Chow Mein, 117
Marengo, 116
Micro-Fried, 105, 111
Milano, 113
Noodle au Gratin, 148
in the Pot, 50
Soy Sherry, 112
Sukiyaki, 114
Supreme, 113
Swiss Coated, 109
Tarragon Grilled, 109
and Vegetables, 116
Veronique, 109
Whole Roast, 112
Whole, defrosting, 202
Wings, Crunchy, 47
Chili, 84
con Carne, 93
in whole meal, 213
Chilled Minted Pea Soup, 54
Chinese Fried Rice, 143

Chocolate
Cherry Bundt Cake, 192
Chip Bars, 188
Choco-Peanut Butter Sauce, 180
Fudge Frosting, 187
Fudge Layer Cake, in whole
   meal, 217
Hot Fudge Sauce, 178
Nut Brownies, 188
-Raisin Nut Clusters, 198
Rich Chocolate Fudge, 181, 196
Choco-Peanut Butter Sauce, 180
Clam(s), 124
Chowder, New England, 56
Clarified Butter, 175
Cocoa, West Coast, 58
Coconut
Chewy Coconut Bars, 188
Squares, 187
Coffeecake, Sour Cream, 76
Coffee, 32, 49
Irish, 57
Cold Eggplant Appetizer, 41
Cold Fresh Tomato Soup, 57
Coney Island Hot Dog, 62
Containers and Utensils, 17-21
Convenience Foods, Automatic
   Cooking Guide, 28
Converting Recipes, 35-36
   see also specific food categories
Cook Control Settings Guide, 26

Cookies, 182, 183; see also Bar
   Cookies
Cooking Guide
for Convenience Appetizers, 40
for Convenience Breads, 70
for Convenience Eggs and
   Cheese, 134
for Convenience Vegetables, 153
for Meat, 80-83
for Poached Eggs, 135
for Poultry, 108
for Scrambled Eggs, 135
for Seafood and Fish, 124
for Vegetables, 151-152
Cooking/Defrosting Guide
for Convenience Desserts, 183
for Convenience Rice and
   Pasta, 142
for Convenience Seafood, 123
Corn, 151, 153, 154
and Pepper Pudding, 158
chips, freshening, 39
Cream of Corn Soup, 52
Honey Corn Bread Ring, 74
Muffins, in whole meal, 213
-Mushroom Scallop, 158
-on-the-Cob, 149, 151, 166
Cornbread Stuffing, Chicken with,
   111
Cornish Hens, 107
with Wild Rice, 116
Country Style Potatoes, 163
Country Style Ribs, 99
Country Vegetable Soup, 51
Covering, 24, 29
Crab
Imperial, 132
Legs, 123, 124
Meat, defrosting, 123, 205
Supremes, 46
Cranapple Jelly, 186
Cranberry
Carrots, 157
Hot Cranberry Punch, 60
Sauce, 171
Cream of Corn Soup, 52
Cream of Mushroom Soup, 51
Creamed Potato Mix, 163
Creamy Cabbage, 158
Croissant
Chicken, 66
Rougemont, 66
S'Mores, 66
Crumb Crust, 181, 194
Crumb Topped Tomatoes, 159
Crunchy Chicken Wings, 47
Crust; see Pie(s), Crumb Crust
Cupcakes, 182
frozen, 183
Pumpkin, 191
Curry Dipper, 46

Custard, Egg, 182
Custard Sauce, Rum, 177
Cut Up Chicken, defrosting, 202

D

Daiquiri, Hot Devilish, 58
Dandy Dumplings, 76
Danish Apple Pie, 195
Date Oatmeal Bars, 190
Defrosting, 199-205; see also
    Cooking/Defrosting Guide,
        Automatic Defrosting
            Guide, 200
    Bread, 205
    Broccoli, 204
    Brownies and other frozen bar
        cookies, 205
    Carrots, 204
    Cauliflower, 204
    Chicken, Cut Up, 202
    Chicken, Whole, 202
    Crab Meat, 205
    Fish Fillets, 204
    Fish, Whole, 202
    Green Peas, 204
    Ground Beef, 79, 200, 201
    Meat, 79-80
    Pork Chops, 202
    Rolled Rib Roast, 201
    Rolls, 205
    Seafood, 123
    Shrimp, 205
    Spinach, 204
    Steak, 201
    Stew Beef, 201
    Vegetables in Sauce, 204
Deluxe Mints, 11, 196
Density of food, cooking time
    affected by, 15
Desserts, 181-198
    Automatic Cooking Guide,
        29, 182
    Cooking/Defrosting Guide -
        Convenience, 183
Devil's Food Cake, 192
Dill Sauce, Hot Lemony, 175
Dinner, Frozen, 201
Dips, heating, 40
Dressing, Best Ever French, 174
Duckling, 31, 107, 108, 118
    Roast Orange, 118
Dumplings, Dandy, 76

E

Easy Gravy, 170
Egg(s), 133-140; see also Omelet,
    Quiche
    Cheddar and Onion, 138
    Cheese Scramble, 136

Cooking Guides, 134, 135
Custard, 182
Festival, 140
Fiesta Scramble, 140
In Nests, 135
Poached, 135, 136
Scrambled, 135, 136
Scrambled, in whole meal, 212
Shirred, 136
Sunny-Side-Up, 133, 138
Eggplant, 151, 155
    Cold Eggplant Appetizer, 41
    Parthenon, 98
    Enchilada Casserole, 89
English Muffin Bread, 74
Entree, Frozen, 204

F

Favorite Meatloaf, 89
Festival Eggs, 140
Fiesta Scramble, 140
Fillet of Fish Amandine, 127
Fish and Shellfish; see also Seafood,
    specific fish
    Arrangement of, 121
    Fillet of Fish Amandine, 127
    Fillets, 124
    Fillets, defrosting, 123, 200, 204
    Fillets with Mushrooms, 124
    Grilled Swordfish Steaks, 125
    Mock Lobster Bisque, 51
    New England Clam Chowder, 56
    Scallops Vermouth, 127
    Steaks, 123, 124, 125, 200
Sticks, frozen, 123
    Stuffed Bass, 121, 130
    Stuffed Mountain Trout, 130
Whole, cooking, 124
    Whole, defrosting, 123, 200, 202
Fluffy Tapioca, 190
Fondue, Swiss, 41
Frankfurters; see Hot Dog
French Onion Soup, 55
Fresh Peaches in Raspberry
    Liqueur, 184
Fresh Strawberry Jam, 186
Fresh Strawberry Sauce, 180
Frosting
    Chocolate Fudge, 187
    Snow White, 192
Frozen Dinner, 201
Frozen Entree, 204
Fruit, 29, 182, 183
Fudge
    Hot Fudge Sauce, 178
    Rich Chocolate, 181, 196

G

Game birds, 106
Garlic
    Bread, in whole meal, 212

Chicken Italiano, 112
    Parmesan Bread, 71
Golden Apple Chunks, 186
Gravy, Easy, 170
Green Beans, 151
    Amandine, 158
    Italiano, 157
Green Peas, see Peas
Green Peppers, see Pepper(s)
Greens; Collard, Kale, 151
Grilled Swordfish Steaks, 125
Grits, 142
Ground Beef, see Beef

H

Ham, see also Bacon, Pork, Sausage
    Baked Ham with Pineapple, 104
    Canned, 82
    Center Cut Ham Slice, 82
    Cherry Glazed Ham Slice, 104
    Hot Ham and Swiss, 62
    Precooked, 31, 82, 102
    Smoked Ham Shank, 100
Hamburger(s)
    Cheeseburgers, 63
    Pizza Burgers, 68
Harvard Beets, 160
Hash, 84
Hearty Cheese and Frank Soup, 55
Height of food, cooking time affected
    by, 15
Herbed Leg of Lamb, 97
High Altitudes, adjusting for, 26
Hollandaise Sauce, 173
Homemade Pie Shell, 181, 194
Honey
    Corn Bread Ring, 74
    -Glazed Chicken, 113
    -Glazed Pork Roast, 102
Horseradish-Onion Beef Roast, 84
Hot Buttered Rum, 58
Hot Cereals, 28, 142
Hot Cranberry Punch, 60
Hot Devilish Daiquiri, 58
Hot Dog, 28, 65, 79, 83
    Coney Island, 62
    Hearty Cheese and Frank Soup, 55
Hot Fudge Sauce, 178
Hot Ham and Swiss, 62
Hot Lemony Dill Sauce, 175
Hot Milk, 28, 57
Hot Toddy, 60
Hot Tuna Buns, 68
Hot Water for Instant Beverages, 28,
    32, 60
Hungarian Goulash, 92

I

Instant Foods, Automatic Cooking
    Guide, 28

Instant Soups, Soup Mixes, 51
Irish Coffee, 57
Italian Meatball Sandwich, 68

J

Jam, Fresh Strawberry, 186
Japanese Cauliflower Soup, 56
Jelly, Cranapple, 186

K

Knockwurst, precooked, 63, 83

L

Lamb
  Chops, positioning, 77
  Cooking Guide, 31, 81-82
  Defrosting Guide, 79
  Eggplant Parthenon, 98
  Herbed Leg of Lamb, 97
  Leg or Shoulder Roast, bone in, 98
  Ragout, 97
  Zesty Lamb Chops, 97
Lasagna
  Frozen, 142
  One-Step, 141, 146
  Zucchini, 92
Lemon
  Butter Sauce, 174
  Dessert Sauce, 177
  Hot Lemony Dill Sauce, 175
  Pineapple Creme, 194
Liver, 16, 25, 80
  and Sausage Pâté, 43
  Chicken Liver Chow Mein, 117
  Venetian Style, 104
Lobster Tails, 123, 124
Low or Reduced Calories, 37
  Chicken and Vegetables, 116
  Cold Eggplant Appetizer, 41
  Cream of Mushroom Soup, 51
  Grilled Swordfish Steaks, 125
  Japanese Cauliflower Soup, 56
  Poached Salmon, 121, 125
  Russian Tea Mix, 57
  Zucchini Lasagna, 92

M

Macaroni
  and Cheese Vegetable Medley, 146
  Mexican, 148
Meat, 77-104
  Automatic Cooking Guide, 31
  Automatic Defrosting Guide, 79
  Cooking Guide, 80-83
  Defrosting Guide, 79-80
Meatball(s),
  à la Russe, 92
  All-American, 95

Barbecued, 84
  Italian Meatball Sandwich, 68
  Soup, 52
  Tiny, 44
Meatloaf, 31, 80
  Favorite, 89
  in Whole meal, 217
Metal utensils, 17, 19, 21
Mexican Macaroni, 148
Micro-Fried Chicken, 105, 111
Microproof Cookware, Guide, 21
Microwave Cooking, see also
  Converting Recipes,
  Food Characteristics
  Arrangement of Food, 15, 22-23,
    37-38, 121
  Cooking Methods, 22-26
  Cooking Recommendations, 38
  Timing, 13-14
  Utensils, 17-21
Microwave Ovens, see also
  Automatic Cooking
  Getting to Know Your Automatic
    Oven, 27-31
  Glass Tray, 20
  How it works, 5-8
  Middle Metal Rack, 8, 20
  Touch pads, 27
  User Instructions, 2
  Uses for, 9-12
  Using the Oven, 32-34
Milk, Hot, 28, 57
Minestrone Soup, 54
Mints, Deluxe, 11, 196
Mixed Vegetables, in whole
  meal, 215
Mock Lobster Bisque, 51
Moisture Content of Food, cooking
  time affected by, 16
Molasses Buttermilk Bread, 71
Muffins
  Blueberry, 76
  Corn, in whole meal, 213
  Oatmeal, 73
  Raisin Bran, 73
Mushrooms, 152
  Corn-Mushroom Scallop, 158
  Cream of Mushroom Soup, 51
  Fish Fillets with, 124
  -Pimiento Rice, 144
  Sautéed, 168
  Stuffed, 11, 39, 47
  Tuna-Mushroom Patties, 125

N

Nachos, 43
New England Clam Chowder, 56
Noodle(s), see also Lasagna, Pasta,
  Spaghetti
  and Cheese, 144

Chicken Noodle au Gratin, 148
  Stroganoff Casserole, 144
Nut(s); see also specific nut
  Caramel Nut Candy, 198
  Chocolate Nut Brownies, 188
  Chocolate-Raisin Nut
    Clusters, 198
  Scotch Nut Oatmeal Cake, 191
  Stuffing, Turkey with, 120
  Zucchini-Nut Bread, 69, 73

O

Oatmeal
  Date Oatmeal Bars, 190
  Muffins, 73
  Scotch Nut Oatmeal Cake, 191
Omelet, 134
  Classique, 133, 136
  Puffy Cheddar, 135
One-Step Lasagna, 141, 146
Onion(s), 152, 154
  Cheddar and Onion Egg, 138
  French Onion Soup, 55
  Horseradish-Onion Beef Roast, 84
Orange
  Ginger Pork Chops, 99
  Roast Orange Duckling, 118
  Sauce, 174
Oriental Beef, 88
Oysters, 121, 123, 124

P

Pan Baked Potato Halves, 160
Parmesan
  Garlic Parmesan Bread, 71
  Potatoes, 165
Parsley New Potatoes, 160
Parsley Potatoes, in whole
  meal, 215
Party Nibblers, 46
Pasta, 141, 142, 144-48; see also
Lasagna, Noodles, Spaghetti
  Cooking/Defrosting Guide, 142
  Macaroni and Cheese Vegetable
    Medley, 146
  Mexican Macaroni, 148
  San Francisco Dish, 144
Pâté, Liver and Sausage, 43
Peaches, Fresh Peaches in
  Raspberry Liqueur, 184
Peanut Brittle, 198
Peanut Butter, Choco-Peanut
    Butter Sauce, 180
Peanut Crispy Bars, 187
Peas, 152, 153, 154
  Canadian Green Pea Soup, 52
  Chilled Minted Pea Soup, 54
  Francine, 162
  Green, 162
  Green, cooking frozen, 204

Green, in whole meal, 216
Pecan(s)
Pie, 195
Toasted Seasoned, 44
Pepper Steak, 88
Pepper(s)
Corn and Pepper Pudding, 158
Stuffed Green, 90
Piercing, 25
Pie(s) 182, 183; see also Crumb Crust
Danish Apple, 195
Pecan, 195
Shell, Homemade, 181, 194
Yogurt Pumpkin, 195
Pineapple
Baked Ham with, 104
Lemon Pineapple Creme, 194
Zucchini Bread, 74
Pizza
Burgers, 68
Quick Appetizer, 39, 46
Poached Egg, 135, 136
Poached Salmon, 121, 125
Polish Sausage, precooked, 63, 83
Popcorn, cooking recommenda-
tions, 38
Pork; see also Bacon, Ham, Sausage
Barbecued Spareribs, 100
Chops, defrosting, 202
Cooking Guide, 31, 82-83
Country Style Ribs, 99
Defrosting Guide, 79, 200
Honey-Glazed Pork Roast, 102
Loin Roast, boneless, 102
Orange Ginger Pork Chops, 99
Seasoned Pork Chops, in whole
meal, 215
Stuffed Pork Chops, 99
Sweet and Sour, 100
Pot Roast in Sherry, 77, 85
Potato(es), 152, 153
Arrangement of, 14
Baked, 163
Country Style, 163
Creamed Potato Mix, 163
Mashed, 150
Pan Baked Potato Halves, 160
Parmesan, 165
Parsley New, 160
Parsley, in whole meal, 215
Salad, 162
Scalloped Potato Mix, 163
Twice-Baked, 157
Poultry, 105-120; see also Chicken,
Cornish Hens, Duckling, Turkey
Automatic Cooking Guide, 31
Automatic Defrosting Guide, 107,
200
Cooking Guide, 108
Precooked Ham, 31, 82, 102
Precooked Sausages, Bratwurst,
Polish Sausage, Knockwurst, 63
Pudding, 29, 182
Corn and Pepper, 158

Fluffy Tapioca, 190
Mix, 191
Raisin Bread, 194
Tapioca, 182
in whole meal, 212
Puffy Cheddar Omelet, 135
Pumpkin
Cupcakes, 191
Yogurt Pumpkin Pie, 195
Punch, Hot Cranberry, 60

Q

Quantity of food, cooking time
affected by, 14-15
Quiche Lorraine, 138
Quick Appetizer Pizza, 39, 46

R

Raisin
Bran Muffins, 73
Brandy Sauce, 173
Bread Pudding, 194
Chocolate-Raisin Nut
Clusters, 198
-Nut Ring, 71
Raspberry
Liqueur, Fresh Peaches in, 184
Sauce, 178
Ratatouille, 164, 165
Rearranging, 23
Recipe conversions, 35-36
for Appetizers, 40
for Baked Goods, 70
for Desserts, 182
for Eggs and Cheese, 134
for Hot Drinks, 50
for Meat, 78
for Pasta, 142
for Poultry, 106
for Rice, 142
for Sandwiches, 61
for Sauces, 170
for Seafood, 122
for Soup, 50
for Vegetables, 150
Red Cabbage, Sweet-Sour, 162
Reheating, 37-38
Automatic Cooking Guide, 28
Reuben Sandwich, 65
Rib Roast, bone in, 77, 86, 87
Rice, 141-45, 148
All Seasons, 148
Artichoke Pilaf, 143
Chinese Fried, 143
Cooking/Defrosting Guide, 142
Frozen, in pouches, 28,
141, 142
Mushroom-Pimiento, 144
Pilaf, 143
Spanish Rice, 143
in whole meal, 214
Wild, Cornish Hens with, 116

Rich Chocolate Fudge, 181, 196
Roast(s), Beef, see also Lamb,
Pork, Veal
Cooking Guide, 29, 31, 81
Defrosting Guide, 79, 200
Horseradish-Onion Beef, 84
Pot Roast in Sherry, 85
Rib Roast, bone in, 86
Rolled Rib, defrosting, 201
Tenderloin of Beef Supreme, 85
Roast Beef 'n Swiss Rolls, 63
Roast Orange Duckling, 118
Rocky Road Candy, 196
Rolled Rib Roast, defrosting, 201
Rolls, see also Bread
defrosting, 205
Sweet, in whole meal, 212
Rotating food, 24
Rum Custard Sauce, 177
Rum, Hot Buttered, 58
Rumaki, 11, 39, 47
Russian Tea Mix, 57

S

Salmon
Poached, 121, 125
Ring, 128
Simple Salmon Ring, 127
Sandwiches, 28, 61-68
San Francisco Dish, 144
Sauces, 169-180; see also Dressing,
Gravy
Sausage, 79, 82, 83, 99
Liver and Sausage Pâté, 43
Precooked, 63
Sautéed Mushrooms, 168
Savory Cauliflower, 149, 159
Scalloped Potato Mix, 163
Scallops, 123, 124
Vermouth, 127
Scampi, 128
Scotch Nut Oatmeal Cake, 191
Scrambled Egg(s), 135
in whole meal, 212
Seafood, 121-132; see also specific
seafood
Automatic Cooking Guide, 29
Cooking Guide, 124
Cooking/Defrosting Guide, Con-
venience Seafood, 123
Defrosting Guide, 123
Seasoned Pork Chops, in whole
meal, 215
Shape and Size of food, cooking time
affected by, 15
Shielding, 15, 17, 19, 24
Shirred Eggs, 136
Shish Kabobs, 96
Short Ribs of Beef, 90
Shrimp, 22, 23, 124
and Artichokes, 44
Chow Mein, 132
Creole, 128

defrosting, 44, 123, 200, 205
Scampi, 128
Veracruz, 130
Simple Salmon Ring, 127
Sloppy Joe, heating, 61
Slow-Cooking, Automatic Cooking
Guide, 29
Smoked Ham Shank, 100
Snails, 124
Snow White Frosting, 192
Soup Mixes, Instant Soups, 51
Soup(s), 28-29, 33, 49-57
Canadian Green Pea Soup, 52
Canned Soup, 55,
Chicken in the Pot, 50
Chilled Minted Pea Soup, 54
Cold Fresh Tomato Soup, 57
Country Vegetable Soup, 51
Cream of Corn Soup, 52
Cream of Mushroom Soup, 51
French Onion Soup, 55
Hearty Cheese and Frank Soup, 55
Instant Soups, Soup Mixes, 51
Japanese Cauliflower Soup, 56
Meatball Soup, 52
Minestrone Soup, 54
Mock Lobster Bisque, 51
New England Clam Chowder, 56
Tomato Soup Piquante, 56
Sour Cream
Coffeecake, 76
dip, heating, 40
Soy Sherry Chicken, 112
Spaghetti
Beef & Spaghetti Casserole, in
whole meal, 216
Squash, 152
Spanish Rice, 143
Spareribs, Barbecued, 100
Spicy Apple Drink, 60
Spicy Barbecue Sauce, 171
Spinach, 154, 159
cooking frozen, 204
Oriental, 168
Squash, 152
Spaghetti, 152
Yellow, in whole meal, 217
Standing Time, 25, 31, 80, 106, 107,
122, 150
Starting Temperature of food, cook-
ing time affected by, 16
Steak(s)
Cooking Guide, 81
defrosting, 201
Defrosting Guide, 79, 200
Pepper, 88
Tomato Swiss, 89
Stew Beef, defrosting, 79, 200, 201
Stew, Beef, 93
in whole meal, 212

Stews, Slow-Cook Guide, 31
Stirring, 23
Strawberry
Fresh Strawberry Jam, 186
Sauce, Fresh, 180
Stroganoff Casserole, 144
Stuffed Bass, 121, 130
Stuffed Cabbage, 93
Stuffed Green Peppers, 90
Stuffed Mountain Trout, 130
Stuffed Mushrooms, 11, 39, 47
Stuffed Pork Chops, 99
Stuffing
Chicken with Cornbread, 111
Mix, 153
Turkey with Nut, 120
Sugar and Fat Content of food,
cooking time affected by, 16
Sunny-Side-Up Eggs, 133, 138
Sweet and Sour Pork, 100
Sweet Potatoes, 152, 166
Candied, 155
Sweet Rolls, in whole meal, 212
Sweet-Sour Red Cabbage, 162
Swiss Coated Chicken, 109
Fondue, 41
Hot Ham and Swiss, 62
Roast Beef 'n Swiss Rolls, 63
Swordfish Steaks, Grilled, 125

T

Tacos, Beef, 62
Tapioca
Fluffy, 190
Tarragon
Grilled Chicken, 109
Sauce, 175
Temperature Probe, 7, 8, 30-31, 33, 49
Guide to Suggested Settings, 31
Tenderloin of Beef Supreme, 85
Timing, Information about, 13-14
Tiny Meatballs, 44
Toasted Seasoned Pecans, 44
Tomato, 22
Cold Fresh Tomato Soup, 57
Crumb Topped, 159
Soup Piquante, 56
Swiss Steak, 89
Warmer, 60
Tongue, 80
Tuna
Hot Tuna Buns, 68
-Mushroom Patties, 125
Turkey, 31, 107, 108, 200; see also
Poultry
Breast of Turkey Jardiniere,
120
with Nut Stuffing, 120
Turning over, 23

Turnips, 152, 154
TV dinners, 19, 21, 28
Twice-Baked Potatoes, 157

U

Utensils, 17-21

V

Veal
Cooking Guide, 82
Cordon Bleu, 96
Cutlets, 82
Defrosting Guide, 80
Parmigiana, 95
Shoulder or Rump Roast,
boneless, 95
Vegetable(s), 149-168; see also
specific vegetable
Automatic Cooking Guide, 29
Blanching, 153-54
Canned, 166
Chicken and, 116
Cooking Guides, 151-153
Country Vegetable Soup, 51
Macaroni and Cheese Vegetable
Medley, 146
Mixed, in whole meal, 215
in Pouches, 150
in Sauce, defrosting, 204

W

Water, Hot, for Instant Beverages, 28,
32, 60
Welsh Rabbit,
frozen, 134
on Toast, 140
West Coast Cocoa, 58, 59
White Sauce, Basic, 169, 171
Whole Chicken, defrosting, 202
Whole Fish, defrosting, 202
Whole Meal, 207-217
Whole Roast Chicken, 112
Wild Rice, Cornish Hens with, 116

Y

Yellow Squash, in whole meal, 217
Yogurt Pumpkin Pie, 195

Z

Zesty Lamb Chops, 97
Zucchini, 152, 154
Lasagna, 92
-Nut Bread, 69, 73
Pineapple Zucchini Bread, 74
Ratatouille, 165